Theology of the
Open Table

Theology of the
Open Table

Eojin Lee

RESOURCE *Publications* · Eugene, Oregon

THEOLOGY OF THE OPEN TABLE

Copyright © 2016 Eojin Lee. All rights reserved. Except for brief quotations in critical publications or reviews, no part of this book may be reproduced in any manner without prior written permission from the publisher. Write: Permissions, Wipf and Stock Publishers, 199 W. 8th Ave., Suite 3, Eugene, OR 97401.

Resource Publications
An Imprint of Wipf and Stock Publishers
199 W. 8th Ave., Suite 3
Eugene, OR 97401

www.wipfandstock.com

PAPERBACK ISBN: 978-1-5326-0830-8
HARDCOVER ISBN: 978-1-5326-0832-2
EBOOK ISBN: 978-1-5326-0831-5

Manufactured in the U.S.A.   OCTOBER 31, 2016

All scripture quotations unless noted otherwise are taken from the New Revised Standard Version of the Bible, copyright 1989, Division of Christian Education of the National Council of the Churches of Christ in the United States of America. Used by permission. All rights reserved.

For the glory of God

Contents

Acknowledgments | ix
Abbreviations | xi
Introduction | xiii

Part I: Reflection on Traditional Eucharistic Practice in the Presbyterian Church of Korea (PCK)

1   Korean Culture and Its Influence on Worship and the Eucharist of the Presbyterian Church of Korea (PCK) | 3
2   The Formation and Development of Worship and the Eucharist of the PCK | 27
3   The Theological Basis of the PCK's Understanding of the Eucharist: The Last Supper as the Origin of the Eucharist | 60

Part II: The Theology of the Eucharistic Open Table

4   The Historical Basis for the Theology of the Open Table (1): The Eucharist in the First Two Centuries | 83
5   The Historical Basis for the Theology of the Open Table (2): The Eucharist after the Third Century | 113
6   The Biblical Basis for the Theology of the Open Table | 137
7   The Theological Basis for the Theology of the Open Table | 163

Part III: A Model of Application of the Open Table Theology in the Uniting Church in Australia (UCA)

8   The Way of the Open Table: The Eucharist of the Uniting Church in Australia (UCA) as a Model | 181

Conclusion | 225
Bibliography | 231
Name Index | 247
Subject Index | 251

Acknowledgments

THIS BOOK IS A revision of my doctoral dissertation. As such, I am greatly indebted to many people for completing this book. I take this opportunity to express my gratitude to the people who have been instrumental in the successful completion of this book.

I would like to express the deepest appreciation to many teachers, colleagues and friends at Charles Sturt University in Sydney. I am grateful to Rev. Dr. Sang Taek Lee, Dr. Gerard Moore, Dr. William Emilsen, Dr. Jione Havea, Dr. Benjamin Myers and Dr. Jeffrey Aernie for their persistent questions, guidance and supports. Also thanks to the staff at Camden Theological Library, the Veech Library and St Mark's Library for their support. I particularly thank Rev. Dr. Stephen Burns of Trinity College Theological School in Melbourne who offered various forms of direct advice and assistance during my first two years for the dissertation.

I like to thank Rev. Dr. Chris Walker at the Assembly of the UCA, Rev. Carolyn Thornley at UTC, Rev. Dr. Ockert Meyer at St. Stephen's Uniting Church in Sydney, and Rev. Leonie Findlay at Strathfield-Homebush Uniting Church in Strathfield for sharing their precious time during the process of interviewing.

I am grateful to my teachers, especially Rev. Dr. Dal Lee, Rev. Dr. Samuel Cheon and Rev. Dr. Yong Hoon Cho of Hannam University for their encouragement and help. I thank Rev. Dr. Joong-Sam Lee and Deadeok Presbyterian Church for their prayer and financial support. I acknowledge with gratitude the generous gift of the editing skills and wisdom of Carolyn Craig-Emilsen at United Theological College.

I am also indebted to Wipf & Stock editors and anonymous reviewers, whose suggestions and comments helped me to make this book a better work in many ways.

I give thanks to my grandmother, parents, the families of my brother and sister in South Korea and my mother-in-law and her family in Sydney for their loving support and prayer. Finally, I would like to thank my wife

Yoonjeong, daughter Yoonjin and son Joowon for their patience, understanding and love.

Abbreviations

Ad uxor.	*Ad uxorem*
Adv. haer.	*Adversus haereses*
BCE	Before the Common Era
BCW 1997	*Book of Common Worship 1997*
BCW 2008	*Book of Common Worship 2008*
BEM	*Baptism, Eucharist and Ministry*
BUC	Bexley Uniting Church
CAFC	Carrington Avenue Faith Community
CE	Common Era
CPC	Canadian Presbyterian Church
De spec.	*De spectaculis*
H. E.	*Ecclesiastical History*
NSW	New South Wales
NT	New Testament
OT	Old Testament
PCA	Presbyterian Church of Australia
PCK	Presbyterian Church of Korea
PCTS	Presbyterian College and Theological Seminary
PCUS	Presbyterian Church in the United States
PCUSA	Presbyterian Church of USA
QS	Qumran Scrolls
Rev.	Reverend
SSUC	St. Stephens' Uniting Church
St.	Saint
UCA	Uniting Church in Australia

UiW	*Uniting in Worship*
UiW2	*Uniting in Worship 2*
UTC	United Theological College
WCC	World Council of Churches

Introduction

1 Context and Rationale

THE PRESBYTERIAN CHURCH OF Korea (PCK) developed its worship and eucharistic tradition after a Presbyterian missionary Horace G. Underwood established the first Presbyterian church in Korea in 1887. The distinctive features of the PCK's worship and eucharistic tradition have been described and expressed in its directories. The first directory of worship of the PCK was published in 1921 and was, in both structure and content, greatly influenced by the *Directory for Worship* produced by the Presbyterian Church in the United States (PCUS) in 1894.[1] Although, as time went on, the directory was edited several times, regarding the concept of worship and the eucharist there were few changes for many decades. One of the characteristics of these early directories was the separation of the eucharist and worship. These directories categorized the eucharist into sacrament and included only the elements of the service of the word such as hymn, prayer and sermon in the section of worship. Although these directories did not provide an actual order of worship, the recognition of the eucharist as a sacrament not part of worship led the PCK to the so-called preaching centered worship tradition. For the theological basis of the eucharist, the PCK simply translated the Westminster Confession of Faith into Korean and used it. Following the teachings of the Westminster Confession of Faith, the PCK began to preserve the traditional eucharistic understanding which emphasizes the paschal meaning of the eucharist and requires participants to prepare baptism and faith for the eucharist. Since then, several further editions have been published, but there was no radical change in terms of either structure or content regarding worship and the eucharist for over 60 years.

---

1. Lee, *Study of History*, 229–34.

Around the early 1980s the ecumenical movement began to influence the eucharistic theology of the PCK. In this process, the World Council of Churches (WCC) documents such as *Baptism, Eucharist and Ministry* (BEM) and the Lima Liturgy played a crucial role in broadening the PCK's eucharistic understanding. The first reflection of the ecumenical movement can be observed in the directory of worship of 1983.[2] While the earlier directories treated the eucharist as a sacrament, the directory of worship of 1983 recognized the eucharist as part of worship. However, even as this change was made in 1983, the eucharistic theology presented in BEM failed to be expressed in the official documents of the PCK.

The first theological reflection of the ecumenical movement in the PCK's directories is found in the *Book of Common Worship* (BCW)[3] of 1997. This directory led the PCK to broaden its eucharistic theology with an introduction of the five key eucharistic understandings of BEM.[4] More recently, in the BCW of 2008[5] (the latest worship directory of the PCK), the recognition of the eucharist as part of worship came to be more clearly expressed than the BCW of 1997. In addition, regarding ecumenism, this book strengthened the relationship between the PCK and other mainline churches by including eucharistic prayers from not only Protestants but also Roman Catholic and Greek Orthodox traditions in its worship resources. One of the most significant contributions of this book to the PCK's eucharistic understanding is an expansion of eucharistic theology. Although basically the eucharistic theology in the BCW of 2008 is still based on the last supper tradition, this book makes a new attempt to view the meal after the resurrection as a eucharist.

Between the late 20th and the early 21st century with this development of eucharistic theology there was an attempt to renew the eucharistic practice in the PCK. In 2001, the Jeonnam Synod belonging to the PCK passed the resolution of an open table which allows unbaptised people to participate in the eucharist. Furthermore, the Jeonnam Synod decided to propose the issue of the open table in the National General Assembly Meeting of the PCK. Before long, however, other synods which came to know the decision of the Jeonnam Synod expressed consistently strong opposition to

---

2. The General Assembly of the Presbyterian Church of Korea, *Constitution* (Seoul: Publishing House PCK, 1983).

3. Committee on the Book of Common Worship, *The Book of Common Worship* (Seoul: Publishing House PCK, 1997).

4. For more details on the five meanings of the Eucharist in BEM, see World Council of Churches, *Baptism, Eucharist and Ministry*, 10–15.

5. Committee on the Book of Common Worship, *The Book of Common Worship* (Seoul: Publishing House PCK, 2008).

the Jeonnam Synod. In turn, the Jeonnam Synod had to retract its plan. The final decision of the Jeonnam Synod was to set up a committee to study a theology of the open table.[6]

After the incident, influential theologians in the PCK began to write editorials in newspapers and articles in journals regarding the issue of the open table. Supporters of the open table expected to broaden their eucharistic perspective with an introduction of a theology of the open table through those studies. However, contrary to their expectations, the theologians uniformly protested against the open table and maintained the justification of the traditional way of practising the eucharist. There was virtually no reflection on the open table but a simple repetition of the traditional eucharistic theology.

Unlike the PCK's response to the open table, the western reformed churches are expanding the practice of the open table. What is the cause of the difference between the PCK and the western reformed churches regarding the issue of the open table? The issue relating to the open table is not limited to the simple question, "who can participate in the eucharist?" Although the key question of the open table is necessarily involved with the matter of inclusion in the eucharist, the process of solving the question embraces a wide range of historical, biblical, theological and pastoral challenges.

One of the critical issues regarding the open table is the question of the origin of the eucharist. Traditionally, most mainline churches have recognized that Jesus instituted the eucharist at the last supper. The traditional belief of the last supper as the origin of the eucharist has had a great influence on the churches' eucharistic theology and practice. As a result, theologically, the churches have come to emphasize the paschal meaning of the eucharist. In practice, the churches have developed the so-called closed table tradition which allows only baptized members to participate in the eucharist, seeking a biblical authority for that regulation from the last supper narrative of the Synoptic Gospels and 1 Corinthians 11 where Jesus shared the meal with his twelve disciples.

However, recent studies on the origin of the eucharist challenge the traditional belief of the last supper. The first meaningful challenge to the traditional eucharistic understanding is found in the book of Smith and Taussig, *Many Tables: The Eucharist in the New Testament and Liturgy Today*. Smith and Taussig note that the last supper tradition in the New Testament is not one but many. In addition, the early Christian communities had

---

6. Park, "Debates on the eucharist," *Gidokgongbo*, June 23, 2001.

various meal formations different from the last supper tradition.[7] A liturgical scholar, Bradshaw suggests that the differences in the institution narratives in the Synoptic Gospels and 1 Corinthians 11, the omission of the story of the last supper from the fourth Gospel, and the diversity of eucharistic form and content in the early churches documents point to the fact that Jesus did not leave a fixed institution or commandment regarding the eucharist, and that eucharists conducted by the early churches were originated from a variety of meals of Jesus rather than the last supper as a supposed single definitive event.[8] Bruce Chilton (a biblical, rather than liturgical, scholar) has also articulated an understanding of the early churches' eucharists as rooted in the meals shared by Jesus throughout his whole ministry, as opposed to a single "last supper." Throughout Jesus' ministry, Chilton argues, his meals depicted a vision of the kingdom of God as a manifestation of the feast for all peoples prophecised in Isaiah 25.[9]

The academic achievements of these new approaches to the eucharistic origin have led churches to rethink their traditional eucharistic theology and practice, and rediscover the significance of the meals of Jesus and the eucharistic diversity of the early church. This shift of the recognition of the eucharistic origin raises the following questions. If the last supper loses its authority as the original, how can the traditional eucharistic theology and practice based on the last supper be understood and used for the eucharist today? What eucharistic theology can the church today draw from the meals of Jesus? How can the eucharistic theology be connected with the open table? These questions will shape the content and direction of the following chapters.

2 Methodology

This book is divided into three parts: three chapters in part one, four chapters in part two, and one chapter in part three. The focus of part one is on the traditional eucharistic understanding of the PCK. For part one, I collect and analyze historical, theological and liturgical resources relating to the eucharist of the PCK. In part two, I establish historical, biblical and theological bases for the open table. For this, the works of biblical and liturgical

---

7. Smith and Taussig, *Many Tables*, 36–69.

8. See Bradshaw, *The Search for the Origins of Christian Worship* (Oxford: Oxford University Press, first published in 1992, 2002). Bradshaw, *Eucharistic Origins* (London: SPCK, 2004), and *Reconstructing Early Christian Worship* (Collegeville, MN: Liturgical Press, 2009). See also Bradshaw, and Johnson, *The Eucharistic Liturgies* (Collegeville, MN: Liturgical Press, 2012).

9. See Chilton, *A Feast of Meanings* (New York, NY: E. J. Brill, 1994).

scholars are collected. Then, I analyze and evaluate their main theories in order to build the open table theology. Part three presents a practical application for the open table. The focus of part three is on the eucharist of the Uniting Church in Australia (UCA). In part three, I collect and analyze historical, theological and liturgical resources regarding the eucharist of the UCA. Also, I include interviews with local church pastors and theologians and a case study of the eucharistic practice of three worshipping communities in the UCA so that readers may have a more exact understanding of the open table theology and practice of the UCA.

Chapter 1, as the first step of the study of the traditional eucharistic understanding of the PCK, explores cultural background and its influence on worship and the eucharist of the PCK. It also outlines the features of the main religions in Korea: Shamanism, Buddhism and Confucianism. Then it analyses how those religious features have affected the PCK's eucharistic theology and practice.

Chapter 2 examines the history of the eucharist of the PCK. One of the distinctive features of the PCK's worship is the preaching centred worship omitting the eucharist. When did the preaching centred worship begin in the PCK? How has the PCK developed the worship tradition? This chapter focuses on the missionaries' eucharistic understanding and practice in the early period of the PCK and the process of development of the eucharist of the PCK. It also highlights the main eucharistic emphases of the PCK.

Chapter 3, the last chapter of part one, deals with the main theories which have led the PCK to preserve its eucharistic understanding. The eucharistic understanding of the PCK is firmly based on the last supper tradition. What theories have influenced the PCK's eucharistic understanding? What are the issues and main points of the theories? This chapter outlines and evaluates the theories of major scholars' influences on the formation and development of the PCK's eucharistic understanding.

Chapter 4, using historical approach to the eucharist, studies the diversity of the eucharistic theology and practice in the early church. This chapter explores the historical evidence that the earliest eucharistic traditions were different from the last supper tradition. Why is the explanation of John of the last supper different from that of the synoptic Gospel? If the last supper is the original, why do the earliest church documents consistently neglect the last supper story? For the study, I will concentrate on the early church documents regarding the eucharist particularly in the first and second centuries.

Chapter 5 also takes a historical approach. While chapter 4 explores the eucharist in the first two centuries, this chapter focuses on the shift of the eucharistic theology and practice after the third century. This chapter examines the eucharistic tendency of standardization under the influence of the last supper tradition. When does the mention of the last supper appear first in church documents outside the New Testament? What affected the eucharistic standardization based on the last supper tradition? I will study the process of development of the traditional eucharistic understanding based on the last supper tradition from the third century through the reformers to John and Charles Wesley in this chapter.

Chapter 6 explores the biblical base for the open table. The results of the historical study of the eucharist in the previous chapters raise a critical question concerning the traditional belief that the origin of the eucharist is the last supper. If the historical evidence challenges the traditional belief of the origin of the eucharist, where did the eucharist come from? This question leads this thesis to rethink the meals of Jesus including the last supper. In this chapter I will try to interpret Jesus' meal practices in the perspective of the kingdom of God and to reinterpret the last supper in the light of the open table theology. I will also seek the eucharistic significance of the meals of Jesus after the resurrection.

Chapter 7 aims at providing the theological base for the open table. There have been some controversial issues in the discussion concerning the open table such as the interpretation of "discerning the body," the relationship between the eucharist and baptism, the tension between traditional eucharistic understanding and pastoral and missional requests for the open table, and the understanding of sacraments. In this chapter I outline these issues and explore how to build the theological basis for the open table. I will also seek to deepen the eucharistic theology through providing the recognition of the eucharist as a means of grace.

In chapter 8, the final chapter of this study, concerning a practical application, I will be seeking a way as to how the open table theology might be embodied in liturgy and practice. For this, I will examine the eucharist of the UCA expressed in its official documents such as Basis of Union, the Minutes of Assembly Meeting and worship resources. The works of theologians and pastors in the UCA will also be explored. For a more exact understanding of the eucharist of the UCA, I will choose three local worshipping communities and study the actual practice of the eucharist in those communities. Then I will try to evaluate the eucharist of the UCA from the perspective of the open table theology.

These eight chapters form the main body of this book. In conclusion, I will draw out key findings of the chapters and try to synthesize them in order to enhance the open table theology. The open table theology which is systematized and embodied in this book is expected to offer a contribution to renewing not only the eucharist of the PCK but also other churches.

Part I

Reflection on Traditional Eucharistic Practice in the Presbyterian Church of Korea (PCK)

Chapter 1

Korean Culture and Its Influence on Worship and the Eucharist of the Presbyterian Church of Korea (PCK)

EVERY CULTURE HAS A religious basis. Religion creates culture, and at the same time culture forms the religion. Before the introduction of Christianity, there were three representative religions which prevailed on the Korean peninsula: Shamanism, Buddhism and Confucianism. These religions have created the uniqueness of Korean culture in its long history.[1] When Protestant missionaries introduced Christian belief in Korea the unique Korean culture influenced the formation and development of worship and the eucharist of Korean church. In this chapter, I will examine the main ideas and features of the three religions. Then I will explore how the Korean culture influenced worship and the eucharist of the PCK.

1 Cultural Background of the PCK

Mu-gyo (Shamanism in Korea)

Mu-gyo is the oldest and the indigenous religion of Korea. *Mu-gyo* is also called *Mu* or *Mu-sok*. The shaman of *Mu-gyo* is called *Mu-dang*. Dan-gun, who is believed to be the founder of Korea's first kingdom Gojoseon (2333–108 BCE), was a political leader and *Mu-dang*. After the era of Gojoseon, Three Kingdoms (Goguryeo, Baekje and Silla) ruled Korean peninsula. Cha-cha-oong, the name of the second king of Silla (57 BCE–935 CE), also meant *Mu-dang*. Likewise, *Mu-gyo* was closely connected with the royal authority and ruled people in the early stages of Korean history. After the fifth century BCE, Buddhism and Confucianism were introduced in Korea, and

---

1. For more details on the relationship between Korean culture and religion, see Yu, "Religious Basis of the Korean Culture," 111–22.

took over the throne of national religion from *Mu-gyo*. However, *Mu-gyo* has not disappeared and has kept influencing a way of life of Koreans.[2]

In *Mu-gyo* faith, there exist countless gods in *Cheonsang-ge* (category of sky), *Jiha-ge* (category of underground) and *Ingan-ge* (category of human).[3] *Mu-gyo* believes that the gods control life and death, the blessings and curses of human beings. However, there are some gods who are more closely connected with the life of human beings. In particular, for a community's wealth and peace, rituals are offered to forty-three kinds of *Dong-shin* (gods of sky, land, the sun, the moon, stars, mountains and the like). For a family business and health, *Ga-shin* (god of house), *Jo-sang-shin* (ancestor god) and *Sam-shin* (three gods governing childbirth) are worshipped.[4] In addition, there is no concept of an absolutely good or evil god in *Mu-gyo*. *Mu-gyo* believes that even the *Sonnim-shin* (the god of disease who suddenly appears in the life of a human, throws the whole of life into disorder and sometimes takes away life from children) will give people fortune instead of illness when the god is well treated. Conversely, if any god is ignored or treated poorly, the god will punish people with misfortune or illness.[5]

Gut or *Pu-dak-geo-ri*, the ritual of *Mu-gyo*, is led by a *Mu-dang*. In *Gut*, only *Mu-dang* owns the power and right to contact with gods. Clients and other people indirectly communicate with gods through *Mu-dang*. Thus, *Mu-dang* has absolute power and influence in *Gut*.[6] Generally *Gut* can be divided into two categories: communal *Gut* and personal *Gut*. Communal *Gut* includes various forms of *Gut* mainly praying for a good harvest and peace of a community. Personal *Gut* has three categories: 1. *Gibok-je*: *Gut* for success of the family business, and the health and fortune of family members. 2. *Saryeong-je*: *Gut* for consoling the soul of the dead and sending the soul to *Jeo-seung* (traditionally Koreans believe that when people die souls have to go to *Jeo-seung*, which can be translated as "beyond world"). 3. *Gubyeong-je*: *Gut* for healing a patient.[7] The contents and orders of *Gut* vary between regions but generally *Gut* comprises twelve *Geo-ri* (elements). The main themes of the twelve *Geo-ri* are the preparation of *Gut*, inviting gods, making wishes to gods, receiving *Gong-su* (answers from gods), and

---

2. Choi, *Joonsik Choi's Proper View*, 38–39.
3. Yu, "Religious Basis of the Korean Culture," 118.
4. Kim, "Realities of Folk Believes in Korea," 71–78.
5. Im, *Mu-ga*, 14.
6. Yu, "Religious Basis of the Korean Culture," 120.
7. Yu, "Religious Character of Korean *Mu-gyo*," 42–43.

farewell to the gods.[8] Likewise, the main purpose of *Gut* is physical health and economic prosperity.

An understanding of life and death in *Mu-gyo* is, also, a crucial element which led Koreans to pursue earthly happiness. *Mu-gyo* believes that people live in *E-seung* (this world) while alive and after death souls go to *Jeo-seung* (beyond world).[9] Especially, the concept of *Jeo-seung* in *Mu-gyo* is quite different from other religions. In *Mu-gyo*, *Jeo-seung* is a vacant place whereas most religions view that after death good souls go to heaven where the souls enjoy a new world. In *Jeo-seung* there is no hope or expectation of new life. There is no salvation or rest of soul. *Mu-gyo* believes that souls having unresolved earthly problems do not want to go to *Jeo-seung* as there is no savior or consoler of soul in *Jeo-seung*. Thus the souls stay in *E-seung* until all problems are resolved. The souls wander about aimlessly in *E-seung* because they do not own a body to settle earthly matters. These wandering souls in *E-seung* are named *Won-gui* or *Won-ryeong*. *Won-gui* is generally considered a harmful ghost. Koreans often connect unfortunate accidents, diseases or death with the work of *Won-gui*. The only method to escape from the affliction of *Won-gui* is to console *Won-gui* and send it to *Jeo-seung* through *Gut*. *Jeo-seung* is the place where all people must go after death but nobody wants to go.

This negative perspective on the afterlife is well presented in *Sangdu-sori* (a farewell song which is sung during the funeral march for a soul leaving for *Jeo-seung*). *Sangdu-sori* does not pay attention to the illustration of life in *Jeo-seung*. The sorrow of parting dominates the song. In the song, the bereaved family cries and pleads with the dead to not leave them. On the other hand, the song describes the mind of the dead person who does not want to depart from the loved ones but has to go:

> Now if you go, when will you come back?
> Please tell me when you will come back. . . .
> Poor and pitiful
> The dead is pitiful. . . .
> Live well. Live well.
> Live well. Don't remember me. . . .
> Going, going, I am going.
> I have finished this world. I am going. . . .[10]

---

8. Yu, "Religious Basis of the Korean Culture," 118.

9. For more details on the understanding of *Mu-gyo* on *E-seung* and *Jeo-seung*, see Kim, "Mu-sok faith and Christian faith," 14–21.

10. Kang, *MBC*, 208–9.

All souls have to go to *Jeo-seung* due to death but there is nothing for the soul to do. In the song, the world after death is a barren land rather than paradise. This concept of *Jeo-seung* leads Koreans to be more obsessed with *E-seung*, that is, the life of this world. The attachment to the realities of this world is a notable feature of Korean indigenous faith.

Buddhism

Buddhism in Korea was introduced from China about 372 CE and grew as the national religion in the period of the Three Kingdoms (about 100 BCE–668 CE), unified Silla (668 CE–935 CE) and continuously Goryeo (918–1392 CE). For nearly one millennium, the upper class used Buddhism for strengthening their reign. *Pal-gwan-hwoe* (a Buddhist festival) clearly shows the close relationship between Buddhism and the ruling class. *Pal-gwan-hwoe* was originally a religious-leaning festival centred at Buddhist temples but as time passed it was transformed into a social and national festival. The dynasties of Silla and Goryeo used *Pal-gwan-hwoe* to enhance bondage between people, especially to raise the status of the royal family and ruling class, and to secure the justification of reign.[11]

The Joseon dynasty (1392–1897 CE) was founded after Goryeo around the late 14th century. In Joseon, Confucianism was the governing ideology and so Buddhism was suppressed. In the early stage of Joseon, according to the policy of *Soong-yu-eok-bul* (meaning "to venerate Confucianism and to restrain Buddhism"), Buddhist temples and lands were forfeited. Buddhist monks were banned from entering cities. They had no choice but to escape deep into the mountains. Although there were some kings such as Se-jo (1455–1468 CE) and Myeong-jong (1545–1567 CE) who tried to revive Buddhism with the policy of *Heung-bul* (meaning "to revive Buddhism"), the basic governing ideology of Joseon was Confucianism. Due to this process, Buddhism in Joseon could be said "to have stepped down from the throne" and thus permeated the life of the people, seeking ways to survive.

Between the 6th and 4th centuries BCE, Buddhism was established in India based on the teachings of Siddhartha Gautama generally known as the Buddha. Since then, Buddhism has grown with various branches such as *So-seung* (Hinayana), *Dae-seung* (Mahayana), *Mil-gyo* (Vajrayana) and so forth. The branch of Buddhism introduced through China into Korea was *Dae-seung*. The early Buddhism verged on *So-seung*, which pursued personal enlightenment through asceticism, but later the faith of *Dae-seung*,

---

11. Gu, "National," 260.

focused on deliverance of others and interest in matters of human life, began to emerge.[12]

In *So-seung* Buddha means Siddhartha Gautama (Sakyamuni) who was enlightened and entered into nirvana (the state of complete absence of sensation). However, *Dae-seung* believes that there exist innumerable Buddhas who are enlightened and *Bosals* (Bodhisattvas) who pursue enlightenment to become Buddha. *Bosals* never seek nirvana for their own sake. They act to help *Jung-saeng* (all living creatures) struggling in this world. Also Buddha is not a god who resides only in heaven but is a being who lives for *Jung-saeng* with *Bosals* to establish *Jeong-to* (the world of Buddha where there is no agony, pain and anxiety). In *Dae-seung*, there are various Bodhisattvas such as *Mun-su bosal* (god of wisdom), *Bo-hyun bosal* (god of practice) and so forth. Among them, *Gwan-se-um bosal* (god of mercy) presents well the spirit of *Dae-seung*. *Gwan-se-um bosal* can "see" the voice of anxiety in the world. The gender of *Gwan-se-um bosal* is neutral. The face is masculine but the body is feminine. The womanish body symbolizes mercy and maternal love. *Gwan-se-um bosal* rushes to the scene of anguish with mercy and love. *Dae-seung* Buddhism enters deep into the human world and tries to solve the matters of life while the interest of *So-seung* is on *Hae-tal* (Buddhist deliverance, that is, emancipation from the world).[13]

Miruk is a Bodhisattva of *Dae-seung* Buddhism. *Miruk*, as a successor of Gautama Buddha, is the future Buddha who will save human beings. *Miruk* was taught by Gautama and was an intellectually and spiritually outstanding disciple. In answering the questions of disciples, Gautama prophesized that *Miruk* would die but he would return to earth to save the world as the future Buddha.[14] According to *Seong Bul Gyeong* which is one of Buddhist scriptures, 5,670 million years after the death of Gautama, *Miruk* will be reincarnated in a figure of a man in his thirties. He will give people sermons three times. While the first Buddha Gautama could not save many human beings, at the first sermon of *Miruk*, 9,600 million people will be enlightened, then 9,400 million and lastly 9,200 million.[15] The incredible number of people delivered by *Miruk* seems to be a symbol of hope rather than to have a literal meaning, and a completion of the unfinished work of Gautama through which only a few people who were enlightened could enter nirvana.

12. Han, *Context of Korean Philosophy*, 68.
13. Lee, *Eastern Philosophy*, 204.
14. Yeo, *The World of Miruk Gyeong*, 182.
15. Ibid., 110.

In *Yongwha Segye* (the new world ruled by *Miruk*), there is no agony or anxiety. The world is full of gold and diamonds and everyone enjoys plenty of food. There is no pain, sickness, aging or death. Here, it would be worth noting that *Yongwha Segye* is situated not in heaven but on earth. Although the *Yongwha Segye* will come in the future, people who are oppressed strongly anticipate that the new age will arrive in their life time. In the early history of Buddhism in Korea, the faith in *Miruk* was often embodied into attempts of transforming the current world. Gyeon-Hweon (867–936) who was born as the son of a poor peasant dreamed of a new kingdom. He gathered his allies to establish *Yongwha Segye,* and claimed himself to be *Miruk*.[16] His revolution was successful but the lives of people under his rule did not improve. He used politically the thought of *Miruk* so that he came to the throne. Around the same time, Gung-Ye (861–918) was born to Hun-An, a king of Silla, and a concubine. In power struggles, he was pushed out to a temple and became a monk. He joined rebels led by General Yang-Gil against the Silla kingdom and attained fame winning several wars. Finally he established the later Goguryeo kingdom asking his people to believe him as *Miruk*. However, in actual life, he was a tyrannical leader rather than *Miruk*.[17] Some rulers used the *Miruk* faith for their political purposes, but it is also a sign that *Miruk* faith had a huge influence on people. On the other hand, in the period of Joseon when Buddhism was restrained, *Miruk* faith continuously influenced the lives of people by blending with shamanism.

The poet Eun Goh tries to connect the *Miruk* faith with the context of people who are oppressed, comparing this to Sakyamuni (Gautama) Buddhism. He gives an interpretation that Sakyamuni is the Buddha for the upper classes in feudal eras but *Miruk* symbolizes the liberation and deliverance of *Minjung* (the mass of the people who are politically oppressed and economically exploited).[18] So *Miruk* is the Buddha for the *Minjung*.[19] The *Miruk* faith means the popularization of Buddhism and at the same time the embodiment of the *Minjung*'s will of establishing an ideal world in their real life. Thus *Miruk* faith flourished especially at the times of social turmoil when the *Minjung*'s suffering was worst. *Miruk* faith consoled the socially oppressed who found little hope in Sakyamuni Buddhism.[20]

---

16. Kim, *Sam-guk Sa-gi*, 401–10.

17. Ibid., 396 – 401.

18. For more details on the concept of *Minjung*, see the section "The Influence of *Mugyo* and *Miruk* Faith on the Eucharist in *Minjung* Theology" of this chapter.

19. Goh, "Miruk and Minjung," 234.

20. Ibid., 226.

The difference between Sakyamuni Buddhism and *Miruk* faith is revealed in Buddhist statues. The Sakyamuni Buddhist statue is set on the highest place in a worship room. The statue is generally of gilt bronze and presents a magnificent and dignified appearance. However, permission to enter the worship room was given to only the royal family and the nobility. The *Minjung* needed the Buddha for their own sake. Thus the *Minjung* put up *Dolbucheo* (a Buddhist statue made of a stone of *Miruk*) in fields and streets where they were not excluded instead of the luxuriously gilded statue for the ruling classes.[21] The figure of *Dolbucheo* was far from being delicate or splendid. Many of these statues were worn away by years of wind and rain. Yet, the pitiful figure of *Miruk* was the symbol of the life of *Minjung* and symbolized consolation and hope for them.

Confucianism

The national ideology of Joseon was *Seong-ri-hak* which is one of the main theories of Confucianism. *Seong-ri-hak* tries to explain the origin and movement of human beings, society and the universe through the concept of *Li* and *Gi*. As the origin of the whole universe, *Li* which is immanent within all human beings is naturally good and equal. Due to *Li* all human beings have a natural morality. When considering only *Li*, all humans are equal and are beings of dignity. On the other hand, as an essential element of the whole creature there is *Gi* within all human beings. Unlike *Li*, each *Gi*, which has a material cause, has a different size.[22] As a result of the dissimilarity of *Gi*, humans are divided into the wise and the foolish.

The ruling class of Joseon, *Yang-ban*, used the theory of *Li* and *Gi* as an instrumental tool for explaining their superiority in social position and justifying the oppression of the lower classes. The social system of Joseon was *Yang-cheon*. The term "*Yang*" in *Yang-cheon* means *Yang-in* (middle class) and "*Cheon*" means *Cheon-min* (lower class). Under the *Yang-cheon* system, only *Yang-in* could take *Gwa-geo* (civil service exam) and become government officials. The leading figures of the establishment of Joseon, *Sinjin-sadaebu* (newly rising scholar-bureaucrats), implemented drastically the policy of expanding the number of *Yang-in* to secure a justification of the foundation of Joseon. Legally there was only a distinction of two classes, *Yang-in* and *Cheon-min*. However in actual life there existed four classes, which are *Yang-ban*, *Jung-in*, *Sang-min* and *Cheon-min*, and there was a very strict distinction between four classes.

21. Lee, *Religion and Social Formation in Korea*, 99.
22. Suh, *Religion and Humans*, 100 – 101.

Yang-ban politically monopolized the high positions of government. Socially they belonged to the highest class. The society of the Joseon Dynasty was led by Yang-ban bureaucracy. Literally Yang-ban means Yang (two) and Ban (branches) of government officials. The government system of Joseon was divided into two parts: Mun-ban (civil administrator) and Mu-ban (martial office holder). The real power of the controlling government was concentrated in Mun-ban. The central government which was comprised of Yang-ban dissolved private armies and controlled landed proprietors by sending local governors to each district. Also Yang-ban became the main body managing Joseon and checking the abuse of royal powers.[23] In the early years of Joseon the original meaning of Yang-ban was men who were qualified to become bureaucrats but later the meaning of Yang-ban was expanded to include all family members and their descendants. Economically almost all Yang-ban were rich landlords having many slaves. Yang-ban intensified the exclusivity and discriminated against Seo-eol (children of the second wife) and Hyang-ri (lower level local officials) in order to keep their political, economic and social privileges. Socially Seo-eol and Hyang-ri were blocked to enter high positions of government.[24] Jung-in was the class between Yang-ban and Yang-in. Jung-in were engaged in entry level administrative positions or as technical civil servants. Jung-in were discriminated by Yang-ban but they played an important role for the maintenance of the Yang-ban system by having close connections with Yang-ban and by ruling the classes of Sang-min and Cheon-min. Generally Yang-in were occupied mainly with agriculture and commerce. They were given a huge burden of tax by the ruling class. Although ostensibly the door of becoming Yang-ban was open to all through Gwa-geo exam, it was quite difficult for the lower classes like Yang-in except Yang-ban families to possess enough time and financial support to pass the exam. Cheon-min was the lowest class of Joseon and basically No-bi (slaves) comprised Cheon-min. For example, a butcher, prostitute, musician, Mu-dang and the like were legally Yang-in but actually were treated as Cheon-min. They did not have any rights as a human being and were seen as possessions to trade and inherit.

Based on the theory of Li and Gi, Joseon justified gender discrimination. The teachings as to the differences between men and women in Joseon are recorded in Ye-gi, one of five classics of the Confucian canon. According to chapter 12 Nae-chik in Ye-gi, a man and a woman are distinguished from birth. When a baby boy is born a bow is to be on the left side of a door and for a baby girl a towel is to be on the right side of a door. In addition, Ye-gi

---

23. Shin and Lee, *A New Understanding of the History of Korea*, 27.
24. Ibid., 30.

says that *Chil-nyeon nam-yeo bu-dong-seok bu-dong-sik*. It means that by seven, a boy and a girl should not sit and eat together.[25] Yutae Lee's book, *Jung-hun*, reflecting the thought of *Ye-gi*, gives instruction about how men and women should behave. Even with family, men should not visit freely the rooms of women. Men fifteen years old and over should not sit or play with their sisters. Even making a joke between them was banned. Sexual distinction was applied to the manner of using public places. Men should not use a well or toilet with women. This rule applied to *No-bi* as well. When *No-bi* broke the rule they were punished by being whipped on the calf.[26]

Nam-jon-yeo-bi thought is a clear example of discrimination against women in Joseon. This term means that the rights and position of men were superior to that of women. The term itself is not from Confucian books but the thought can be easily found in Confucianism in Korea. It would be worth observing an excerpt from the books, *Nae-Hun* and *Ge-Nyeo-Seo*, which were used for teaching women Confucian ideology in Joseon:

> The only one thing that a woman has to wish for one hundred years is her husband and to serve him. A woman has to allow her husband to do what he wants to do except one thing that cannot be accepted by the world because it is extremely wrong. Do not ignore even a word of your husband. The most outstanding service that a woman can do for her husband is to not be jealous. If your husband keeps one hundred concubines, overlook his deed. Although your husband loves too much his concubine, respect more him, and do not be offended by his deed.[27]

Sam-jong-ji-do (three principles that women have to keep) was also a widespread thought in Joseon society. The core of the thought is that women have to obey men because women's inferiority is determined by the law of nature. Three principles are to obey your father before a marriage, your husband after marriage, and then your son after the death of husband.[28]

The core of *Dae-hak* and *Jung-yong*, the representative books of Confucianism for men, is *Su-sin Je-ga Chi-guk Pyeong-cheon-ha*. It means that the goal of life for a man is to cultivate himself, to regulate family, to govern the state, and to make the entire world peaceful. While the level of the goals of men's lives presented in the books is quite high, *Yeo-gye*, one of the Confucian books for women, compels women to expect quite a low level of life goals. *Yeo-gye* has as its premise that women are by nature weak and

25. Ji, *Ye-Gi*, 123–70.
26. Lee et al., *Yeh-hak Philosophy*, 123–24.
27. Han, *Shin-Wan-Yeok*, 200–201.
28. Mun, "The Change of Women's Position in Family," 61.

humble. Thus the social position of women is low. Women should not try to gain a reputation by good works. Women have to bear a shame and tolerate disgrace. Women have to live as if they were afraid of something.[29]

Likewise, the patriarchal social system based on Confucian ideology undermined the dignity and values of women. Especially in the period of Joseon women lost most of the freedom that they enjoyed before, and came to have a restricted sphere of activity. In Goryeo (918–1392 CE) men and women were free to communicate each other and there was not a strict regulation concerning women's travelling. However, in Joseon (1392–1897 CE), the women's sphere was limited to the inside of the house, and they were banned from visiting a temple or *Mu-dang*'s shrine. When a woman wanted to go out of her house, she had to wear *Jang-ot* (a long hood with which she covered her face). Around the turn into the 17th century women's right to own property was considerably weakened. Until the 16th century, sons and daughters inherited equal property but in the middle of the 17th century the discrimination between men and women became worse and then women's property rights were remarkably diminished. Thus financially women became more reliant on men.[30]

In the West, a shift in the perception of the right and worth of children started from the 16th century. The consideration of children as human beings with full human rights among people from all levels of society became widespread in the 19th century which echoed the end of the feudal era and the beginning of the modern capitalism. However, the 19th century Joseon was still under the dominant patriarchal feudal system. In the feudal Joseon, adults forced children to obey. And children were considered as objects to control not as whole people.[31]

Children, except those who belong to *Yang-ban* families, could not have an opportunity to go to school. They had to participate in economic activities and take care of their little siblings. Girls were more discriminated against than boys with regard to the opportunity of education. Almost all the parents recognized that it was useless to educate their daughters. The parents' only wish for their daughters was that they meet a good husband, serve well him and raise healthy children. One of the worst systems for girls in Joseon was early marriage. Early marriage was still widespread even in the early 20th century in Korea. Gijeon Kim gives an illustration of the life of girls who were married early, criticizing the system:

---

29. Ewha Institute for the Humanities, *Landscape*, 208–15.
30. Mun, "The Change of Women's Position in Family," 62–64.
31. Bae, "Society and Child," 195.

At such an early age to grow, girls are separated from their parents and sweet home, and have to work in a strange kitchen of their husband who they have never met with. They cannot enjoy life and wear good clothes. They suffer from maltreatment by husband's family.[32]

Children's disobedience to the adults' will was considered as destructive to the order of society. One of the Confucian ethics, *Jang-yu-yu-seo*[33] developed into the thought that young people should obey and respect the will of old people. In the period of Joseon which stressed hierarchical order, children were recognized as a being lower than an adult, and as just a family member rather than an independent being.

The hierarchical perspective of Confucianism also influenced on the understanding of the world after death and religious life in Joseon. In Confucian teaching, sons and daughters have to respect their parents. The respect of descendants continues even after the death of their ancestors. The respect for the dead is embodied in *Je-sa* (ancestor worship). Generally, *Je-sa* is held on the anniversary of the ancestor's death and traditional holidays. In *Je-sa*, descendants prepare cordially food and hold memorial rite in reverence for their ancestors.

Confucianism understands the world after death as a hierarchy. According to feudal hierarchy in Joseon, the procedure and object of *Je-sa* were strictly distinguished. Only *Cheon-ja* (literally son of sky, that means a king) was able to worship *Cheon* (god of sky). *Cheon-ja* and *Je-hu* (feudal lords) could hold sacrificial rites for *Sa-jik* (god of land and grain). *Je-sa* for Confucian saints such as Confucius and Mencius, were held only in *Munmyo* (Confucian shrine) by *Cheon-ja* in capital city and by *Je-hu* in local communities. Ordinary people could offer *Je-sa* to only their ancestors.[34] In *Je-sa* where the family is concerned, the hierarchical system is also well-founded. In the *Je-sa* for a father who died, the eldest son of the first wife offers *Cho-heon* (the first cup given to the soul of father), the first wife offers *A-heon* (the second cup), and a man among the family offers *Jong-heon* (the last cup). The order of *Bu-bok* (a deep bow to the soul) and *Um-bok* (eating food used for Je-sa), according to ages and distance of kin relationship, starts from the highest man and continues to the lowest.[35]

---

32. Kim, "Mit-myeo-neu-ri," 541–44.

33. Originally it means that brothers should respect each other. But this term was literally interpreted and applied in Joseon society as the meaning that there is an order between adults and children.

34. Gum, *Ghost and Ancestor Worship*, 87.

35. Lee, "Ju-Ja-Ga-Rye," 58.

For *Yang-ban*, *Je-sa* was part of their life. The family of Hee-mun Oh (1539–1613), a Confucian scholar of Joseon, is recorded to offer 25 times of *Je-sa* a year.[36] However, conducting *Je-sa* frequently does not mean that descendants respect well their ancestors who died. As I stated before, *Je-sa* is offered on the days having special meanings such as seasons and the day of death of an ancestor not an ordinary day. *Ye-gi*, a Confucian book, explains the reason why people should not conduct frequently *Je-sa*:

> It is not proper to conduct *Je-sa* frequently. If you conduct frequently *Je-sa*, you might be less respectful towards *Je-sa*. Yet, it is, also, not proper to do not conduct *Je-sa* for too long time. For, you would forget *Je-sa*.[37]

A Confucian scholar, Yutae Lee (1607–1684) says in his book, *Jeong-hun* that *Si-je* (seasonal ancestor worship) should be held 4 times a year, *Chun-bun* (spring), *Chu-bun* (fall), *Ha-ji* (summer) and *Dong-ji* (winter).[38] A sincere attitude, the thorough preparation and keeping properly the procedures are essential in *Je-sa*. On three days before the *Si-je*, all should clean their body and mind, and one day before the *Si-je*, all family members should clean house, clothes, dishes and utensils used for *Je-sa*. As to the food of *Je-sa*, three or four kinds of *Jeok* (fried meat with vegetables), six kinds of fruits, a bowl of *Poh* (dried slices of meat) and *Hae* (rice nectar), and a bowl of *Cheong-jang* (bean-paste soup) between vegetables are to be arranged.[39]

A crucial function of *Je-sa* is to maximize the affinity between family members. Basically, only the direct descendants of the dead can participate in *Je-sa* and eat the ritual food. Through *Je-sa*, the living descendants are connected with the dead ancestors. The scattered family members gather for *Je-sa* and solidify a family membership. It would be worth observing *Je-sa* in terms of family membership.

Who can lead *Je-sa*? Who can participate in *Je-sa*? These questions were very controversial issues in the period of Joseon. For, to become *Bong-sa-ja* (the leader of *Je-sa*) meant having priority to inherit property, and to participate in *Je-sa* meant verifying family membership. Until the 16th century, *Bong-sa-ja* was decided by various methods. *Yoon-hoe-bong-sa* was that sons and daughters took turns holding *Je-sa*. *Woe-son-bong-sa* was the *Je-sa* which was held by the descendants of the daughter of the dead. *Chong-bu-bong-sa* was conducted by the wife of the eldest son of the dead.

---

36. Lee, *Yeh-hak philosophy*, 116.
37. Lee, "Ju-Ja-Ga-Rye," 38–39.
38. Lee, *Yeh-hak philosophy*, 98.
39. Ibid., 116–119.

Sometimes, the concubine's son was able to hold *Je-sa*.[40] However, since the middle of Joseon, distinctions between paternal and maternal lines, the eldest son and other sons, the first wife's sons and concubine's sons, and sons and daughters were emphasized. These distinctions meant restructuring family membership centering on the eldest son of the first wife. From the middle of the 17th century, *Je-sa* for the father who died was held by only the eldest son of the first wife and his family, and spontaneously other family members were excluded from the *Je-sa*.[41]

2 Cultural Influences on Worship and the Eucharist of the PCK

Mu-gyo's Influence on Worship and the Eucharist

Mu-gyo, as the indigenous religion, has affected many aspects of worship and the eucharist of the PCK. First of all, the passion and devotion for religious life found in not only the PCK but also other Korean churches seem to be influenced by *Mu-gyo* faith.[42] In *Mu-gyo*, women were used to praying at dawn every day or during a certain period for their family or private wishes. They believed that a god would be impressed by their prayers which were fervently and repeatedly conducted and would lead to their wishes being fulfilled. Religious commitment and sincerity were the crucial values in *Mu-gyo*. Similarly, almost all Korean churches hold early morning prayers every day. On Friday late at night, *Cheol-ya Gido* (a prayer meeting at night) is held for about two hours. Also, there is *Jak-jeong Gido* (a planned prayer). For this prayer, many Korean Christians decide to pray for one month or 1000 days for a certain purpose. During *Geum-sik Gido* (fasting and prayer) people do not have food and sometimes even water. As well as prayer, in the early period of Korean Christianity, many Christians used to decide to offer their time for voluntary preaching in a heathen village. In 1905, Rev. Carl E. Kearns reported:

> We were very much surprised to see 625 days subscribed in a few minutes and a considerable number of additional subscriptions came in after the service closed. To distinguish this service from the daily witnessing to our believers which each Christian does as a matter of course, the terms of subscription required that the volunteer preacher leave home and spend the specified

---

40. Lee, "Ju-Ja-Ga-Rye," 50.
41. Ibid., 58.
42. Kim, *Biblical View on Blessing*, 65.

number of days at this own expense in a heathen village. Subscriptions were for five or ten days, or a week or a fortnight, to be fulfilled within six weeks after the class closed. One man who subscribed 150 days had to have this time limit extended. . . . Personally I know of about 3,000 days of volunteer preaching that has been done in all parts of the province.[43]

The religious passion led the PCK to emphasize more thorough preparations for the eucharist. In the PCK, it is not a strange experience of hearing an announcement that the eucharist will be held on the next Sunday service, therefore participants should prepare for the eucharist during week days with prayer and leading a holy life.

Another effect of *Mu-gyo* on worship and the eucharist of the PCK can be found in *Sa-kyeong-hoe* (a revival meeting or Bible study meeting).[44] *Sa-kyeong-hoe* has been one of the core growth engines of the PCK and other Korean churches. *Sa-kyeong-hoe* consists mainly of hymns, prayer and preaching without the eucharist. Originally *Sa-kyeong-hoe* was a special meeting different from the Sunday service.[45] However, gradually the *Sa-kyeong-hoe* style of worship came to prevail in the Sunday service. As a result, the recognition of the eucharist as a sacrament different from worship began to be embedded in the PCK.

In the process, *Mu-gyo* faith contributed to the spread of *Sa-kyeong-hoe* style of worship. Harvey Cox, exploring the reason for the growth of Pentecostalism in Korea, notes that many features of the worship in Pentecostal churches reflect *Mu-gyo*.[46] Although his focus is on Pentecostal church, he finds for a fact that other churches growing fast in Korea also have similar styles of worship to the Pentecostal church.[47] The shamanic features in the worship of those churches observed by Cox are the main elements of *Sa-kyeong-hoe*. Thus it is not difficult to find shamanic features in *Sa-kyeong-hoe*. One of the similarities between *Sa-kyeong-hoe* and shamanic practices is that participants seek personal benefits such as physical health, material blessings and peace of mind. The climax of *Gut* of *Mu-gyo* is invocation and ecstasy through which *Mu-dang* invites and makes contact with a god respectively. There is a general faith in *Mu-gyo* that *Mu-dang* has an ability

---

43. Kearns, "A Collection in Days of Preaching," 7–8.

44. In Korea, *Sa-kyeong-hoe* is also called *Bu-heung Sa-kyeong-hoe* or *Bu-heung-hoe*.

45. For more details on the origin and development of *Sa-kyeong-hoe* in the PCK, see chapter 2.

46. Cox, *Fire from Heaven*, 222.

47. Ibid., 222.

to heal those who suffer from illness through making contact with a god in ecstasy.[48] People share certain feelings of happiness and freedom from worries with *Mu-dang* in ecstasy, albeit temporally. Similarly, in *Sa-kyeong-hoe*, the main theme of participants' prayers is earthly blessings. Also, with mystical experiences such as speaking in tongues, prophecy and healing in *Sa-kyeong-hoe*, they feel spiritual satisfaction and freedom from life's worries and pain.[49] The attraction of the consolation gained from *Sa-kyeong-hoe* led the PCK to pursue a more emotional and enthusiastic style of worship rather than liturgical worship including the eucharist.

The Influence of Mugyo and Miruk Faith on the Eucharist in Minjung Theology

Minjung theology emerged in the 1970s with a theological reflection on "the oppressed in the Korean political situation."[50] Literally, *Minjung* can be translated as "the mass of the people."[51] However, Byung Mu Ahn who is considered the father of *Minjung* theology tried to connect *Minjung* with the ὄχλος (crowd) in the Gospel according to Mark. Ahn determined five characteristics of the ὄχλος:

> 1 Wherever Jesus went, there were always people who gathered around him. . . . 2 These people were the so-called sinners, who stood condemned in their society. . . . 3 There are cases where they (the *ochlos*) are differentiated from the disciples. . . . 4 The *ochlos* are contrasted with the ruling class from Jerusalem who attack and criticize Jesus as their enemy. . . . 5 Because the *ochlos* were against the rulers, the rulers were afraid of them and tried not to arouse their anger.[52]

Furthermore, Ahn distinguished the ὄχλος (crowd) in Mark from the λαος (people) in Luke. According to him, the λαος in Luke refers to the people of God who repent their sins and are baptized, but the ὄχλος in Mark "belong to a class of society which has been marginalized and abandoned."[53] Then, Ahn identified the ὄχλος with *Minjung* in Korea who were suppressed

---

48. Eliade, "Shamanism," 202.
49. Joon-sik Choi suggests a possibility that there would be the connection between the ritual of Mu-gyo and *Bu-heung-hoe*. See Choi, *Korea's Customs People's Faith*, 49–51.
50. Suh, "Minjung and Theology in Korea," 18.
51. Ibid., 17.
52. Ahn, "Jesus and the Minjung in the Gospel of Mark," 138–39.
53. Ibid., 149.

by an exploitative class. Ahn insisted that "God's will is to side with the *Minjung* completely and unconditionally."⁵⁴ In the 1980s, one of the goals of *Minjung* theology was the liberation of *Minjung* from the oppression of a dictatorial regime. Now, the *Minjung* theology of Korea, leading a social transformation movement, has developed into a representative theology of the Third World along with Liberation theology in Latin America.⁵⁵

One of the key understandings of *Minjung* theology concerning the eucharist is the recognition of the eucharist as an act of sharing a meal with *Minjung* rather than simply a ritual. Jesus' meal sharing with *Minjung* was an act of realizing the kingdom of God in this unequal world.⁵⁶ *Minjung* is a politically and economically oppressed class. The upper class extorts money and food from *Minjung*. As a result, the poor and hungry *Minjung* comes to be poorer and their starvation is worse. *Minjung* theology views that the salvation of *Minjung* includes not only spiritual but also political and economic liberation. For the salvation of *Minjung*, Jesus invited *Minjung* to his table and provided them with food. Also, in the eucharist, Jesus becomes the food for *Minjung*. Through the eucharist, the act of meal sharing with *Minjung*, Jesus presented a way of delivering *Minjung* and restoring the kingdom of God.⁵⁷

The equality of human beings, one of the foundations of *Minjung* theology, is found in *Mugyo*. Historically, *Mugyo* was the religion for *Minjung*. Especially in Joseon which made a severe discrimination according to age, class and sex, *Mugyo* was instrumental in consoling a weary body and soul of those seen to be of lower status especially women. Generally, in most religions a priest is male but the priest of *Mugyo*, *Mu-dang*, is female. In *Mugyo*, of course, there are male shamans but they are called *Baksu Mu-dang* and the number of *Baksu Mu-dang* is remarkably lower than *Mu-dang*. In addition, in *Gut*, the role of the male is mainly a helper, playing musical instruments such as *Buk* (drum) and *Jing* (gong) while *Mu-dang* leads the ritual practice.⁵⁸

The *Minjung*-oriented characteristic of *Minjung* theology is also observed in *Miruk* faith of *Dae-seung* Buddhism. *Yongwha Segye* which will be established by *Miruk* is a paradise on earth not in heaven. As *Miruk* faith takes a keen interest in the life of *Minjung*, social justice and economic and political liberation of *Minjung* are major themes of *Minjung* theology.

---

54. Ibid., 150.
55. Jo, "Several Tasks of Minjung Theology," 286.
56. Ahn, *Galilee Jesus*, 146.
57. Park, *Jesus Movement and Table Community*, 248–65.
58. Kim, *Study on Shamanism of Korea*, 16.

Minjung churches in the PCK have tried to participate in activities for *Minjung*. Almost all the churches are founded in industrial areas and slums and the main members of the churches are those who are politically oppressed and socially marginalized. During Sunday services, the churches more often conduct the eucharist than other protestant churches. Sometimes, they celebrate the eucharist before participating in an antigovernment campaign or a meeting for human rights of laborers. For them, participation in the eucharist means a union of participants with Jesus' body and blood. It, also, means the participants' decision to join the way of suffering and to live for *Minjung* in history and society following Jesus.[59] Another reason why they conduct the eucharist before participating in the meetings for *Minjung* is that doing so is to follow what Jesus did at the last supper. Under the military regime in South Korea between 1970s and 1980s, *Minjung* churches participated in meetings for the liberation of *Minjung* after the eucharist. The hostile government kept an eye on them. During or after the meeting, there was much suffering of participants such as forcibly being taken to the police station or imprisonment. Thus, just like Jesus who was arrested and suffered after the eucharist they joined the life of Jesus through the eucharist.[60] The more frequent celebrations of the eucharist in the Sunday service and active participation in social and political matters for *Minjung* through the eucharist offered a meaningful challenge to the PCK's traditional understanding of the eucharist which is appreciated as just a sacrament and not part of worship. However, this new approach to the eucharist attempted by *Minjung* theology failed to be widely accepted by the PCK.

The Influence of Confucianism on the Eucharist

Social Influence

The concept of *Li* and *Gi* of Confucianism not only explained the reason of differences between human beings but also was employed to justify the right of the ruling classes, men and adults to control the lower classes, women and children. This Confucian ideology permeated and formed the social system, culture and religion in Joseon. Christianity which rooted in the soil of Joseon came to spontaneously have Confucian characteristics.

There was a strong distinction between men and women in Joseon. The distinction of sex was applied to Christian worship and life. Until the early 20th century, many churches during worship divided men and women

---

59. Park, "Jesus' Table Community Movement and Church," 87–120.
60. Park, *Worship in the Presbyterian Church in Korea*, 131.

into different seats. Geumsan Church in Gimje and Dudong Church in Iksan which are preserved as historical relics show clearly the circumstances of that time's worship and culture. Both churches have a specific design of the worship place in an "L" shape. The goal of this design of building is so that men and women cannot see each other but a preacher can see all. Today, there is no Korean church which separates men from women in worship. Ostensibly the distinction between men and women in a place seems not a big issue. However, there have been many cases, where the distinction has led to a number of serious instances of discrimination against women in church policy. Some Protestant denominations in Korea such as *Hapdong* and *Gosin* ban women from becoming an ordained presbyter or pastor. It was not until the 1990s that the PCK allowed the ordination of women.[61] As a result, in the eucharist of the PCK, the roles of the pastor and the committee for the eucharist came to be occupied by men. The duties for women were mainly to prepare bread and wine before the eucharist, to become a receiver of bread and the cup from men during the eucharist, and to clean bread crumbs and utensils after the eucharist.

Confucianism also influenced the installation system of Korean churches. According to Scripture, the installation system never means a hierarchy. There are different kinds service and working in a church. Each one of us serves the body of Christ by the gifts from God (1 Cor 12). However, the idea of Confucianism which is deeply rooted in the consciousness of Koreans led church members to recognize the installation system as a hierarchy. Many church members who are accustomed to a Confucian hierarchical social system recognize a change of position from lay through deacon to presbyter as an upgrade of social status.[62] They also consider *Dang-hoe* (Session) which consists of presbyters and pastors as not a meeting to serve the church but the supreme decision making body with power and authority. It is typical in big Korean churches that candidates for a presbyter fight a fierce battle to win the election.

In such a hierarchical understanding of the installation system, Korean churches discern strictly between the baptized and the non-baptized. The non-baptized might not feel discriminated in ordinary church life. For, they would think that they could participate if they wished to. However, there is a service which prohibits the non-baptized from participating in. The service is the eucharist. As an example, the PCK bans people who are not baptized from coming to the table of the eucharist. Of course, such a

---

61. In 1994, the 79th Assembly of the PCK passed the bill regarding the ordination of women. In 1996, the PCK produced the first woman ordained presbyter and minister. Kim, *A Brief History of the Christian Church in Korea*, 257.

62. Lee, *New Church New Land*, 118.

eucharistic practice is not the special eucharistic characteristic of the PCK. Many mainstream churches in the world keep that eucharistic tradition. However, recently other Presbyterian Churches that had contributed to the formation of the PCK have changed stance on the issue of the participation of the non-baptized in the eucharist. There were four denominations which had influenced the formation of the PCK: the Presbyterian Church in USA, the Presbyterian Church in US, the Presbyterian Church of Australia (PCA) and the Canadian Presbyterian Church (CPC).[63] In these denominations, the open table practice, which allows the non-baptized to take part in the eucharist, is widespread today.[64] In contrast, the PCK keeps the traditional eucharistic regulation, which opens the eucharist to only the baptized, and repeatedly expresses a strong aversion to the open table. Compared to the western churches' perception of the open table, the PCK's robust inflexible response to the open table can be regarded as a key feature of the PCK's Eucharistic tradition that has been influenced by Confucian thought.

Confucianism also affected the PCK's view on the age of the participant in the eucharist. The idea of *Jang-yu-yu-seo* in Confucianism is a representative characteristic of Korean society. Children are generally recognized as those who should follow the plan and will of their parents in a family and the rules installed by adults in society. In addition, all have to respect someone who is older than them and even between twins hierarchical order by birth time is considered as an important ethical rule to be kept. The strict boundary and division by ages is also found in the eucharist. The constitution of the PCK says that only the baptized members who are over fifteen years old have the right to participate in the eucharist.[65] It is possible that the consideration of a certain age as a prerequisite for the eucharist would be to echo the reformed tradition which recognizes the significance of participants' confession of faith and knowledge of the eucharist. However, when considering other reformed denominations in the west which allow children to participate in the eucharist, this eucharistic regulation of the PCK seems to be influenced by Confucianism.

---

63. Park, "Legacy," 214–17.

64. In 1998 and 2004, regularizing the open table practice was proposed to the General Assembly of the Presbyterian Church of USA (PCUSA) but the bills remain unresolved. As to the recent discussions on the open table in the PCUSA, see Stubbs, *The Open Table*, 9–24. However, in practice, the PCUSA holds the open table policy. See Presbyterian Church (U.S.A.), *Invitation to Christ: A Guide to Sacramental Practices* (KY, Louisville: Office of Theology and Worship, 2006). For more details on the open table policy of the UCA and the CPC, see chapter 8 of this book.

65. The General Assembly of the Presbyterian Church of Korea, *Constitution*, 172.

Cultural Influence

In the early Joseon, whether a person's life succeeds or not depended on knowledge of Confucianism. The more knowledge of Confucianism a man had, the more he had a chance to become a government official and get a high position. Around the middle of Joseon, the number of Confucian scholars increased rapidly. They believed that the highest good was to learn and follow the teachings of Confucianism. As time went on, the teachings of Confucianism became the social norms and tradition. People in Joseon considered an attempt to break the norms and tradition as a sin and gradually turned into a conservative society which was afraid of challenge and change. Joseon society was led by conservatism as to tradition and rigorism as to norms. Today South Koreans still live under the influence of Confucian culture.

The conservatism and rigorism of Confucianism would affect the understanding of the PCK on church tradition and regulation of the eucharist. As observed before, the four Presbyterian Churches which deeply influenced the formation of the PCK are all support an open table whereas the PCK holds strongly to the traditional way of practicing the eucharist. In 2001, there was an attempt to discuss the issue of an open table in a synod in the PCK. I will explore this incident in detail in the next chapter. At that time, however, other synods in the PCK regarded even a discussion of an open table as a challenge to church tradition. After the incident, there was no further official discussion on the open table in the PCK. The four Presbyterian Churches and the PCK have shared the traditional eucharistic understanding, which allows only the baptized to participate in the eucharist, for a long time. What are the great differences between the four Presbyterian Churches and the PCK? The only difference among those churches is whether they are influenced by Confucianism or not.

Additionally, the PCK permits only those who are over the age of fifteen the participation in the eucharist. Chronological age restriction is also found in the eucharistic teachings of John Calvin, the founder of Presbyterianism. However, in recent decades there has been a tendency that Presbyterian churches in the west remove the age limit for the eucharist from their eucharistic regulations. In actual practice, pastors give not only children but also the non-baptized an opportunity to participate in the eucharist with a missional purpose. Unlike the churches in the west, the PCK still keeps the traditional eucharistic requirements, baptism and the age of fifteen. The PCK's conservative attitudes towards church tradition of the eucharist can be explained by Confucian influence on Korean churches.

Religious Influence

In terms of religion, Confucianism is embodied in *Je-sa* (ancestor worship). For centuries, religious beliefs and regulations based on *Je-sa* affected every aspect of Koreans' consciousness and life style. When Christianity was introduced into Korea, the eucharist was not a concept entirely unfamiliar to Koreans. The eucharist reminded Koreans of *Je-sa* because the two rituals shared many similarities. Spontaneously, religious characteristics which were included in *Je-sa* influenced the eucharistic theology and practice of Korean churches.

The first influence of *Je-sa* on the PCK can be found in the PCK's emphasis on the meaning of the death of Jesus in the eucharist. *Je-sa* is held on the date of death of an ancestor. The core of *Je-sa* is a remembrance of deceased ancestors. Koreans who are accustomed to *Je-sa* would understand, without great difficulty, the eucharist as a rite of memory of the death of Jesus. As a result, the meaning of the death and sacrifice of Jesus is the focuse rather than other themes in the eucharist of the PCK.

Secondly, Koreans' perspective of *Je-sa* affected the frequency of the eucharist in the PCK. Traditionally, the PCK holds the eucharist three or four times a year. The frequency was originally caused by the preaching centered worship tradition which was inherited from the early missionaries. Since the 1980s, however, the PCK has begun to recognize the eucharist as part of worship and stipulate the recognition in its constitution and worship books. Nevertheless, most churches in the PCK do not try to increase the frequency of the eucharist. Rather, they seem to be satisfied with the quarterly practice of the eucharist. This situation is well explained by the connection between the eucharist and *Je-sa*. In Korea, *Je-sa* is to be held on special days such as the anniversary of ancestor's death and the first days of the four seasons. A reason why *Je-sa* must not be frequently held was related to thorough preparations for *Je-sa*. Confucianism taught that *Je-sa* which is inadequately prepared disgrace ancestors and the whole family. When considering many Koreans who find similarities between the eucharist and *Je-sa*, it is possible for them to think that it is not proper that the eucharist is held every Sunday.

The attitude of thorough preparation in *Je-sa* seems to affect the emphasis on a pious and moral living of the participants in the eucharist in the PCK. In the early stage of Korean church history, people who wanted to receive baptism had to be a catechumen for at least six months to one year. Also, for baptism, they had to stop smoking and drinking. And to keep a moral life style and the Lord's Day was essential.⁶⁶ Even after being baptized, church members should keep a rigid church regulation. If there were some church members who did not keep the Lord's Day, they were banned from participating in the eucharist.⁶⁷ Likewise, a pious life and moral strictness were considered to be essential requirements for people who want to come to the table.

Thirdly, it is possible that the distinction between the baptized and the non-baptized in the eucharist of the PCK is further justified by the emphasis on membership in *Je-sa*. Who can participate in *Je-sa*? This question has been a very sensitive issue in *Je-sa* because to participate in *Je-sa* means not only to get family membership but also to share the heirship of family property. It seems that the emphasis on membership in *Je-sa* affected the PCK's strict distinction between the baptized and the non-baptized in the eucharist.

3 Summary and Evaluation

This chapter has explored the cultural background of Korea and its cultural influence on the eucharist of the PCK. Three main religions have been considered before the introduction of Protestantism into Korea: *Mu-gyo* (Shamanism), Buddhism and Confucianism.

Mu-gyo, as the oldest and indigenous religion of Korea, has deeply affected the lives of Koreans. In *Mu-gyo*, the role of *Mu-dang* (Shaman) is decisive. When people meet problems in life, they seek *Mu-dang* to solve the problems. Then, *Mu-dang* holds *Gut* (the ritual of *Mu-gyo*) where people pray their wishes to a god invited by *Mu-dang*. The main concerns of *Mu-gyo* are earthly blessings such as healing, exorcism, and the success of family business. *Mu-gyo*'s attachment to earthly happiness is caused by its negative concept of the life after death. In *Mu-gyo* faith, *Jeo-seung* (the place where after death souls have to go) is a hopeless and barren place. This faith of *Mu-gyo* has led Koreans to be more obsessed with the life of this world than the afterlife.

Buddhism was introduced into Korea around the fourth century CE. Until the period of Goryeo (918–1392 CE), Buddhism had been mainly used for the upper class as a ruling ideology. During the Joseon era (1392–1897 CE), however, Buddhism was suppressed under the policy of *Soong-yu-eok-bul* (meaning "to venerate Confucianism and to restrain Buddhism"). The Joseon Dynasty restrained Buddhist monks from coming into cities and forfeited Buddhist property. As a result, Buddhist monks had to move their

66. Ryu, *Early American Missionaries in Korea*, 111–12.
67. Ibid., 123.

temples deep into the mountains. Although politically Buddhism lost its position as the national religion, that situation came to be an opportunity to attain the position of the religion of people. In the process, *Miruk* (Maitreya) faith of Buddhism came to prevail particularly in the *Minjung* (lower class) of Joseon. Originally *Miruk* meant a Bodhisattva who will save the world in the future. However, *Miruk* faith blended with *Mu-gyo* faith which is closely connected with earthly life. Then, the *Minjung* came to equate *Miruk* with a god in *Mu-gyo* faith and pray to *Miruk* for their earthly blessings.

Confucianism was the national ideology of Joseon. *Seong-ri-hak* (one of the main theories of Confucianism) enabled Joseon to maintain its strong hierarchical social system, providing a theoretical basis for the division between the upper class and the lower class, men and women, and children and adults. Socially, there were four classes in Joseon and the distinction between the classes was strictly kept. Many Confucian scholars argued that women are inferior to men and should obey men, trying to maintain the patriarchal system of Joseon. Moreover, in Joseon children were not considered as human beings with full human rights. The inferiority of women, children and low classes was supported by Confucianism.

These cultural features have affected the eucharist of the PCK. The religious passion of *Mu-gyo* faith influenced the attitudes of the PCK towards the eucharist. The PCK viewed that participants in the eucharist need more thoroughgoing preparation because the eucharist is more important than the ordinary Sunday service. This perspective led the PCK to keep more strictly its eucharistic regulation regarding the prerequisites for the eucharist. On the other hand, *Mu-gyo*'s attachment to earthly life influenced the development of *Sa-kyeong-hoe* style of worship, which omits the eucharist, in the PCK. *Sa-kyeong-hoe* which shared many similarities with *Gut* (the ritual of *Mu-gyo*) comforted participants with enthusiastic prayer and preaching. Various mystical experiences such as healing, speaking in tongues, and exorcism also helped participants forget worries and see their lives more positively. *Sa-kyeong-hoe* style of worship came to prevail in the PCK and spontaneously the frequency of the eucharist decreased.

Mu-gyo and *Miruk* faiths influenced the eucharistic understanding of *Minjung* theology. The similarity between *Mu-gyo* faith and *Miruk* faith is the interest in the lower class, *Minjung*. This feature contributed to the appearance of *Minjung* theology and enabled it to interpret the eucharist as a tool for the liberation of *Minjung*. However, the new concept of the eucharist attempted by *Minjung* theology failed to influence deeply the PCK's traditional eucharistic understanding.

Confucianism has had the biggest influence on the eucharist of the PCK. The influence of Confucianism on the eucharist of the PCK can be divided into three dimensions. The first is social influence. Socially, Joseon which was based on Confucianism had a hierarchical system, distinguishing people by class, sex and age. Even though times have changed and the Joseon Dynasty disappeared a long time ago, the social characteristics based on Confucianism still linger in South Korea. As a result, the Confucian hierarchical system affected the church system and deepened distinction between the baptized and the non-baptized, men and women, and adults and children in the eucharist of the PCK. The second is cultural influence. Confucian culture is conservative as to tradition and strict as to norms. These cultural characteristics led the PCK to be reluctant to change church tradition and eucharistic regulations. The third is religious influence. The core of the Confucian rite, *Je-sa*, is a remembrance of the death of an ancestor. This characteristic would lead the PCK to focus the meaning of the sacrifice of Jesus in the eucharist. *Je-sa* is held on the date of the death of an ancestor and seasons. This perspective would affect the frequency and preparation of the eucharist of the PCK. As a result, most churches in the PCK hold the eucharist three to four times a year and ask participants to prepare thoroughly the eucharist.

While cultural features have mainly affected the PCK's attitudes towards the eucharist, the eucharistic tradition of the early American missionaries had a more direct impact on the formation of the eucharist of the PCK. In chapter 2, I will explore the eucharistic legacy of the missionaries and its influence on the PCK's eucharist. And I will also examine how the PCK has developed its eucharist theology, practice and particular emphases.

Chapter 2

The Formation and Development of Worship and the Eucharist of the PCK

GENERALLY, ALMOST ALL CHURCHES in the PCK celebrate the eucharist three to four times a year although recently the frequency has kept increasing. Likewise the PCK's worship could be characterized as the worship concentrating on the service of the word omitting the eucharist. Then, when did the preaching centred worship of the PCK begin? And in about 120 years of history of Korean Protestantism, how has the PCK preserved the eucharistic tradition? In this chapter I will explore through historical study the process of formation and development of worship in relationship to the eucharistic tradition and focal points of the eucharistic theology of the PCK.

1 The Formation of Worship and the Eucharist of the PCK

Worship Communities in Manchuria and Japan

The first Korean protestant worship community began not in Korea but in Manchuria.[1] John McIntyre and John Ross were sent as missionaries of the Scottish Bible Society into China in January and August 1872, respectively. The main region of their mission was Manchuria. When gauging the possibility of mission in Korea they met young Korean sellers in Manchuria. The missionaries tried to introduce Christianity to those young sellers, learning Korean language from them. Eventually, in 1879, John McIntyre baptized four youths who were Eung-chan Lee, Hong-joon Baek, Sung-ha Lee and Jin-gi Kim. Although not in Korea, the baptism was a historic moment when the first protestant Koreans were baptized. In the same year John Ross baptized Sang-ryoon Suh and Chung-song Kim. The youths who were sellers travelling between Korea and China became colporteurs and helped the ministry of the missionaries. They not only taught the missionaries the

---

1. Manchuria is a historical name of a large region of Northeast China.

Korean language but also supported John Ross in translating the whole New Testament into Korean. Later, the young Koreans became the leaders of the first Korean worship community in Manchuria and the northern territory of Korea. In 1879 Hong-joon Baek formed the first Christian community with his son-in-law Gwan-geun Kim and E-ryeon Kim, who was Gwan-geun's father, in Euiju of Korea and they ran a catechism class. This community grew into a worship community that had eighteen members by 1885. On 27 April 1889, the eighteen members included thirty-three men and women who were baptized by Horace G. Underwood in the Yalu River and later became the leaders of Euiju church.[2]

Sang-ryoon Suh returned to his home in Euiju with his little brother Kyeong-jo Suh who later became one of the first seven ordained pastors but soon they had to flee to Sorae because of their hometown's hostility towards Christians.[3] When considering that the Christian community formed by Hong-joon Baek in other regions of Euiju grew well, the receptivity to Christianity seems to have varied between villages. In 1885 the brothers began teaching about twenty seekers the Bible and catechism in their homes. It is assumed that around the end of 1886 they began to arrange a place to start regular Sunday worship. Later the worship community developed into the Sorae church.[4]

In Manchuria young Korean sellers from Euiju converted to Christianity. In Japan there was also contact between a Korean man Soo-jeong Lee and Christianity. As an unofficial secretary of Young-Hyo Park who was a member of the Korean delegation, Soo-jeong Lee arrived in Japan in September 1882. Soo-jeong Lee met Tzdasen who was a Japanese Christian and agriculturist, and learned the Bible from him. In April 1883 Soo-jeong Lee was baptized by G. W. Knox, a missionary from the United States at Noh Weol Jeong church in Tokyo. Soo-jeong Lee became the first baptized Korean protestant in Japan. In 1884 he translated the Gospel of Mark from Japanese into Korean at the request of Rev. Henry Loomis. When Horace G. Underwood and Henry G. Appenzeller arrived at Jemoolpo of Korea in 5 April 1885, the book brought by them was the Gospel of Mark translated by Soo-jeong Lee. In 24 June 1883, Soo-jeong Lee began Sunday school where Korean students studying in Japan were taught catechism. The Sunday school grew and formed the first Korean worship community in Tokyo at the end of 1883. Soo-jeong Lee and his worship community in Japan made a contribution to the formation of the worship of Korean church in a

2. See The Institute of Korean Church History, *A History of Korean Church*, 142–54.
3. Clark, *History of the Korean Church*, 46.
4. The Institute of Korean Church History, *A History of Korean Church*, 155–56.

quite different way from the church in Manchuria. Even though the Korean church in Japan was not involved directly in forming the worship of the Korean church as in Manchuria, Soo-jeong Lee and his community requested churches in America to urgently dispatch missionaries for the mission to Korea in 1883 and 1884. The repetitive appeals of Korean Christians in Japan helped move the Presbyterian and Methodist Boards of Mission of the United States. As a result, Horace G. Underwood and Henry G. Appenzeller who might be called the founders of Korean Protestant church were able to come to Korea.[5]

Missionaries and Worship

The first protestant missionary was Horace N. Allen sent by the Northern Presbyterian Church of the United States. He arrived in Korea in September 1884 as a medical missionary. A Presbyterian missionary, Horace G. Underwood and a Methodist missionary, Henry G. Appenzeller arrived at Jemoolpo on Easter Sunday April 5, 1885. After that, many missionaries of diverse denominational backgrounds from the United States, Canada, Australia and Europe came to Korea.[6] However, at that time the missionaries' public ministry was forbidden by the Korean government. Thus, in the early stage, missionaries had to gather for worship in their homes only with their family. The first worship of the missionaries was held in Horace Allen's house in 28 June 1885. In spite of different worship traditions, Methodist and Presbyterian missionaries led prayer meetings and Sunday services together in an ecumenical spirit. In 11 October 1885, eleven participants who were missionaries and their families celebrated the first eucharist in Korea.[7]

In 1886, Korea and France established a multi-article treaty. This treaty not only allowed Roman Catholic priests of France to stroll the street freely wearing their vestments[8] but also gave protestant missionaries some leeway for mission.[9] The meetings and worship of missionaries were gradually introduced to Koreans, and from January 1886 a few Koreans began to participate in a Week of Prayer and around August 1886 in Sunday service.[10] However, even after the condition for the mission improved, the missionaries still conducted a simple style of worship omitting the eucharist. The di-

5. Ibid., 157–62.
6. Kim, *Korean Church History*, 91.
7. Brown, *The Mastery of the Far East*, 505.
8. Ryu, *Early American Missionaries in Korea*, 87.
9. Ibid., 220.
10. Brown, *The Mastery of the Far East*, 505–6.

rect reason for that situation might be found in the worship tradition of the churches the missionaries were sent from. As previously discussed, there were four Presbyterian Churches which had an influence on the formation of the PCK. In the 1900s, the worship tradition of all these denominations was preaching centered worship.[11] Especially in the case of the Presbyterian churches in America which had most affected the formation of the constitution and worship books of the PCK, the recognition of the eucharist as part of worship was not expressed in an official document until the 1970s.[12]

The first Presbyterian church in Korea, Jeongdong Church (the predecessor of Saemoonan Church) was established by Horace G. Underwood in his house with fourteen men on September 27, 1887. On Christmas of the same year, the first eucharist was celebrated in Jeongdong Church. The participants of the eucharist were only seven.[13] The number was small but it was a historic event that represents the first Presbyterian eucharist with Koreans.

A Methodist missionary Henry G. Appenzeller used his house as a worship place. On Sunday afternoon July 24, 1887, he baptized the first Korean convert, Jungsang Park. On October 2, he baptized the second Korean convert Yong-Gyeong Han and immediately the eucharist was held.[14] Wilbur C. Swearer evaluated the sacraments as the beginning of "the evangelistic work of the Methodist Episcopal Mission."[15] On 9 October 1887 Appenzeller organized the first Methodist church in his house and named it Bethel Church.[16] The component of the first service of Bethel church was very simple. The service was commenced with the prayer of Appenzeller and then went on to a Scripture reading from the Gospel of Mark 1. After that, without preaching, the service was concluded by the prayer of a Korean, Mr. Chang.[17]

The simple style of worship in the early stages which was composed of prayer and Scripture readings began to have more liturgical figures with the construction of church buildings and the growth of indigenous

---

11. Although John Calvin recommended conducting the eucharist every week, most Reformed churches followed the Zwinglian tradition in terms of the frequency of the eucharist. See Vischer, *Christian Worship in Reformed Churches Past and Present*, 22–23.

12. The first official recognition of the eucharist as part of worship is observed in *The Worshipbook: Services* published in 1970 by the United Presbyterian Church in the U.S.A., the Presbyterian Church in the U.S., and the Cumberland Presbyterian Church. See ibid., 136–37.

13. Brown, *The Mastery of the Far East*, 506.

14. Lee, *Appenzeller*, 496.

15. Hulbert, *The Korea Review*, 256.

16. Bethel Church is the predecessor of Jeongdong Methodist church.

17. Joo, *Korean Methodist Worship*, 25–26.

church leaders who were not yet ordained. It is worth observing the order of worship which was presented in *Wi Won Ip Kyo In Kyu Do* (*For Teaching Doctrine to the Inquirers*) of an American Presbyterian missionary, Samuel Moffett. The order of worship suggested by Moffett for Korean churches was as follows: 1 Hymn; 2 Prayer; 3 Scripture Reading; 4 Prayer by one or two church members; 5 Hymn; 6 Lesson; 7 Prayer; 8 Offering; 9 Hymn.[18] In this service, the reason for the omission of the benediction is that the liturgy was made for family worship and small size worship without an ordained pastor.

The early form of worship around 1890s is also found in a Christian newspaper, *Joseon-Grisdoin-Hoebo* (*Joseon Christian Newspaper*). The order of worship suggested by the World Methodist Council for Korean churches was introduced by Appenzeller is as follows: 1 *Poongryu Sori* (Prelude); 2 Hymn (with Hymn book congregation stands); 3 The Apostles' Creed; 4 Prayer (Pastor and Congregation Kneel down. After the prayer chant the Lord's Prayer); 5 Anthem; 6 Reading from the Old Testament (Responsive reading is possible in reading Psalms); 7 Doxology (Glory is to the Father and the Son, from the beginning, this time forth and forever. Amen); 8 Reading from the New Testament; 9 Offerings and Announcement; 10 Hymn (with Hymn book congregation stands); 11 Preaching; 12 Prayer (a short prayer for becoming the sermon beneficial for congregation); 13 Hymn; 14 Apostolic benediction.[19]

These forms show a liturgical development when compared with the earliest form of worship. However, the distinctive character of these early forms of worship is preaching centred worship. Except for special seasons such as Christmas and Easter, ordinary Sunday services were conducted with only the service of the word omitting the eucharist.

2 Evangelization and Preaching Centred Worship

From the early stage in the history of the Korean Protestant church, the preaching centred worship was introduced by missionaries and became a typical worship style. For more concrete understanding on the worship tradition of the Korean protestant church, it would be helpful to investigate the reason why the missionaries passed down the preaching centered worship to the early Korean church in relation to historical context.

---

18. Moffett, *Wui Won Ip Kyo In Kyu Do*, 13–14.
19. Joo, *Korean Methodist Worship*, 177–78.

John L. Nevius' Mission Methods

In the late 1800s the priority of protestant missionaries was to evangelize Koreans and to establish churches. For missionaries, the evangelization and church growth were believed to be the most important reasons why they were sent to Korea. Although they devoted their lives to establish modern schools and hospitals in Korea, the main reason for all the exertions was to gain Korean converts. For the early missionaries, to introduce a theology or liturgy of the West would be considered as important but not an urgent matter. The purpose of all meetings and services of the missionaries was "one, the Christianization of the Nation."[20]

For the Christianization of Korea, missionaries did not hesitate to abandon not only their theological belief but also liturgical tradition. The style of worship chosen by the missionaries for the evangelization of Korea was a non-liturgical and preaching centred worship. This worship style came to be strengthened by John L. Nevius' Mission Methods. Nevius' mission methods developed over by his career and experience as a Presbyterian missionary to China for twenty-five years and influenced the Korean protestant church to form the preaching centered worship tradition. Nevius' articles and his *Methods of Mission Work* (1886) influenced the minds of young and inexperienced missionaries such as H. G. Underwood and H. G. Appenzeller. Presbyterian missionaries in Korea continuously requested John Nevius to visit Korea. Finally in June, 1890 Nevius arrived at Seoul and for two weeks he taught missionaries about his experience in China and mission methods. As a result, Presbyterian missionaries adopted Nevius' mission methods, with a few alterations, as official Presbyterian mission policy in 1891. Soon, Methodist missionaries also did not hesitate to follow Nevius' mission methods.

Regarding worship, one of the main contributions of Nevius' mission methods which might be summarized as "Self-Propagation, Self-Government and Self-Support" to the early Korean churches was to cultivate an independent spirit in order that each local church could worship in the circumstances where there was a lack of missionaries and ordained pastors. In unorganized Christian communities, a lay man led worship and ministry except baptism and the eucharist. Thus, for ordinary Sunday services, there was no choice but to worship in a quite simple order. Although all church members respected worship leaders, it was difficult for them to provide a subtly crafted sermon, as they did not have the necessary training or education for preaching. In that situation, a lesson replaced the sermon

---

20. Underwood, *The Call of Korea*, 188.

and the service was concluded with a hymn not a benediction.[21] Generally, local churches were able to have a chance to hold sacraments one or two times a year when a missionary visited them. A church leader disciplined candidates for baptism in advance and on the day of the appointment a missionary officiated at baptism and the eucharist after a catechism.[22] In the situation of a lack of ordained pastors, missionaries had to visit villages as many as possible. In the early stage of Korean church history, the journey of the missionaries to visit local churches was necessary and played a crucial role for the growth of Korean church.

The emphasis of Nevius' mission methods on Bible study also influenced the formation of Korean protestant worship.[23] Korean Christians were well known for their devotion in studying the Bible. Thus the missionary, Charles Deming named Koreans "student of the Bible."[24] Bible study came to be adopted under the name of *Sa-kyeong-hoe* (a revival meeting or Bible study meeting) in the Korean church. *Sa-kyeong-hoe* was held in winter, the agricultural off-season, for one to two weeks. The main purpose of *Sa-kyeong-hoe* was Bible study but participants were taught rules for church organization and catechism as well. At most, hundreds of people gathered for *Sa-kyeong-hoe*. In the early stage *Sa-kyeong-hoe* was held at a big church in a city and the host church provided accommodation for participants from the countryside. Generally, the order of *Sa-kyeong-hoe* was as follows. According to accommodation, they began the day with prayer and hymns in the early morning. After breakfast, they gathered in the church building and had a time for meditation for 30 minutes, and then they studied the Bible in groups. In the afternoon, again they studied the Bible and had time to learn hymns. In the late afternoon, they visited house by house for propagation and invited people to the evening meeting. In the evening, a large scale service which had a style similar to Frontier Worship was held with all participants of *Sa-kyeong-hoe* and non-Christians who were also invited.[25] *Sa-kyeong-hoe* reached its peak at the meeting held at Jang Dae Hyeon church in Pyeong Yang from 6 to 15 January 1907. The climax of the *Sa-kyeong-hoe* was the time of prayer after the sermon in the night meetings. All participants prayed aloud but there was "a subdued, perfect harmony"[26] in the prayer.

21. Ohk, "The Early Mission Policy of Korean Presbyterian," 175.
22. Kearns, "Itineration," 225.
23. Nevius, *Methods of Mission Work*, 40–41.
24. Deming, "The Korean Christian," 153.
25. See Cho, *Korean Church and Renewal of Worship*, 33–69.
26. McCune, "The Holy Spirit in Pyeng Yang," 1.

The missionary G. Lee at the same scene portrayed the atmosphere of the night after the prayer:

> After the prayer there were a few testimonies, and then the leader announced a song, asking the audience to rise and stating that all those who wished to go home could do so, as we intended to stay until morning, if there were men who wished to remain that long and confess their sins. A great many went, but between five and six hundred remained. These we gathered into one ell of the building, and then began a meeting the like of which none of us had ever seen. After prayer, confessions were called for, and immediately the Spirit of God seemed to descend on that audience. Man after man would rise, confess his sins, break down and weep, and then throw himself to the floor and beat the floor with his fists in a perfect agony of conviction.[27]

Even though the meeting at Jang Dae Hyeon church concluded on 15 January 1907, the fervor of the meeting spread throughout the whole country and gave impetus to the emergence of Revival Movement in Korea. The worship style of the revival meeting composed of hymns, prayers and sermons came to be spontaneously embedded in the worship tradition of Korean church.

3 The Development of Worship and the Eucharist of the PCK

The Inauguration of the PCK

In the early period of Korean church, the missionaries' ecumenical spirit for the Christianization of Korea was much stronger than the distinctiveness of their denominations. The missionaries' ecumenical cooperation came to be enhanced in *Sa-kyeong-hoe*. They believed that the *Sa-kyeong-hoe* was the most effective season for the revival of the Korean church. Transcending the denominational boundaries, they gathered all their abilities and strengths for the revival of Korea. In 1905, ahead of the *Sa-kyeong-hoe*, the General Council of missionaries offered a suggestion to the missionaries in Korea:

> . . . as far as possible, during the revival season, the entire missionary body withdraw from literary work, country itineration and other lines not bearing directly on the work in hand, so that

---

27. Lee, "How the Spirit Came to Pyeng Yang," 34.

the entire thought, prayer, and effort may be directed to this one supreme end.[28]

However, from the early of 1900s the mood of ecumenism among missionaries began to change. Each denomination established a seminary to produce Korean pastors. Not only the theology but also the worship style began to reflect each denomination's colour. At the same time, constitutions or books of worship which contained denominational characteristics were published.

In 1901 a Presbyterian missionary, Samuel A. Moffett established the first seminary of the PCK in Pyeong Yang. He began to teach two students, Jong-sup Kim and Gi-chang Bang, and the number of students increased more as time went by. In 1907, 38 missionaries and 40 Korean elders organized the Independent Korean Presbyterian Church. At the same year, seven Korean students, Sun-joo Gil, Jeon-baek Yang, Keong-jo Suh, Seok-jin Han, In-seo Song, Gi-chang Bang and Gi-poong Lee who had just graduated from Pyeong Yang Presbyterian Theological Seminary were ordained.[29] In the history of worship of the PCK, 1907 was the turning point. The leader of worship came to be changed from a lay man to an ordained pastor. As a result, the style and content of worship began to develop more liturgically.

The PCK's Worship and the Eucharist in the Early 1900s

Charles Allen Clark's *Moksa Jibup* (*Pastoral Theology*) shows the development of worship from the early simple style composed of hymn, prayer and lesson or sermon to a more liturgical one. From 1908 Clark became a professor of Preaching and Ministry at Pyeong Yang Presbyterian Seminary. In *Moksa Jibup* he suggested a new order of worship led by an ordained pastor. The order of worship included Confession of Sins and Word of Pardon, which were the traditional orders of the liturgies of John Calvin and the Presbyterian Church. The church was persuaded to use the Psalms more frequently during worship. In addition, Clark strongly suggested using both methods of Scripture Reading which were *Lectio Selecta* and *Lectio Continua* in worship. The Apostles' Creed and recitation of the Ten Commandments were also added to the order of worship.[30]

28. The General Council, "A Call to A Special Effort," 30.
29. Clark, *History of the Korean Church*, 144.
30. Clark, *Moksa Jibup*, 179–80. Sunday Service order suggested by Clark: Introduction (Biblical verses, prayer or hymn) – Confession of sins (Psalm 51; 32; 6; 38; 102; 130; 143 – Hymn – Scripture Reading: Lectio Selecta – The Apostles' Creed, the Ten Commandments or the Creed of each church – Hymn – Scripture Reading – the text relating to Sermon – Prayer of Congregation – Hymn – Offering and Prayer

The introduction of liturgical worship by Clark in 1919 seems to not only be a pastoral and liturgical consideration but also be related to the historical context of Korea. After the Eulsa Restriction Treaty of 17 November, 1905 as a result of which Japan deprived Korea of diplomatic sovereignty, missionaries' political stands were divided. Missionaries such as Gale and Scranton supported pro-Japanese activities. J. S. Gale argued for the justification of the Eulsa Restriction Treaty, saying that if the treaty was not agreed to Korea would have been crushed by Russia.[31] Scranton dismissed the Epworth League which was the only youth organization of the Methodist church in Korea because it participated in political activities of opposing Japan's colonial rule.[32] On the contrary, missionaries such as Noble[33] and Hulbert[34] supported actively the independence of Korea, criticizing pro-Japanese missionaries and the United States government sympathetic to Japan's violation of the sovereignty of Korea.

However, many missionaries moved towards a politically centrist stance upholding the division of religion and state. The main reason for the missionaries' decision was to protect the church from Japan's oppression. Considerable numbers of the participants in the anti-Japanese independence movement were Christians and Japan regarded churches as the base of the operation for the movement.[35] In 1911 following the 105-Man Incident which was fabricated by Japanese government for the suppression of Korea's independence movement, over seven hundred Koreans who were mostly Christians and twenty-four Presbyterian and Methodist missionaries were arrested. Worship in churches and the life of missionaries were monitored by Japanese policemen.[36] Under this situation, missionaries had to make urgent decisions for the Korean church. It seems natural that they, as missionaries, came to focus on the evangelization rather than political independence of Korea. C. A. Clark's basic concern as a missionary would also be the growth of Korean church amid stability. On February 15, 1908 C. A. Clark insisted that the most important thing was that the church should not participate in political matters because the church was a

---

– Announcement – Hymn – Sermon – Prayer after sermon – Hymn – Benediction – Meditation. See ibid., 195–97.

31. Gale, *Korea in Transition*, 38–39.

32. Methodist Episcopal Church Board of Foreign Missions, *Annual Report*, 322.

33. Presbyterian Church in the U.S.A. Board of Foreign Missions, *The Annual Report*, 269.

34. Hulbert, *The Passing of Korea*, 222–24.

35. Clark, *History of the Korean Church*, 129–30.

36. Yoon, *The Study on The 105-Man Incident and Sinminhoe*, 6–27.

spiritual organization.³⁷ This view was developed further by Clark in 1919 with the publication of his liturgical book, *Moksa Jibup*. For, in the same year, the Samil Movement, the Korean resistance movement to Japanese colonial rule, occurred. In the process of suppression of the movement, the Japanese government persecuted severely churches as most leaders of the movement were Christians. In this situation where the survival of Christianity was threatened by persecution, Clark was worried about the future of the Korean church. He wanted to shift the attention of Christian leaders from political involvement to worship and church life. This was the intention behind the publication of his book, *Moksa Jibup*.

On the other hand, Clark, as an expert in the practical theology of the only Presbyterian seminary at that time, tried to recover the Presbyterian tradition in worship through his *Moksa Jibup* but his efforts to establish a Presbyterian worship style in Presbyterian churches seem to be in vain. About 10 years after *Moksa Jibup* was introduced, Korean Presbyterian churches still followed Moffett's simple worship structure³⁸ which was influenced by Nevius.³⁹ The order of Andong Church's Sunday service in 1928⁴⁰ seems to basically follow the order of Moffett's liturgy. In Andong Church's worship, the Hymn is sung three times like Moffett. In addition, the order of Offering following the Sermon is the same as Moffett contrasting with Clark's order where the Offering is before the Sermon. The Prayer before the Scripture Reading is also the same pattern as Moffett. It is worth observing that in Andong Church a presbyter or deacon leads the Prayer like Moffett. In contrast, Clark suggests that an ordained pastor takes charge of the Prayer of Congregation: "A pastor ought to prepare the Prayer of Congregation because the prayer is not for his own sake but for church. This prayer of pastor will be a standard of prayer of church members."⁴¹

An interesting observation is the use of Psalms in Andong Church's Sunday Service. The Psalms which is not present in Moffett, is added in Andong Church's Sunday Service. Regarding the Psalms, did Andong

37. Paik, *The History of Protestant Missions in Korea*, 402.

38. Sunday Service worship order suggested by Moffett: Hymn – Prayer – Scripture Reading – Prayer – Hymn – Lesson – Prayer – Offering – Hymn. See Moffett, *Wui Won Ip Kyo In Kyu Do*, 13–14.

39. For more details on the development of the PCK's worship in early period, see Kim, "The Early Korean Presbyterian Church Worship," 535.

40. The worship order of Andong Church Sunday Service on January 1, 1928 : A silent prayer – Hymn 4 – Psalms 1 – The Lord's Prayer – Announcement – Hymn 32 – Prayer Deacon Chun Bae Kim – Scripture Reading (Acts 7:1–8) – Sermon – Offering – Prayer: Deacon Seong Man Kim – Hymn 3 – Benediction. See Andong Church History Committee, *Andong Church History 90 Years*, 101.

41. Clark, *Moksa Jibup*, 182.

Church follow Clark? The use of the Psalms was possibly influenced by the Methodist tradition rather than by Clark. For Clark emphasizes the use of the Psalms in worship for the Confession of Sins, while the early order of worship introduced by a Methodist missionary, in *Joseon-Grisdoin-Hoebo* (*Joseon Christian Newspaper*)[42] provides proof of the use of the Psalms in worship as in Andong Church. Furthermore, the Lord's Prayer located in the first part of the worship of Andong Church also seems to echo the Methodist worship tradition. The Lord's Prayer is a representative element of early Methodist worship. In the Christmas Service of 1887 held in Bethel chapel, Appenzeller gave his first Korean sermon. The order of the service was as follows: 1 Baptism (Myeong-ok Kim); 2 Hymn; 3 Prayer (in Korean, Scranton); 4 Scripture Reading (Matt 2); 5 Scripture Reading (Luke 2, Scranton); 6 Sermon ("Give him the name Jesus," Matt 1:21, Appenzeller); 7 The Lord's Prayer; 8 Hymn; 9 Benediction.[43] In 1910, the Methodist Church in Korea published *Daegangryeong Gwa Gyucheuk* (*Doctrine and Discipline*) which became a guide for the Methodist Sunday service. This book is presumed to be translated from the Discipline 1908 of the Methodist Episcopal Church.[44] The order of the Lord's Prayer introduced into the Sunday service in *Daegangryeong Gwa Gyucheuk* is after the Prayer for Congregation.[45] These Methodist features which are found in the Andong Presbyterian Church Sunday Service order indicate an ecumenism in the early period of the Korean protestant church. At that time, there was little distinction between denominations. Churches exerted their efforts to evangelize Korea. It was never strange that Presbyterians and Methodists worshiped together. In such a cooperative atmosphere, the Methodist worship tradition which was translated into Korean at least 9 years earlier than Presbyterian worship book by Clark would spontaneously be introduced and used in the Presbyterian church.[46]

The Saemoonan Church Sunday service on 30 October 1932 depends highly on Moffett with a few alterations in order.[47] Regarding the structure,

---

42. Appenzeller, *Joseon-Grisdoin-Hoebo*, 12 January 1898.

43. Appenzeller, *Diary*, December 25, 1887. See Joo, *Korean Methodist Worship*, 28.

44. Kim, *The Study of Formation of Sunday Service Presented in Worship Book*, 177.

45. Methodist Episcopal Church, *Methodist Church Doctrine*, 52–55.

46. Park, "Understanding on Holy Communion of the Early Methodist Church in Korea," 138–39.

47. The order of Saemoonan Church Sunday Service held on October 30, 1932: A silent prayer – Hymn – Prayer (Presbyter or church member) – Psalms – Scripture Reading – Hymn – Sermon – Prayer – Offering – Prayer – Announcement – Hymn – Benediction. See Saemoonan Church History Committee, *Saemoonan Church History 100 years*, 239.

the Saemoonan Church worship is almost the same as Moffett. The Hymn is offered three times and the Offering is placed after the Sermon reflecting Moffett. Like the Andong Church, the use of the Psalms which seems to be influenced by the Methodist tradition is presented in Saemoonan worship. A special feature is the Announcement placed between the Offering after the Sermon and the Benediction. More than 10 years after that Clark's *Moksa Jibup* which contained the Presbyterian worship tradition was introduced in 1919, the majority of Korean Presbyterian churches still followed Moffett's order of worship and the Methodist tradition.

Directories of Worship in the Early 1900s

The first directory of worship of the PCK was included in the draft of the first constitution that C. A. Clark completed in 1919. The book was published officially in 1921. Yet, almost all the contents of the directory of worship 1921 were taken from the *Directory for Worship* of the Presbyterian Church in the United States 1894.[48] The directory was edited several times and in 1934 it came to be equipped with the most similar contents to the recent editions. The directory of worship 1934 deals with worship from chapter 2 to 6.[49] Chapter 2 explains the preparation of worship. Chapters 3 to 6 contain an explanation of Scripture Reading, Psalms and Hymns, Prayer, and Sermons respectively. Chapters from 9 to 11 deal with the eucharist in the section on sacrament with baptism, not part of worship. Although the book did not present an actual order of Sunday service it could be inferred from the order of chapters of the book that, undoubtedly, the order of worship was the preaching centered worship composed of hymn, prayer and sermon. Since then, several further editions have been published, but there has been no conspicuous change with regard to either structure or content for over 60 years. For much of its eucharistic theology, the PCK simply translated the Westminster Confession of Faith into Korean and used that as the basis of its beliefs.

---

48. Lee, *A Study of History and Prospect on Presbyterian Worship Model*, 229–34.

49. The General Assembly of the Presbyterian Church of Korea, *Constitution*, 218–30.

The Liturgical Movement and Its Influence on the Eucharist of the PCK

From the early 1980s the influence of the Ecumenical Movement, revealed in documents such as *Baptism, Eucharist and Ministry* (BEM), slowly began to be absorbed into some of the PCK's thinking about worship. The Ecumenical Movement led Korean liturgists, focusing on the preaching centered worship, to have an interest in liturgical worship of various denominations. The Lima liturgy, a precious product of the Ecumenical Movement, laid a cornerstone for the Liturgical Movement in Korea in the 1980s. Those who led the Liturgical Movement were the professors of worship and preaching at seminaries. The Liturgical Movement had strong repercussions on the protestant worship tradition in Korea that is preaching centered worship. The Liturgical Movement unfolded in various ways. One of the most notable changes was the introduction and publication of church year calendars, lectionary and worship books in protestant churches. In 1981, *Calendar for the Plan of Worship and Preaching* by Jang-bok Jung, a professor of worship and preaching at Presbyterian College and Theological Seminary, was published. In 1984 as, firstly, a similar form of worship book, *85 Handbook of Worship and Preaching* was published. After that, other denominations began to publish worship books such as *Worship and Pulpit* and the *Worship Book*.[50]

Another reflection of this influence in the PCK can be seen in the directory of worship of 1983. In 1982 the 67th General Assembly had passed the revised bill so as to worship and the result came to be contained in the directory of worship included in the *Constitution* of 1983.[51] Compared to the former eucharistic theology kept from the early of 1900s to before the directory of worship of 1983, the most distinctive change observed is in the place of the eucharist in worship. While in the earlier directories, which stood firmly in a preaching-centered worship tradition, the eucharist was treated in a section of the book on "sacraments," alongside baptism, separate from the Sunday service material, the directory of worship of 1983 began to place the eucharist as part of the Sunday service. In addition, the book gives an instruction that worship including the eucharist should be frequently conducted because worship itself consists of the Word of God and the Eucharist. In 1980s, BEM had success in changing the PCK's recognition of the eucharist as part of worship but the theology and shape of the eucharistic

---

50. See Jung, *Calendar for the Plan of Worship and Preaching*; Jung, *85 Handbook of Worship and Preaching*; Park, *Worship and Pulpit*; The Korean Methodist Church Mission, *The Korean Methodist Church Worship Book*.

51. See The General Assembly of the Presbyterian Church of Korea, *Constitution*, 1983.

service presented in BEM failed to influence the official documents of the PCK until the 1990s.

The Book of Common Worship 1997

It was only with the *Book of Common Worship* (BCW) 1997[52] that more radical change, reflecting BEM, was made to the shape of the PCK's eucharist. Whilst former worship directories had relied deeply on the teachings of the Westminster Confession of Faith, the BCW 1997 enriched the content and theology of the eucharist by introducing the influence of the five key understandings of the eucharist articulated in the ecumenical consensus gathered in BEM.[53] First of all, the BCW 1997 gives more clearly an understanding of the eucharist as part of worship, explaining the order of Sunday service more fully than in the former editions.

Furthermore, the BCW 1997 presents as a sample eight orders of Sunday service in order that the church can choose one of them according to circumstances. Among them, five are made of only the service of the Word and three, Sunday Service 6, 7, and 8, include the eucharist as part of worship.[54] Also, as to the frequency of the eucharist, chapter 3 of the BCW 1997 urges the church to celebrate as frequently as possible the eucharist in remembrance of the death and resurrection of Jesus.[55] Nevertheless, there appears to be a limitation in embodying the five key understandings of BEM in actual practice of the eucharist. The samples of Sunday service including the eucharist keep preserving the former understanding of the eucharist, that emphasizes the death of Jesus and sacrificial meaning of the last supper.

A central theme penetrating the actual practice of the eucharist in the BCW 1997 is the sacrifice of Jesus. The eucharist is the place of remembering the death of Jesus and of representing the Lord's flesh which was injured and torn and the blood which was shed from Jesus' precious body. Concerning the emphasis on the death of Jesus, it would be worth observing the addresses for the eucharist presented in Sunday Services 6, 7, and 8 respectively:

---

52. See Committee on the Book of Common Worship, *The Book of Common Worship*, 1997.

53. BEM contains five meanings of the Eucharist: The Eucharist as Thanksgiving to the Father; as *Anamnesis* or Memorial of Christ; as Invocation of the Spirit; as Communion of the Faithful; as Meal of the Kingdom. For more details, see World Council of Churches, *Baptism, Eucharist and Ministry*, 10–15.

54. Committee on the Book of Common Worship, 1997, 42–74.

55. Ibid., 84.

> Dear friends, this Holy Communion is, in remembrance of Christ, the rite of remembering his death and resurrection until his coming again.[56]
>
> Brothers and sisters who have been bought at the price of the holy blood of the Lord, Holy Communion is the rite to remember the death of the Lord in remembrance of Christ until his return.[57]
>
> Today's Holy Communion given by the Lord is not just for a celebration but the place where we deeply commemorate and reenact the flesh of the Lord which was wounded and torn and the blood which was shed from the precious body for us. We must remember the scene and make a decision of the new covenant so that the Lord's flesh becomes my flesh and the Lord's blood flows in our veins.[58]

The act of breaking the bread is also considered as having an important meaning in the PCK's eucharist, because it is through the moment the death of the Lord might be dramatically shown to all participants. Through this moment, participants remember the Lord who was torn and injured for themselves. Furthermore, the eucharist is recognized as the last paschal meal shared with disciples whom Jesus loved. In other words, Jesus was the paschal lamb, and the bread and wine were the flesh and blood of the lamb. Before distributing the bread and the cup, the following statement is made by the pastor:

> Now, when you receive the Lord's bread, ponder upon the Lord's flesh injured for us, and have it with thanksgiving sincerely offered to God. . . . Now, receive the Lord's cup, and ponder upon the Lord's precious blood shed to the last drop for us, and have the cup with thanksgiving sincerely offered to God.[59]

---

56. Ibid., 53.
57. Ibid., 59.
58. Ibid., 70.
59. Ibid., 72.

The Book of Common Worship 2008

A Broad Eucharistic Understanding

More recently, the latest worship directory of the PCK, the BCW 2008 shows a drastic change in the eucharist especially in actual practice.[60] The BCW 2008 has entirely removed a separate category on "sacraments" and has instead included both baptism and the eucharist amongst its resources for Sunday worship. As a result, the appreciation of the eucharist as part of Sunday worship has been more deeply embedded in the worship of the PCK.

Compared with the BCW 1997, one of the most significant changes found in the BCW 2008 is an effort to contain the various meanings of the eucharist in actual practice. The eighth sample of the Sunday service includes the liturgy of the eucharist and expresses the eucharist as a feast in "Invitation to the Eucharist":

> This is a feast of joy of people of God. All peoples will come from north and south, and from east and west and sit at table of the Kingdom of God. This is the Lord's table. Our Lord invites those who believe in him to the feast he has prepared. Let us participate in the feast of heaven the Lord has prepared for us.[61]

Additionally, the BCW 2008 provides as a guide nine sample services for the seasons: Advent, Christmas, Epiphany, Lent, Passion/Palm Sunday, Good Friday (1), Good Friday (2), Easter Vigil Service, Day of Pentecost. All, except the services of Lent, Good Friday (1) and (2), include the eucharist. Among the six services including the eucharist, while the service of Epiphany preserves the traditional understanding of the eucharist that is sacrifice, others express various meanings. First of all, in "Invitation to the Eucharist" of Advent the festive and communal meanings of the eucharist are well presented:

> Beloved brothers and sisters, this Holy Communion is a joyful event which has been prepared by God. In the Kingdom of God, people of the Lord will come from north, south, east and west and sit at the table of the Lord. The Lord has provided this Holy Communion. Our Lord invites those who believe in him to the feast offered by him.[62]

---

60. See Committee on the Book of Common Worship, *The Book of Common Worship*, 2008.
61. Ibid., 77.
62. Ibid., 120.

The focus of the thanksgiving prayer for the eucharist is also on other reasons rather than deliverance through the sacrifice of Jesus. The reasons for thanksgiving include created in the image of God, giving life and breath, choosing us as God's children and sending Jesus into the world. Especially, in illustrating the life of Jesus, the death on the cross is mentioned but the event of death is recognized as just a moment in the whole life of Jesus from the incarnation to the ascension. The more important theme than the death is the expectation of the second coming of Jesus:

> The Lord, following the will of God, carried the cross and was killed by people whom Jesus loved. However, we praise the Lord who resurrected from the dead, reigns over this world and now becomes the friend of sinners. When the kingdom that the Lord has promised will come, we will celebrate the victory with the Lord. In remembrance of the Lord Jesus, now we will share the bread and cup. We will convey to all people the news of your death and resurrection. Holy God, we pray that send us the Holy Spirit, make us be grafted in Christ the Lord by sharing the bread, provide us new life, and let us live as people who are his very own until we participate in the feast with the Lord in glory.[63]

In the Christmas service, the diversity of the eucharist is well presented. The time of holding the eucharist is the day full of glory of heaven and the peace of world. Those who gather to worship after hearing the good news of the birth of Christ come to the holy table with thanks and joy. Also, in prayer of the eucharist, the focus is not the sacrifice of Jesus but Jesus Christ who came into the world through incarnation. Therefore, Jesus Christ is the gift of God given to human beings.[64]

The Easter Vigil Service also shows a considerable development. Firstly, in the "Invitation," the eucharist is the place of grace that the risen Lord has provided. More interestingly, there is a new illustration of Jesus as the bread of life. In the eucharist of Easter Vigil Service there is an attempt to view the eucharist from the perspective of the Fourth Gospel by calling Jesus the bread of life, forming a contrast to the PCK's traditional understanding of Jesus of the last supper as the paschal lamb based on the institution narratives which are from the Synoptic Gospels and 1 Corinthians 11. The next distinctive feature is found in the "Epiclesis" of the Easter Vigil.[65] The definition of the eucharist illustrated in the prayer is the meal after resurrection shared by Jesus with two disciples on the way to Emmaus (Luke 24), not

---

63. Ibid., 121.
64. Ibid., 126-28.
65. Ibid., 162–63.

the last supper (Matt 26, Mark 14, Luke 22 and 1 Cor 11). Again, in "Lesson before Communion" the Emmaus story is mentioned:

> The risen Lord first of all met his disciples at table. The risen Jesus shared a meal with the disciples on the way to Emmaus and also by the Sea of Tiberias with Peter and other disciples. The disciples realized that Jesus really rose again in participating in the same table with Jesus. Now we are across from the holy table which the risen Lord has prepared for us. The Lord today gives for us the bread and cup of the Lord. Now we will receive the bread and cup according to the will of our Lord.[66]

Ecumenical Association

The BCW 2008 also provides a variety of eucharistic prayers which draw on sources not only in other reformed churches but also the Roman Catholic, Greek Orthodox and Lutheran traditions. First of all, the BCW 2008 uses a new type of prayer such as the Litany and *Kyrie Eleison* which are very familiar to Roman Catholic and Lutheran but foreign to the PCK. The BCW 2008 does not use the Greek term *Kyrie Eleison* but, instead, translates it into Korean language. In addition, *Kyrie Eleison* is not recited but sung. The lyrics of the song are as follows:

> *Juyeo, Juyeo, Woorirul Bulssanghee Yeogisoseo* (Lord, Lord, have mercy on us).
> *Grisdoyeo, Grisdoyeo, Woorirul Bulssanghee Yeogisoseo* (Christ, Christ, have mercy on us).
> *Juyeo, Juyeo, Woorirul Bulssanghee Yeogisoseo* (Lord, Lord, have mercy on us).[67]

In chapter 1, the addition of the Creed in the order of worship could be, also, considered as an effect of the ecumenical movement on the PCK worship. In mentioning the Creed, the BCW 2008 introduces the Nicene Creed (CE 325) along with the Apostles' Creed (CE 404). Traditionally, the PCK has confessed the Apostles' Creed (CE 404) as a confession of faith. The BCW 2008 notes that not only the Apostles' Creed (CE 404) but also the Nicene Creed (CE 325) were officially and historically chosen by church.[68]

---

66. Ibid., 163.
67. Ibid., 73.
68. Ibid., 34–35.

A distinctive feature of the BCW 2008 is to add the Peace as part of the order of worship. The Peace goes back to the Kiss of Peace of the early church and is found in the service of the Roman Catholic Church, Orthodox Church and some protestant churches preserving the liturgical tradition as well. In the PCK worship, a simple greeting between participants is generally placed in the order of announcement after sermon has replaced the Peace.[69] Seeking to shed light on the origin and meaning of the Peace, the BCW 2008 places it as a crucial part of the order of worship.

The blessing of baptismal water has been traditionally placed as a crucial element in baptism in the Eastern Orthodox and the Roman Catholic churches but in the reformed tradition the order had been banned by reformers due to a different theological perception of the nature of baptismal water.[70] However, recently through conversations between denominations the PCK has been able to have a new understanding of the blessing of baptismal water and to engage with valuable meanings of this element which had been erased by the passion of reformers. The BCW 2008 gives six baptismal rites. Among them, "Thanksgiving Prayer for Baptismal Water" is placed in "Baptism for Infant and Child" and in "Baptism for Those Who Have A Mental Disability" even though the PCK's theological appreciation of the blessing is still different from the Roman Catholic and the Eastern Orthodox churches.

Renewal of Baptism was newly introduced into the Easter Vigil Service of the BCW 2008. The purpose of the Renewal of Baptism, which is conducted after baptizing candidates, is to make all church members who have already been baptized remember the meaning and promise of baptism. The pastor, followed by an elder holding a baptismal font, sprinkles baptismal water on a congregation by using palm branches and proclaims the words "remember your baptism."[71] The Renewal of Baptism presented in the BCW 2008 seems to be indebted to that of the Roman Catholic Church in terms of form and the practice of the rite being conducted in Easter Service.

While the Roman Catholic and the Pentecostal churches have treated healing as significant in worship, in the Sunday worship of the PCK healing was not a matter of grave concern. Occasionally, through sermons the message with regard to healing was proclaimed but the worship was not specially designed for healing but as a normal Sunday service. Instead, the PCK has developed services focused on healing through the Friday prayer or special

69. Ibid., 34.

70. Regarding the Eastern Orthodox and the Roman Catholic churches' understanding of the blessing of baptismal water, see Thurian and Wainwright, *Baptism and Eucharist Ecumenical Convergence in Celebration*, 12–22.

71. Ibid., 161.

meetings. The healing service introduced in the BCW 2008 is conducted as a Sunday service and is quite liturgical. The focus of the service as a whole is on healing. Songs, prayers and sermons in all the orders of worship contain the theme of healing. In particular, the service includes the eucharist. The climax of the service is a prayer with the placing of hands on the sick after the eucharist.[72] Regarding healing, chapter 8, Rite of Traditional Holidays, also contains a service of caring for patients. Notable is that the centre of the service is the eucharist. Generally, the PCK's traditional rite for the pastor's visitation for a patient is composed of a song, a simple lesson and prayer for healing. However, the BCW 2008 introduces the rite, focusing on the eucharist, for patients who cannot participate in Sunday service due to their illness so that the patients feel and experience that they are part of the body of Christ.[73]

The clearer expression of the meal after the resurrection as central to the eucharist in the BCW 2008 is also evidence of the PCK's active participation in the ecumenical movement. In 1995, the WCC working group made a proposal for celebrating the eucharist in ecumenical contexts. The working group based the proposal on three eucharistic texts: Luke 24:13–35, Justin Martyr's *First Apology* 67 and Eusebius' *Ecclesiastical History* 5:24. In particular, the working group's explanation of the first text gives a significant eucharistic perspective which recognizes the meal after the resurrection as a eucharist:

> ... the account in Luke 24:13–35 of the risen Christ transforming two despairing disciples and sending them on mission by means of his living interpretation of the scriptures and his presence in the breaking of bread.[74]

It took over a decade for the PCK to express the WCC's recognition of the meal after the resurrection as the eucharist in the BCW 2008. Moreover, the interpretation of the meal in Luke 24 as a eucharist is included only in the Easter Vigil Service in the BCW 2008. However, in spite of all these limitations, this expansion of the PCK's eucharistic understanding indicates that the PCK keeps trying to have conversations with ecumenical partners.

Response to Pastoral Needs

The BCW 2008 also shows an effort to respond to more varied and complicated pastoral needs according to the change of pastoral circumstances. As the BCW 1997 gives eight samples of a Sunday service only for adults,

72. Ibid., 205–13.
73. Ibid., 507–12.
74. See Best and Heller, *Eucharistic Worship in Ecumenical Contexts*, 29.

the need for guidelines regarding services for various generations and communities already conducted in church has been continuously raised. For this, the BCW 2008 provides directions for "Worship for Youth," "Modern Worship or Contemporary Worship," "Intergenerational Corporate Worship" and "Healing Service."

First of all, "Worship for Youth" and "Modern Worship" consist of contemporary songs, testimony, skit drama, dance and video as materials for praise and sermons.[75] These two services do not contain the eucharist. The majority of the participants of the services are young people and seekers. According to the PCK's eucharistic regulation, children under 15 years old and the un-baptized are banned from participating in the eucharist. Thus, the PCK would recognize that the services do not need the eucharist.

On the other hand, "Intergenerational Corporate Worship" is designed for families in order to overcome the limitation of the recent PCK's worship style divided by generation.[76] One of the unique aspects of this worship is that the eucharist is conducted despite children who are not baptized participating in. However, even in this worship, the PCK tries to keep the principle of the eucharist by providing a guide as below:

> Those who are baptized come in a row and take the bread and cup. Pastor and distributors of bread and the cup receive firstly the elements. It could be possible that participants receive bread and the cup respectively, or bread dipped in wine or grape juice. For children, it is meaningful that they are in the place of Holy Communion and even may observe those who take bread and the cup, although they cannot receive the elements. For infants who cannot understand the eucharist, it would be acceptable to prepare special food for the infants.[77]

Regarding baptism, there have been concerns in the pastoral field about those who are marginalized because the law of church keeps silent about them. The BCW 2008 shows a theological struggle and development for the marginalized. While the BCW 1997 provides only two types of baptism, "Infant Baptism" for babies under two years old and "Adult Baptism" for those who are over fifteen years old, the BCW 2008 adds "Baptism for Children" for those who are three to fourteen years old. In addition, the BCW 2008 gives two types of baptism for the mentally disabled who can express their will, and for those who cannot.[78]

---

75. Committee on the Book of Common Worship, 2008, 186–99.

76. Ibid., 200–205.

77. Ibid., 205.

78. Ibid., 90–98.

There are many services which are not treated in the BCW 1997 but have traditionally been conducted by the PCK. The BCW 2008 contains the services such as "Sunday Service for Independent Day," "Sunday Service for Thanksgiving Day" and "New Year's Eve Service." A drastic change of the BCW 2008 is found in the establishment of worship for communities beyond local churches. For this, the book provides guides of service related to General Assembly, Presbytery, institutions and chapel as well.[79]

The BCW 2008 shows an effort in hearing the voice of the pastoral field as to not only worship but also rites. A rite for dispatch of a missionary is added in "Rites for Installation." "Family Rites" includes "Thanksgiving Service for Birth," "Service for Baby Dedication" which is held when a baby participates in worship for the first time, and "Service for Blessing Children" which is conducted to celebrate children's entrance into a school. For marriage, considering the recent social change that international marriages have become more frequent, the BCW 2008 adds "Outline of International Marriage" and also gives a sample service for wedding anniversaries. In rites, a significant change is found in the rites of funerals. The BCW 1997 focuses on funeral rites in ordinary circumstances but the BCW 2008 provides funeral rites which might be used in various situations such as the death of a child or non believer, body donation, cremation and natural burial.[80]

It is true that the paschal understanding of the eucharist and traditional eucharistic regulations still prevail in the PCK's actual practice, but the number of churches, which try more often to celebrate the eucharist in the Sunday service with well balanced eucharistic theology, is gradually increasing. Crucially the PCK is demonstrating an effort to broaden the eucharistic theology and practice through the BCW 2008.

The First Step towards the Open Table

Around the turn of the 21st century, the PCK gave some expression of a desire to enlarge its traditional understanding of the eucharist. In 2001, it was resolved in a session of Yanglim Church, which belongs to the Jeonnam Synod, to practise an "open table." This meant that the age restriction of 15 would be dropped, with its links to views about a person's capacity or need for faith and repentance, and so would the requirement for baptism before the eucharist.[81] The Yanglim Church proposed to bring its resolution to

---

79. Ibid., 236–49.

80. Ibid., 277–445.

81. It is clearly stipulated in the constitution of the PCK that only baptized persons who are 15 years old or more are allowed to participate in the eucharist. See The

the Jeonnam Synod Meeting. Therefore, the 112th Meeting of the Jeonnam Synod, held from the 17th to 18th of April 2001, passed the resolution that those who are not baptized could participate in the eucharist. Furthermore, the meeting decided to introduce a bill on theology of the open table to the national General Assembly Meeting of the PCK. However, as the decision of the Jeonnam Synod became known to other Synods, strong opposition was raised from others. As a result, the Jeonnam Synod had to hold an extraordinary meeting and finally changed its plan. Its final decision was to retract the resolution passed and the plan to introduce the bill regarding the open table to the General Assembly Meeting, and to set up a special committee to study a theology of the open table.[82] So although the bill on the open table was *not* introduced in the General Assembly Meeting, the decision of the Jeonnam Synod became the first *official* discussion on the open table in the PCK, and it also became a catalyst that made not only theologians but pastors think afresh about the theology of the eucharist.

However, contrary to a general expectation that, with the first official discussion, various studies would be conducted and theological understanding of the eucharist could be deepened and enlarged, editorials in newspapers and various published liturgical studies repeated simply the church's traditional position on the eucharist. What were the grounds for the PCK's traditional understanding of the eucharist? This question is the basis for a discussion in the last section of this chapter.

4 The Authority Sought by the PCK in Understanding the Eucharist

Scripture

The PCK has upheld the principle of *Sola Scriptura* of the Reformers. Thus, in the PCK, Scripture has become the most important authority in evaluating the eucharist. As a result, Matt 26, Mark 14, Luke 22 and 1 Corinthians 11 (the so-called "last supper" stories) which are believed by the PCK as directly reflecting the historical Jesus' institution of the eucharist have played a crucial role in forming the eucharistic practice and theology although recently the Easter Vigil Service of the BCW 2008 has tried to interpret the meal in the Emmaus story in Luke 24 as the eucharist after the resurrection of Jesus. The BCW 2008 fixes only the four last supper stories for

---

General Assembly of The Presbyterian Church of Korea, *Constitution*, 172.

82. Park, "Debates on the eucharist, decided as one year study in Presbytery," *Gidokgongbo*, June 23, 2001.

"the Words of Institution" in an explanation of the order of worship.[83] The PCK's traditional understanding of the eucharist based on the last supper stories penetrates the PCK's eucharistic theology and practice. Thus, the PCK's eucharistic view extracted from the PCK's worship books could be reconstructed as follows: Jesus instituted the eucharist on the night before his arrest (Matt 26, Mark 14, Luke 22 and 1 Cor 11); Jesus gave his disciples the commandment that Jesus' death, resurrection and coming again should be remembered through the eucharist (Luke 22 and 1 Cor 11); The eucharist was the paschal meal (Matt 26, Mark 14 and Luke 22); In the eucharist, Jesus is recognized as the paschal lamb, the bread as the body, and the cup as the blood of Jesus all of which are connected with the death on the cross (Matt 26, Mark 14 and Luke 22); The action of "the breaking of bread" is an essential part of the order of worship (Matt 26, Mark 14, Luke 22 and 1 Cor 11).

Early Church Documents from the First and Second Centuries

The eucharistic directions which are recorded in the early church documents have been accepted as reliable sources by the PCK in preserving its traditional eucharistic theology. In recognition, the PCK has offered the texts of the early church's regulations regarding the eucharist as an evidence against challengers of the traditional eucharistic theology, which, at least in the PCK, has become quite an effective way to preserve its eucharistic tradition.

Among ancient church documents the *Didache* is known as the earliest containing a primitive regional church's life and worship. In the PCK, the *Didache* is recognized as inheriting historically the teachings of Jesus. Jangbok Jung who has led the PCK's worship and liturgy since the 1980s, gives an understanding on the *Didache* in his article as to prayer of the Korean church:

> A lesson of prayer taught by apostles shows well us that the Lord's Prayer was crucially used as a prototype of prayer in the early church. The apostles of Jesus made and used *Didache* as a guide of ministry with a sense of duty that the church established by them had to develop on a sound basis. This guide book, *the Teaching of the Twelve Apostles*, was used with an authority equivalent to the Scripture.[84]

Here, it would be worth noting shortly about the contents of the *Didache*. The *Didache* made up of 16 chapters demonstrates how, after Jesus'

---

83. Committee on the Book of Common Worship, 2008, 36.
84. Jung, "A New Understanding," 139.

death, resurrection and ascension, the Didache's community in the early Jewish Christian setting separated from the influence of Judaism and kept and developed not only the Christian identity but also the eucharist. In the *Didache*, the first instruction of the eucharist appears in chapter 9. The order of the eucharist is firstly the cup and then bread. In the prayer for both the cup and the bread, thanksgiving and glory to the Father is expressed along with the anticipation of the *Parousia* (the *Didache* 9:1–4).[85] Then, chapter 9 adds a quite special instruction related with baptism as follows:

> Let no one eat or drink of your thanksgiving [meal] save those who have been baptized in the name of the Lord, since the Lord has said concerning this, "Do not give what is holy to the dogs" (the *Didache* 9:5).[86]

The *Didache* seems to offer part of Matthew 7:6 as a proof for supporting the so-called fenced table: "Do not give what is holy to dogs" (Matt 7:6).[87] In this text, it can be read that Didache's community is worrying about staining the holy cup and bread by those who are not baptized. To the Didache community the non-baptized seems to be recognized as people who do not have an understanding of the meaning and value of the eucharist and, thus, are unworthy to receive the eucharist.

The *Didache*'s teaching as to who can receive bread and the cup has been referred to as a crucial authority to preserve the traditional understanding of the PCK on the eucharist. Around the early years of the 21st century, when there were debates on whether the non-baptized can receive bread and the cup or not, Jang-bok Jung refers to the *Didache* 9:5, arguing that the PCK's eucharistic tradition which allows only the baptized to participate in the eucharist inherits the early church tradition which was from the eucharist of Jesus.[88]

The *Apostolic Tradition*, generally believed to be written by Hippolytus of Rome in the PCK, has played an important role in preserving the PCK's eucharistic tradition. Jang-bok Jung finds four values from his study on *the Apostolic Tradition*. Firstly, through this book, the content and reality of worship in the post-apostolic period can be discovered. The second value

---

85. Bradshaw, *Eucharistic Origin*, 24.

86. Niederwimmer, *The Didache*, 144.

87. It is unsure that *Didache* quoted directly this verse from Matthew as the *Gospel of Thomas* includes also this verse. In addition, Niederwimmer suggests a possibility of a quotation from an oral tradition or an unknown apocryphal gospel. See, Niederwimmer, *The Didache*, 153.

88. Jung, "The Original Sacrament of Presbyterian Church," *Gidokgongbo*, vol. 2321, May 26, 2001.

is a finding that the "Consecration Prayer" traditionally conducted without recognition of its root by Anglican and Roman Catholic churches inherits this book. Thirdly, this book confirms the roots of Christian worship which has developed and altered as time goes on. Finally, *the Apostolic Tradition* is the most reliable text book for reconstructing the root of worship.[89] Such a generous view of *the Apostolic Tradition* seems to be the result of neglecting the recent academic achievement in studies on the early church documents.[90]

Jang-bok Jung finds authority for the PCK's eucharistic tradition from *the Apostolic Tradition*. He insists that recently many protestant churches lost important values which can be recovered in *the Apostolic Tradition* because of the eucharist being wrongly conducted due to an attempt to open the table to those who are not baptized:

> This teaching [of the *Didache*, that the eucharist should be open to the only baptized] which was given from apostles was inherited by Apostolic Fathers. Around the third century, when churches were severely persecuted, *the Apostolic Tradition* edited by Hippolytus teaches rigorously regarding the qualification of the participants in the eucharist that "a catechumen shall not sit at the Lord's Supper," preserving fully the teaching [of the *Didache*] received around 100 AD. The early church's worship was divided into two parts which are the liturgy of the Word and the Eucharist. In the first part, the liturgy of the Word, everyone who wants to participate in to do so, but in the eucharist only those who are baptized conduct the eucharist letting catechumen go home.... This church tradition shows well that since the early period of church history the qualification of participant has been rigidly kept.[91]

John Calvin (1509–1564) and the Westminster Confession of Faith and Catechisms (1647)

The PCK uses as a doctrine the Westminster Confession of Faith and Catechisms which reflect the reformation faith of John Calvin. The PCK

---

89. Jung, "The Current Illumination," 278–79.

90. Bradshaw estimates that *the Apostolic Tradition* dates from the fourth century or later. He criticizes those who wrongly attribute the book to Hippolytus of Rome. For more detail, see Bradshaw, *Eucharistic Origin* and Bradshaw et al., *The Apostolic Tradition*, 1–17.

91. Jung, "The Original Sacrament of Presbyterian Church," *Gidokgongbo*, vol. 2321, May 26, 2001. Brackets are added by this author.

contains these books in its constitution book. In addition, the Westminster Directory, which derives from the John Knox liturgy influenced by John Calvin, has been used as the most influential guide in the formation and development of the PCK's directories for worship. Thus, the PCK highly depends on John Calvin and Westminster Confession of Faith, Catechisms and Directory in considering matters related to the eucharist.

With regard to the relationship between baptism and the eucharist, the PCK seeks authority from Calvin. For the PCK recognizes Calvin as not only the founder of the Presbyterian Church but also a reformer who recovered the early church tradition which preserved the eucharist of the historical Jesus but was misunderstood by the churches in the Middle Ages. Calvin gives a clear expression of the formula that is baptism before the eucharist in *Catechism of the Church of Geneva*:

> Baptism is for us a kind of entry into the Church. For in it we have a testimony that we, while otherwise strangers and aliens, were received into the family of God, so that we are reckoned among his household. But the Supper testifies that God himself manifests to us as Father by feeding our souls.[92]

In order to disclose the reasons why Calvin preserves the closed table, it would be worth exploring the full range of Calvin's eucharistic theology relating to baptism. Calvin strongly emphasizes two preparations for worthily receiving the eucharist. Firstly, participants should repent their sins.[93] In the Roman Catholic Church, participants were led to take part in the eucharist for their forgiveness of sins but Calvin urged participants to repent their sins in order to receive the eucharist. Hence, White names Calvin's eucharist the "penitential eucharist"[94] because of the emphasis on the thorough preparation. Calvin's penitence includes not only words but a whole life marked by passion for emulating Christ and desires "to cherish, defend, and assist"[95] brethren of Christ (*Institutes of Christian Religion*, IV, 17. 40).

Secondly, participants should inspect whether their faith in the Lord Jesus Christ is true or not. The inspection of individual faith embraces self-examination. Calvin, in his *Short Treatise on the Holy Supper of our Lord Jesus Christ*, mentioned the qualification of participants for the eucharist, enjoining them to thoroughly prepare themselves. For this instruction, Calvin depends on Paul's teaching in 1 Corinthians 11:29: "For all who eat and

---

92. Reid, *Calvin*, 133.
93. Calvin, *Short Treatise on the Holy Supper of our Lord Jesus Christ*, 1540, para. 24.
94. White, *Protestant Worship*, 66.
95. Calvin, *Institutes of Christian Religion*, Vol. 2, 1418.

drink without discerning the body, eat and drink judgment against themselves." For Calvin, bread and wine consecrated by the word of God are no longer ordinary food and wine but are believed as spiritually holy flesh and blood of the Lord Jesus. As eating and drinking the holy food and wine is the holiest act on earth, to participate indifferently in the eucharist is "intolerable blasphemy."[96] The reason for Calvin's emphasis on the participants' careful preparation for the eucharist is not only that the eucharist itself is holy but that people who eat and drink unworthily are judged by God. Thus Calvin says that for the worthy participants the sacred food becomes the food nourishing their body and soul but for people who are with "a soul corrupted by malice and wickedness" the eucharist becomes "a deadly poison"[97] (*Institutes of Christian Religion*, IV, 17. 40).

However, Calvin evidently recognizes the limitation of human effort. Faith begins from the realization of sins and faith is trusting in God's great love which invites even sinners to the eucharist that is the place of grace.[98] Calvin confesses that no matter how much humans try to be holy, they cannot escape from the being sinful:

> For if it is a question of our seeking worthiness by ourselves, we are undone; only despair and deadly ruin remain to us. Although we try with all our strength, we shall make no headway, except that in the end we shall be most unworthy, after we have labored mightily in pursuit of worthiness (*Institutes of Christian Religion*, IV, 17. 41).[99]

We are still unworthy and are sinners. Nevertheless, the Lord bestows the holy food by kindness on us and allows us to participate in the feast by His mercy. Calvin recognizes that the eucharist is "not for the perfect, but for weak and feeble" (*Institutes of Christian Religion*, IV, 17. 42).[100] From this point of view, while Calvin emphasizes self-examination for the eucharist, at the same time he opposes the eucharist recognized as a sacrifice accompanying human's effort. Calvin clearly notes that the subject of the sacrifice of the eucharist is God not humans. The eucharist is totally concerned with the sacrifice of Jesus Christ. For Calvin, it is an error that human sacrifice joins in the sacrifice of Jesus. Calvin says:

---

96. Calvin, *Short Treatise on the Holy Supper of our Lord Jesus Christ*, 1540, para. 20.
97. Calvin, *Institutes of Christian Religion*, Vol. 2, 1417.
98. Calvin, *Short Treatise on the Holy Supper of our Lord Jesus Christ*, 1540, para. 24.
99. Calvin, *Institutes of Christian Religion*, Vol. 2, 1418.
100. Ibid., 1420.

> For if we do not recognise the death of the Lord Jesus, and regard it as our only sacrifice by which he has reconciled us to the Father, effacing all the faults for which we were accountable to his justice, we destroy its virtue. If we do not acknowledge Jesus Christ to be the only sacrifice, or, as we commonly call it, priest, by whose intercession we are restored to the Father's favour, we rob him of his honour and do him high injustice.[101]

The sacrifice of Jesus is not repeated continuously in the eucharist. The eucharist is the "memorial" of the sacrifice which was accomplished once by Christ Jesus. Refusing papists' understanding of the eucharist as the repetitive sacrifice, Calvin maintains that the benefit from the eucharist is "not by the merit of the act, but because of the promises which are given us, provided we receive them in faith."[102]

Similarly, recognizing the limitation of human preparation, Calvin at the same time focuses on penitence and faith as the two prerequisites for the eucharist. Furthermore, in Calvin, the two prerequisites are closely linked with baptism. Baptism is a sign and seal of forgiveness of sins and a "token of confession," (*Institutes of Christian Religion*, IV, 15. 13)[103] which means that the candidates for baptism can publicly confess their sins before a congregation. Moreover, baptism is a confirmation of faith. For that, Calvin gives as an explanation the story of Cornelius the centurion, in Act 10, who is baptized after receiving the Holy Spirit. The baptism he received is for "an ampler forgiveness of sins . . . but a surer exercise of faith" (*Institutes of Christian Religion*, IV, 15. 15)[104] Thus, for Calvin, baptism is a sacrament accompanying faith and repentance. In other words, baptism is the most confidential proof to confirm publicly faith and repentance. Yet, in the case of infants, Calvin allows an exception. Infants can also receive baptism without their confession of faith and sins but after growing when they reach an age to be able to confess it they should do it by the Confirmation.[105]

The Westminster Confession of Faith contained in the PCK's Constitution follows Calvin's view on baptism. In the Westminster Shorter Catechism, baptism is a seal through which we are engrafted into Christ and no one can be baptized without faith and the profession of obedience

---

101. Calvin, *Short Treatise on the Holy Supper of our Lord Jesus Christ, 1540*, para. 34.

102. Ibid., para. 51.

103. Calvin, *Institutes of Christian Religion*, Vol. 2, 1313.

104. Ibid., 1315.

105. Calvin, *Catechism of the Church of Geneva: Being a Form of Instruction for Children, 1545*, n. d.

to Christ.[106] Calvin's emphasis on faith and repentance is slightly changed here into faith and obedience to Christ. But, that does not mean that in the eucharistic theology of the PCK the place of repentance is weakened or neglected. Actually, all liturgies for the eucharist presented in the BCW 1997[107] and the BCW 2008[108] include the Confession of Sins as an essential worship order.

In the Westminster Confession, also, Christ in the eucharist is not a sacrifice offered to God the Father following Calvin. Refusing sacrificial understanding of the eucharist, the Westminster Confession states that the eucharist is the memorial of Jesus who offered himself at once on the cross.[109] Here, the "memorial" is understood by the PCK as not Zwingli's Memorialism but Calvin's Pneumatic Presence.[110]

As to the preparation for the eucharist, like Calvin, the Westminster Confession enjoins participants to "examine themselves of their knowledge to discern the Lord's body, of their faith to feed upon him, of their repentance, love, and new obedience."[111] For, to participate in the eucharist unworthily is eating and drinking the judgment of God.[112] The Constitution of the PCK, Part 4, Worship and Ceremony, states clearly the formula that is baptism before the eucharist:

> We who became a member of church by baptism proceed to the eucharist, that is, the word of God that we can see through grace. The Lord of the eucharist is Jesus Christ in the Holy Spirit.[113]

Based on these theological principles, the Constitution of the PCK instructs that the eucharist should be delivered to the baptized 15 years and over. In the case of the infant baptized, when they become 15 years old, after the Confirmation, they can participate in the eucharist.[114] This means that the PCK interprets 15 years as the proper age of a young person able to discern and believe the eucharist as the body and blood of Jesus. Given

---

106. The General Assembly of The Presbyterian Church of Korea, *Constitution*, 2001, 56.

107. Committee on the Book of Common Worship, 1997, 39–78.

108. Committee on the Book of Common Worship, 2008, 56–83.

109. The General Assembly of The Presbyterian Church of Korea, *Constitution*, 2001, 126.

110. Committee on the Book of Common Worship, 2008, 55.

111. The General Assembly of The Presbyterian Church of Korea, *Constitution*, 2001, 57.

112. Ibid., 128.

113. Ibid., 243.

114. Ibid., 172.

those facts, the PCK seems to make an effort to preserve more thoroughly the eucharist through the dual safeguard which is baptism and the age of 15, compared with Calvin who thought the ideal age as ten (*Institutes of Christian Religion*, IV, 19. 13).[115] However, a development with regard to baptism is found in the most recent directory for worship, the BCW 2008. The BCW 2008 newly introduces Baptism for Children and attempts to embrace those between three to fourteen years old who had been previously excluded from baptism.[116] Although the PCK still preserves the eucharistic principle of "the baptized 15 years and over" according to Constitution, the change in the recognition of baptism could potentially bring a change in the eucharist as well.

5 Summary and Evaluation

This chapter has studied the history and theology of the eucharist of the PCK. In the late nineteenth century, the tradition of worship passed on by the Presbyterian and Methodist missionaries was preaching centered worship. At that time, the eucharist, which was recognized as a sacrament along with baptism, was conducted three or four times a year. This tradition was preserved for over ninety years and began to change only with the influence of the ecumenical movement in the early 1980s. The PCK's understanding of worship slowly began to shift from preaching centered worship to the worship including the eucharist. The PCK positively accepted the five understandings of the eucharist outlined in the BEM document in the BCW 1997. The recognition of the eucharist as part of Sunday service is more enhanced in the BCW 2008. In addition, the BCW 2008 broadens the PCK's appreciation of the eucharist by providing various eucharistic prayers from not only other Protestant churches but also the Roman Catholic and Greek Orthodox churches.

While the PCK expanded its eucharistic understanding through participating in the ecumenical movement, there was a significant challenge to the PCK's traditional understanding of the eucharist in 2001. The Jeonnam Synod passed the resolution supporting the open table, and it was the first official discussion of the open table in the PCK. The resolution created repercussions for many churches in the PCK. Influential theologians and church leaders in the PCK began to write articles and editorials regarding the origin of the eucharist and the PCK's eucharistic tradition. However, most liturgists within the PCK tended to accept literally eucharistic directions

---

115. Calvin, *Institutes of Christian Religion*, Vol. 2, 1461.
116. Committee on the Book of Common Worship, 2008, 90–94.

recorded in Calvin's works and the liturgies of the Church of Scotland which they presumed to be in continuity with the eucharistic practice in the early church. The early church documents such as the *Didache* and *the Apostolic Tradition* of Hippolytus were assumed by the PCK liturgists to be in continuity with Jesus' practice. This was especially so with respect to the relationship between baptism and the eucharist, because they regarded the manuscripts' ruling that baptism precedes the eucharist to be authoritative; they argued that the "closed table" (open only to those of a certain age, and after baptism) was the church tradition preserved since the early church.

This traditional understanding of the eucharist of the PCK has been enhanced by some influential theories such as those of Dom Gregory Dix and Joachim Jeremias. The next chapter will explore their methodologies and the main ideas which have affected the PCK's traditional understanding of the eucharist.

Chapter 3

The Theological Basis of the PCK's Understanding of the Eucharist

The Last Supper as the Origin of the Eucharist

As observed in the former chapters, the PCK's eucharistic theology and practices are based primarily on the biblical accounts especially related to the so-called last supper stories. There is a presupposition found in the PCK's approach to the eucharist that at the last supper Jesus conducted the original eucharist in a certain form, and then the apostles and the early church preserved and developed it in various ways. For the PCK, thus, the diverse eucharistic orders and content presented in the early church documents which are far different from the last supper tradition were created in the process of later ritual development. The core of this presupposition is that it is possible to reconstruct the original, even if it is not a complete reconstruction, at least in terms of basic structure or essential elements. This is done through comparing the early church documents and then seeking "something in common" in structure or terms. The "something in common" is believed to be the original. The rest of the texts are regarded as later addition or regional alteration. I will use "traditional" as the term for such an approach to the eucharist based on the presupposition that the PCK takes. Therefore the traditional approach's foremost issue has been to reconstruct the original form of the eucharist by which the traditional church attains the authority of its eucharistic tradition. Until even the early 20th century, almost all the studies concerning the eucharist were done on the basis of such a presupposition, and the PCK has been served by the results of the "traditional" studies. In this chapter I will explore some representative theories contributing to the solidity of the traditional eucharistic understanding of the PCK.

1 Seeking the Origin of the Eucharist

In the middle of 19th century, there were revolutionary discoveries of the documents of the early church. Starting with J. W. Bickell's short treatise *The Apostolic Church Order* in 1843, many books, introducing the early church's discipline, worship and dogma, such as Paul de Lagarde's *Didascalia Apostolorum* in 1854, Philotheos Bryennios' *Didache or Teaching of the Twelve Apostles* in 1883 were published.[1] The results of these studies ushered the Christian community into a new era of observing more clearly the early church worship which had been in the doldrums since the first publication of *the Apostolic Constitutions* in 1563.[2]

The main methodology used by the 19th century pioneers of liturgical study was the philological method.[3] The presupposition of this method was that Jesus gave his disciples clear teachings regarding the eucharist which the church had to follow. Then there was the development of the rite of the eucharist but the core of Jesus' teachings of the eucharist was preserved in the liturgies of the early church. Based on this presupposition, scholars tried to reconstruct the prototype of the eucharist through comparison between manuscripts of the early church. The method of discerning the original from the later alteration was to find what was common to all documents. For, they believed that what was common would be the essential parts of the eucharist preserved by the early church. Even until the late of 20th century, this methodology dominated the majority of scholars searching the original eucharist.

During the early period of searching for the original eucharist, scholars focused too much on finding a single original apostolic rite which was believed to inherit the eucharist of Jesus in the early church documents, attributing naively those works to the author presented in the title of the documents. For example, among the discoveries of the nineteenth century, a good number of manuscripts had a strong resemblance to *the Apostolic Constitutions* published in 1563. One of the documents was the so-called *Canons of Hippolytus*, first published in 1870. Hans Achelis believed that *Canons of Hippolytus* was the original work of Hippolytus and *Egyptian Church Order* derived from it. The main reason for his belief was Hippolytus, the name given as the author of the book in the title.

The sudden discoveries of the early church documents which were similar with *the Apostolic Constitutions* led scholars to compete to seek the original work of Hippolytus. In 1891, Franz Xaver Funk challenged Achelis

---

1. For a summary of the 19th century's discoveries regarding the early church orders, see Bradshaw, *The Search for the Origins of Christian Worship*, 73–75.

2. Ibid., 73.

3. For more details on the philological method, see ibid., 1.

with the opposite order that *Apostolic Constitutions* 8 was the original source, and *Egyptian Church Order* and then *Canons of Hippolytus* derived from it. In 1899 Ignatius Rahmani argued that the original was the *Testamentum Domini* and other manuscripts were descendents of it.[4] An interesting fact is that at this stage there was no suggestion that *Egyptian Church Order* was the original. However, in 1906 Eduard von der Goltz proposed that *Egyptian Church Order* might be the *Apostolic Tradition*, which was believed to have vanished, written by Hippolytus of Rome.[5] This idea was developed by Eduard Schwartz in 1910 and much fully elaborated by Richard H. Connolly in 1916.[6] Since then this recognition of *Egyptian Church Order* as the original *Apostolic Tradition*, from which other manuscripts derived, came to prevail among the majority of scholars who have led the traditional understanding of the eucharist. Suggesting that the *Apostolic Tradition* is the genuine work of Hippolytus of Rome, Burton Scott Easton argues that it dates back to 217 CE after Hippolytus' parting with Callistus. Even though largely agreeing with Easton, Gregory Dix dates it "within a year or two either way of A.D. 215."[7] However, a limitation of these studies is to neglect the nature of liturgy and to overestimate its historicity. These theories have been challenged by several scholars, Rudolf Lorentz in 1929, Hieronymus Engberding in 1948, Marcel Metzger in 1988, and more recently Paul Bradshaw, Maxwell Johnson and L. Edward Phillips in 2002.[8] Bradshaw suggests:

> the so-called *Apostolic Tradition* is actually an aggregation of material from different sources, quite probably arising from different geographical regions and almost certainly from different historical periods, from perhaps as early as the middle of the second century to as late as the middle of the fourth.[9]

2 A Structural Approach to the Origin of the Eucharist

Aiming to overcome the limitations found in the early philological method, in 1945, Gregory Dix (1901–1952) attempted to reconstruct the shape of the archetypal eucharist by focusing on the structure of the eucharist, through

4. Bradshaw et al., *The Apostolic Tradition*, 1–2.
5. Bradshaw, *The Search for the Origins of Christian Worship*, 76.
6. Bradshaw et al., *The Apostolic Tradition*, 2.
7. Dix and Chadwick, *The Treatise on the Apostolic Tradition of St Hippolytus of Rome*, xxxvii.
8. Bradshaw et al., *The Apostolic Tradition*, 13–14.
9. Bradshaw, *Reconstructing Early Christian Worship*, 50.

trying to find common content or patterns in the diversity of the early material. Despite some criticisms, for over a half century Dix's eucharistic understanding and methodology have influenced many liturgists and played a role in enhancing the traditional eucharistic understanding.

Dix tried to formulate the primitive core of the liturgy. Dix's view was that the primitive worship was originally divided into the *Synaxis* (literally means a meeting) and the eucharist. According to Dix, the *Synaxis* derived from the Jewish synagogue service but the eucharist, although he did not deny entirely a possibility of the influence of the Kiddush (the blessing with which the Sabbath or the great feasts began) or the Passover sacrifice meal, directly derived from the last supper more particularly influenced by Chaburoth (plural of a Chabura or Habura, from Chaber meaning a friend: the common meal with a devotional purpose or fellowship).[10] Around the second century the *Synaxis* began to precede the eucharist in regular Sunday service, and since the fourth century the *Synaxis* and the eucharist have been considered as inseparable elements of Christian worship.[11]

According to Dix, the original shape was the seven-action scheme inaugurated by Jesus at the last supper: (1) taking bread (2) giving thanks (3) breaking (4) distributing it with certain words (5) taking the cup (6) giving thanks (7) distributing it with certain words. Yet, the seven-action scheme, at a very early stage with the disappearance of the meal divided by the cup, was transformed to fourfold action, that is, the eucharist taking bread and the cup together:

> (1) The offertory; bread and wine are 'taken and placed on the table together. (2) The prayer; the president gives thanks to God over bread and wine together. (3) The fraction; the bread is broken. (4) The communion; the bread and wine are distributed together.[12]

Dix believed the four-action shape to be "the absolutely invariable nucleus of every eucharistic rite"[13] conducted by the early churches. Dix recognized that from the first to the third century, there existed various forms of the eucharist comprising bread and cup, bread alone, bread and salt, bread and water, or cup and bread. He argued that, although these

---

10. Dix believes that the last supper was not the Passover but the evening meal, a *Chabura*, twenty-four hours before the actual Passover. Thus, he trusts more the Fourth Gospel's account than the Synoptic Gospels. For more detail on Dix's understanding of the last supper as the *Chaburoth*, see Dix, *The Shape of the Liturgy*, 50–70.

11. Ibid., 37.

12. Ibid., 48.

13. Ibid., 48.

eucharists were irregular and heretical, the universal fourfold action was still kept in them. Also, regarding the account of the *Didache* concerning the cup-bread order which might have become the biggest challenge to his conviction of the fourfold action, Dix considered it an exception with his interpretation that the rite of the *Didache* was the *agape* meal not the eucharist proper.[14]

Dix tries to reconstruct the origin of the eucharist based on the last supper story in Luke. The last supper in Luke 22: 17–20 gives the "cup – bread – cup" order:

> 17 Then he took a cup, and after giving thanks he said, 'Take this and divide it among yourselves; 18 for I tell you that from now on I will not drink of the fruit of the vine until the kingdom of God comes.' 19 Then he took a loaf of bread, and when he had given thanks, he broke it and gave it to them, saying, 'This is my body, which is given for you. Do this in remembrance of me.' 20 And he did the same with the cup after supper, saying, 'This cup that is poured out for you is the new covenant in my blood.'[15]

For Dix, however, the first cup was a preliminary course, not the supper, and Jesus did not drink it. Then the supper began with bread taken and broken in sequence by Jesus. Next, Jesus gave thanks over it. Although the actual words of the thanksgiving were not recorded in the New Testament, Dix is convinced that the prayer was the thanksgiving of Chabura: "Blessed be Thou, O Lord our God, eternal King, Who bringest forth bread from the earth."[16] When Jesus distributed it to his disciples, he gave them something special which was unusual in an ordinary Chabura: "This is my body that is for you. Do this in remembrance of me." (1 Cor 11: 24). After then, there was the incident of Judas' abrupt departure and the prophecies of betrayal and denial, when spontaneously the mood of the supper was suddenly changed into sorrow and anxiety. The meal was over and the next order of Chabura would have been the rinsing of hands. Here, Jesus changed the usual way of Chabura to his own way. Instead of washing the hands, Jesus washed the feet of the apostles from the youngest to Peter who was the eldest. After then, a long monologue of Jesus continued. As the night grew late, the time of the end of the meeting was getting close. Jesus took the cup, containing wine mixed with water.[17] Jesus then gave thanks and distributed it to them. While the

---

14. Ibid., 48–49.
15. Luke 22: 17–20.
16. Dix, *The Shape of the Liturgy* (1947), 54–55.
17. In *Chabura* traditionally water was mixed with wine for drinking and thanksgiving while unmixed wine was generally recognized more suitable for washing.

cup was being passed to all, Jesus again made the astonishing remark, "This cup is the new covenant in my blood. Do this, as often as you drink it, in remembrance of me." (1 Cor 11: 25). Finally Dix sets the "hymn," which was the closing order of every Chabura, in the last part of the supper: "When they had sung the hymn, they went out to the Mount of Olives." (Mark 14: 26).[18]

From the so-called last supper stories, Dix finds the double institution in bread and wine, and his emphasis seems to be more on the latter than the former. The reason is that in Chabura the breaking of bread was generally conducted at every meal even when a Jew ate alone, but the blessing of the cup marked a corporate occasion. Thus, while the former can be conducted in a private rite, the latter must be done only by the Christian community. Furthermore, the significance of the cup is doubled when the meaning of the cup is connected with the new covenant which is redemption through the blood of Jesus:

> The institution in bread alone might have sufficed to 'provide holy communion' (like a priest communicating himself from the reserved sacrament when in the absence of a congregation he cannot celebrate). The association of the bread with the cup provided the basis from which would spring the whole *sacrificial* understanding, not only of the rite of the eucharist but *of our Lord's 'atoning' death* itself, in time to come.[19]

One of the Dix's contributions to the study on the eucharistic origin is the recognition of the eucharist, which is reconstructed on the basis of the New Testament accounts, as "the source," not "the model, for its performance" that must be kept by church.[20] Dix provides the change from the seven to the four action shape as proof that the early churches used the New Testament accounts as a guide not a mandatory rule for their eucharistic practice. He notes:

> Evidently, liturgical practice was not understood by the primitive church to be in any way subject to the control of the N. T. documents, even when these had begun to be regarded as inspired scripture.[21]

However, compared with the former methodology, while Dix made remarkable progress in the study of the original eucharist, his method did not entirely escape from the shade of the philological method but merely

18. Ibid., 56–58.
19. Ibid., 59.
20. Ibid., 48.
21. Ibid., 49.

moved the focus from the original apostolic rite to the original eucharist of Jesus.[22] Moreover, Dix had a strong belief that it is possible to reconstruct an original shape of the eucharist by finding a general principle in the early church manuscripts, that is the exactly same presupposition of the philological method.[23]

Dix's idea was challenged by the nine-fold theory of Bryan Spinks[24] and the alteration of Richard Buxton[25] into two major actions which are thanksgiving and reception accompanied by two minor ones, namely the offertory and the fraction. However, these structural approaches to the origin of the eucharist are based on the presupposition of the philological method. In the case of Dix, an important presupposition used for reconstructing the archetype was that early eucharistic types found in different geographical regions contained one original form instituted by Jesus. Then, over time churches expanded and developed and spontaneously the diversity resulted in regional characteristics, and the content and form were transformed from brevity and simplicity in the original eucharist to longevity and complexity in the later church's eucharist. Thus, Dix believed that the archetypal shape of the eucharist could be reconstructed by removing all attachments and additions and by recognizing the brevity rather than the longevity as the original. However, as Bradshaw indicates, the diversity and irregularity of the liturgies of the early church were too broad and complex to set in a fixed framework. Eventually, Dix responded to the results contradictory to his presupposition by treating them as exclusions, sometimes neglecting them, and even considering them as the creations of heretical groups.[26]

3 A Comparative Approach to the Origin of the Eucharist

The comparative method was originally used for the study on culture from the second half of the 19th century. Anton Baumstark (1872–1948) borrowed this methodology and applied it in his book *Vom geschichtlichen Werden der Liturgie* (On the Historical Development of Liturgy) first published in 1923 and later developed in *Comparative Liturgy*.[27] Compared to the philologi-

22. According to Bradshaw, Dix revised the philological method with "the Structural Approach" rather than overcoming it. For the details, see Bradshaw, *The Search for the Origins of Christian Worship*, 6.

23. Dix, *The Shape of the Liturgy: NEW EDITION*, xxxi.

24. Spinks, "Mis-Shapen," 167.

25. Buxton, "The Shape of the Eucharist," 85.

26. Bradshaw, *Eucharistic Origins*, vii.

27. Baumstark, *On the Historical Development of the Liturgy*, xv.

cal method which is a somewhat mechanical approach to documents, the comparative method's contribution is to recognize liturgy as a living organism. Baumstark writes that prayer which is a living activity never can "be paralysed into the rigour of an immobile and dead formalism" and in prayer which is offered to God, "the fullness of Sacramental Grace" descends on the faithful.[28] For Baumstark, in liturgy, all that is unchanged is the exchange of prayer and grace. The forms of the liturgy continue to evolve.[29]

With the recognition of liturgy as a living organism, Baumstark's contribution to the understanding of liturgy is to perceive the difference between text and practice in liturgy. In other words, he recognized that there were gaps between the liturgical documents and actual worship. Although congregations follow liturgies in conducting worship the liturgies do not tell everything what worshippers would do in the worship. The best way of understanding the worship of a community is to participate in the worship but in the case of worship in the past doing so is impossible. In this sense, Baumstark says:

> ... genuine humility is the only ethical stance to assume before the recognition that – on any given subject – one can only know what falls within comparatively narrow parameters, which – sooner or later – will crimp the relentless pursuit of scientific knowledge.[30]

Compared with the early traditional understanding of the eucharist, a stark difference of the comparative method was the alteration of viewpoint on the process of the development of liturgy. The former believed that there was a single original liturgy from which all liturgies derived and as time went on liturgies developed with variation. Thus, from this perspective, the later liturgy is the more varied and the earlier liturgy is the more unified and simple. However, Baumstark challenged this traditional view. He observed that in the course of liturgical development the earliest liturgies were the most varied but with the lapse of time liturgies had a tendency to uniformity.

Baumstark discerns two crucial meanings embedded in the final chapter's title of the book of Ferdinand Probst (1816–1899), "*Una Sancta Catholica et Apostolica Liturgia*" (One holy catholic and apostolic liturgy). First of all, this phrase discloses the intrinsic solemnity of the liturgy. The core value is shared with all liturgies and thus the solemnity is perpetually and invariably found in all liturgies. However, this phrase might be misunderstood with regard to the forms of liturgy. For this, Baumstark gives an explanation:

---

28. Baumstark, *Comparative Liturgy*, 1.
29. Ibid., 3.
30. Baumstark, *On the Historical Development of Liturgy*, 246.

> On the other hand, this phrase would be fundamentally mistaken if it implied a *complexus* of forms created by the apostles, which were originally uniform but then underwent a process of increasing differentiation. In actual fact, the historical development of the liturgy does not proceed from uniformity at its earliest to an increasing local diversity, but rather from local diversity to an increasing standardization.[31]

Here, Baumstark presents clearly the laws of evolution of liturgy. The originally uniform liturgy, in the earliest stage, became varied. As a reason for the suddenly varied forms in the earliest stage, his suggestion seems quite convincing that the way the original form was handed down from Jesus to the apostles was via oral tradition not by text.[32] Continuously, he argued that in the course of time the early variety was changed into uniformity, and simplicity or brevity into richness and prolixity.

However, Baumstark's law of evolution which is "from variety to uniformity" has a serious weakness in trying to seek the originally uniform liturgy. For, "the uniformity of the original" runs counter to the law of "from variety to uniformity." Is the uniformity in a liturgy the original or a later development? Actually, Baumstark made an opposing statement to the law of evolution of liturgy:

> Moreover, we shall have to regard as primitive phenomena which are found with the same meaning, the same function, and in the same area, in all Christian Rites, or at least in a sufficiently large number of such Rites, and especially so if they have parallels in the Liturgy of the Synagogue. We shall pronounce the same verdict where anything has a Jewish parallel, even when it is limited to a few Christian Rites or it may be only to one. On the other hand, we shall consider as recent all phenomena peculiar to a single Rite or to a few Rites, but without parallel of any kind in the Synagogue. The same verdict must be pronounced on those which, although absolutely or almost universal, change their meaning, place or function from one Rite to another.[33]

In addition, regarding the law suggested by Baumstark, it was impossible to explain fully the variety and complexity found in the later history of liturgy. Recognizing the limitations of the law, in turn, he tried to make up for the exceptions by suggesting supplementary laws. A time went on the movement toward uniformity was continuously obstructed by the regional

---

31. Ibid., 89.
32. Ibid., 95.
33. Baumstark, *Comparative Liturgy*, 31–32.

churches' tendency toward variation, and the movement toward prolixity was disturbed by the later abbreviation. However, as Bradshaw correctly indicates, according to Baumstark's laws, the variety of a liturgy cannot be simply judged as early. Conversely, a liturgy characterized by uniformity cannot be hastily concluded as late.[34]

Although the comparative method took a major step forward compared with the philological method, indicating the diversity of the early liturgies and the uniformity in later stages, it seems to stand on a similar basis to philological method. For, the presupposition of the comparative method is that there existed a root for liturgies, that is, the originally uniform liturgy.[35] Moreover, the provenance of the original eucharist still adheres to the last supper. Baumstark, in spite of his prudent approach to the characters of the liturgy, believed that it was possible to observe the worship in the past through his comparative method. For Baumstark, liturgies, like living creatures which have roots, were derived from the origin, Jesus, and thus the liturgies contained genetic markers identical to the origin.[36] Through the comparative method, he was able to explore which element was contained in a certain liturgy but had disappeared in others or how a prayer developed. Yet, he failed to give a clear answer of the origins of the eucharist. For, in nature, the comparative method needs enough material for comparison. In other words, the comparative method was nearly useless where there was a dearth of sources. For example, Baumstark's comparative method was quite effective in studying the liturgies from the fifth to the seventh century due to there being enough material for comparison. Conversely, Baumstark's study explained little about the original eucharistic form and elements of Jesus due to lack of sources. These features of the comparative method led Baumstark to pay attention to the process of the formation or development of liturgies rather than the roots of a liturgy.[37]

4 An Exegetical Approach to the Origin of the Eucharist

Basically, as we observed, the PCK recognizes the last supper as the origin of the eucharist although the recent worship book BCW 2008 contains an effort to include the meal of Jesus after his resurrection in the eucharist. Such a traditional understanding of the origin of the eucharist has been supported and reaffirmed by the absolute majority of theologians. Higgins,

34. Bradshaw, *The Search for the Origins of Christian Worship*, 12.
35. Baumstark, *On the Historical Development of the Liturgy*, 94–95.
36. Ibid., 11.
37. Ibid., 62–88.

in his work *The Lord's Supper in the New Testament*, expresses clearly the last supper as the origin of the eucharist:

> The Christian sacrament of the Eucharist, called in different branches of the Church by a variety of names (Holy Communion, the Lord's Supper, the Mass) and celebrated and understood in widely different ways, is the direct descendant of the Last Supper of Jesus with his disciples.[38]

This close identification of the eucharist and the last supper which seems to be evidently endorsed by the accounts of the New Testament and exactly the same as the traditional church's confession today regarding the eucharistic origin is profoundly influenced by Joachim Jeremias' achievement, *The Eucharistic Word of Jesus*. As Bruce Chilton indicates, although Jeremias too easily concludes that *ipsissima verba* (the original words) of Jesus are to be found in the New Testament accounts especially regarding the eucharist, the data and insight brought by his study are still meaningful and predominate in the traditional churches.[39]

The belief that the origin of the eucharist is the last supper led Jeremias to be engrossed in exploring the central feature of the last supper. Jeremias asserts that the last supper as the origin of the eucharist was a Passover meal. He raises a question concerning why instead of staying in Jerusalem in the day time and going to Bethany in the evening (Mark 11:11, 19; Luke 21:37; Mark 14:3; Luke 22:39) Jesus remained in Jerusalem for the last supper. Jeremias finds an answer in Jesus' recognition of himself as the paschal lamb. Namely, the reason why Jesus did not leave Jerusalem was that he, the Passover lamb, "must be eaten within the gates of Jerusalem."[40] In addition, Jeremias finds reasons why the last supper was a Passover meal. The last supper was held at night contrary to the custom that the main ordinary meals were held twice a day in the late morning and late afternoon. The number of participants and the action of reclining at meals recorded in the accounts of the last supper were the same as for the Passover meal. Then Jeremias focuses on wine. For, in the days of Jesus, while wine was generally used for medical purposes in everyday life, the drinking of wine was considered appropriate in the seven days of mourning, the three pilgrimage festivals (Passover, Pentecost and Tabernacles) and the meals for the sanctification

---

38. Higgins, *The Lord's Supper*, 9.
39. Chilton, *A Feast of Meanings*, 2.
40. Jeremias, *The Eucharistic Words of Jesus*, 43.

and the dismissal of the Sabbath.[41] Furthermore, Jeremias asserts that the wine used at the last supper was red wine, which signifies blood.[42]

According to the Synoptic Gospels, Jesus held the last supper with his twelve disciples on Thursday night and was put to death on Friday afternoon (Matt 27:62; Mark 15:42; Luke 23:54; John 19:31, 42). In terms of the modern way of measuring a day based on midnight (12 pm), the days of the last supper and the death of Jesus are obviously different. In the first century, through the method of the Jews' calculation that a day was from sunset (6 pm) to sunset (6 pm), both incidents occurred in the same day.[43] The day was the Passover (Matt 26:17-19; Mark 14:12-16; Luke 22:7-13). However, John's account is different from the synoptic chronology. According to John, the incidents from the last supper to the death on the cross occurred not on the Passover but the day before the festival of the Passover (John 13:1; 18:28; 19:14; 19:31-42). The discord in the four gospels has led to considerable debates on the date of the last supper.

Jeremias insists that the chronology of the Synoptic Gospels is more reliable than John, designating the date of the last supper as the Passover. Furthermore, as to the Johannine chronology in contrast to the synoptic view, he argues that the account of John shows an inconsistency with regard to the date of the last supper.[44] I. Howard Marshall who inherits a considerable eucharistic understanding from Jeremias tries to recover the reliability of the Johannine chronology which was damaged by Jeremias, while emphasizing the authenticity of the synoptic chronology. For this, Marshall is indebted to the theory of P. Billerbeck.[45] Billerbeck says that in the time of Jesus the Jewish religion and society were divided into the Sadducaic and Pharisaic traditions. At that time, while Sadducees held a position of political superiority, Jews generally followed the Pharisaic tradition in ordinary life, especially regarding religious regulations. Sadducees constantly tried to achieve a dominant position in religious laws ruling the life of Jews. Billerbeck found evidence of such attempts of the Sadducees in the alteration of the date of offering of the first fruit. One of the differences between the Pharisaic and Sadducaic religious traditions was the interpretation on the day of offering of the first fruit in Leviticus 23:11: "on the day after the Sab-

---

41. Jeremias provides fourteen reasons that the last supper was a Passover meal. For more details, see ibid., 41–62.

42. Ibid., 53.

43. Ibid., 15–16.

44. Ibid., 80–81. Providing an example of "high Sabbath" in John 19:31, Jeremias insists that John wavers between the synoptic account and his own chronology.

45. For more details on Billerbeck's idea, see Jeremias, *The Eucharistic Words of Jesus*, 21–23; Marshall, *Last Supper and Lord's Supper*, 69–73.

bath the priest shall raise it." The Sadducees offered the first fruit on Sunday, the day after the Sabbath, interpreting the text literally but the Pharisees appreciated it as the day after the feast of the Passover and thus offered the first fruit on Nisan 16/17 regardless of days. The Sadducees had political power enough to change the calendar. The Sadducees frequently changed the calendar to keep their tradition by delaying or advancing the beginning of the month by one day. In the year of Jesus' death, originally Nisan 16/17 fell on Saturday, but Sadducees made Nisan 16/17 fall on Sunday by fabricating the calendar so that they could offer the first fruit on that day designated by their tradition.

Billerbeck believed that the Pharisees obviously would try to keep their tradition with an unmodified calendar. In order to avoid conflict, the Sadducees, in turn, allowed the Pharisees to have the Passover meal one day earlier than the Sadducaic calendar. Jesus and his disciples following the Pharisaic calendar had the last supper on the night of Thursday and the Synoptic Gospels reported it, while John the Sadducaic reported the incidents occurred on the same days but on different dates. Marshall, of course, recognizes that there is an element of conjecture in the theory of Billerbeck. Nevertheless, Marshall, praising the idea of Billerbeck as the most plausible among all theories, supports the chronological harmonization between the synoptic and Johannine points of view.[46]

On the other hand, some scholars seek the origin of the last supper in relationship to other meals of the Jewish tradition rather than the Passover meal. G. H. Box[47] argues that the last supper was from the Sabbath-Kiddush. With regard to formal characters, the last supper seems to be more similar to the meal of the Sabbath-Kiddush which is a meeting of preparation for the Sabbath/festival than the Passover meal. The Sabbath-Kiddush was the gathering of a small number of men, who used leavened not unleavened bread; only one cup not many cups; did not read the text relating to Exodus which is a crucial character of the Passover; held the gathering once a week not annually; and had wine mixed with water. These characteristics are all found in the last supper account. Also, William D. Maxwell, suggesting several reasons similar to Box, maintains that the last supper was the Sabbath-Kiddush.[48]

However, the Sabbath-Kiddush theory was criticized that the Sabbath-Kiddush meal was held always on Saturday evening, but the last supper was

---

46. Marshall, *Last Supper and Lord's Supper*, 74–75.
47. Box, "The Jewish Antecedents of the Eucharist," 357–69.
48. Maxwell, *An Outline of Christian Worship*, 5–6.

held on Thursday evening.⁴⁹ The weakness of the Sabbath-Kiddush theory was complemented by the Passover-Kiddush meal of W. O. E. Oesterley. According to him, the last supper was a ritual sanctification of the Passover held on the evening before the feast.⁵⁰ However, his idea had the same deficiency with the Sabbath-Kiddush. Generally the ritual sanctification of the Passover was conducted with the opening of the Passover meal not twenty-four hours before the Passover meal. Thus, Jeremias criticizes that the idea of a Passover-Kiddush which was held "twenty-four hours before the beginning of the feast as *pure fantasy*."⁵¹

There were other attempts to connect the last supper with an evening meal, that is, Chaburoth (plural term of a Chaburah). As observed before, Dix insists that the last supper was a Chaburah meal held twenty-four hours before the Passover.⁵² According to him, in respect of the composition of order, there are considerable similarities between a Chaburah and the last supper. Both have a leader, relish (a preliminary course) which is served before the meal proper, the breaking of bread, the thanksgiving over bread and wine, and at the close of the meeting singing a psalm.⁵³ This theory seems to have an advantage over the ideas related to the Kiddush in view of the fact that a Chaburah meal has no limitation on the date and time, and so it is possible to solve the riddle of twenty-four hours.

Prior to Dix, Lietzmann in his great achievement *Mass and Lord's Supper* first published in 1926 insisted that the last supper was an ordinary meal, resisting the traditional understanding of the last supper as the Passover meal. Lietzmann points out that the peculiar features of the Passover meal are not at all found in the last supper.⁵⁴ On many occasions, Lietzmann, through the investigation of the meals recorded in the Talmudic sources, found that "the breaking of bread" and "the blessing of bread and wine" were general elements of meals in Jewish society not a peculiar distinction of the Sabbath-Kiddush.⁵⁵ For this argument, he provides cogent proof in various sources such as the ritual for the ceremony of the "ushering in of the Sabbath," the inclusion of Sabbath-Kiddush in the modern prayer-book of the German rite which is believed to be preserving the primitive form of the

---

49. Jeremias, *The Eucharistic Words of Jesus*, 28; Higgins, *The Lord's Supper*, 14.
50. Oesterley, *The Jewish Background of the Christian Liturgy*, 167–79.
51. Jeremias, *The Eucharistic Words of Jesus*, 29.
52. Dix, *The Shape of the Liturgy* (1947), 51–52.
53. For more details on Dix's study as to the relationship between the last supper and a Chaburah, see ibid., 50–58.
54. Lietzmann, *Mass and Lord's Supper*, 172.
55. Ibid., 168.

Sabbath-Kiddush in the Talmudic age, the Babylonian Talmud Pesachim, the Jerusalem Pesachim, the Mishnah Berakoth and Pesachim, and the Tosephta.[56] Finally, he insists that "these Jewish table-customs represent in all points the exact prototype of the last meal of Jesus with his disciples"[57] and the meal was a Chaburah.[58]

In addition, Lietzmann, in exploring the early churches' documents such as the *Didache*, the liturgy of Serapion (from fourth-century Egypt) and the third-century Roman liturgy of Hippolytus, suggests that there were two eucharistic traditions. Firstly, he maintains that the liturgy of Serapion which was influenced by the *Didache*, making no mention of the death of Jesus, can be traced back to "the breaking of bread" in Acts. The breaking of bread, of course, traces back to the fellowship at meals of Jesus. The characteristics of this tradition are the joyful sense of the Lord's spiritual presence and an enthusiastic anticipation of *Parousia*. The other tradition is the Pauline type of the eucharist. Lietzmann considers Paul as the originator of this tradition which focuses on the eucharist as a memorial of the death of Jesus and the last supper as provenance.[59]

However, Lietzmann immediately had to face criticism. First of all, Jeremias criticized him that the Chaburah meal was exclusively associated with obligations such as betrothal, weddings, circumcisions and funerals.[60] Furthermore, in the Chaburah, the observance of the Torah was emphasized but there is no evidence of it in the last supper, and it is, also, not sure whether Jesus and his disciples actually did "form a regular association" of a Chaburah.[61]

Another possible interpretation of the last supper might be sought in the communal meals of Qumran. K. G. Kuhn argued that the ritual meals of the Essenes affected two aspects of the last supper. Firstly, Kuhn pays attention to the similar way of gathering for meals between the Essenes and the early church. He insists that the Essenes came together for the meals in a certain place and the early church developed the eucharist in a communal way, echoing the Essenes' meal practice. However, Jeremias refutes Kuhn's theory, mentioning several differences between the two meal practices. For example, whereas at Qumran the monks had meals twice daily at eleven o'clock and in the late afternoon, the early church generally held

---

56. For more detail on the texts of the Talmudic era, see ibid., 165–70.
57. Ibid., 171.
58. Ibid., 185.
59. Ibid., 250–55.
60. Jeremias, *The Eucharistic Words of Jesus*, 30.
61. Higgins, *The Lord's Supper in the New Testament*, 16.

the eucharist at evening. The participants in the communal meal of Qumran were only men but in the eucharist women joined in. Additionally, the only place of the meals at Qumran was the monastery whereas the early church came together not only in the church building but also in private houses.[62] Another influence of Qumran on the eucharist of Christian community suggested by Kuhn is that the records of the last supper in Mark and Matthew which have the bread-word ahead of the wine-word during the supper are different from Lukan/Pauline accounts which insert "after supper" (Luke 22:20; 1 Cor 11:25) between the bread and wine. Kuhn found evidence of the immediate sequence of the bread and wine in the meals of the Essenes.[63] Furthermore, he suggests that the blessing of the priest over the bread and the drink and the phrases "the bread of life" and "the cup of blessing" recorded in 1 Qumran Scrolls (QS) 6:4–6 and the Jewish tale of Joseph and Asenath are closely connected with the last supper.[64] However, such characteristics are general elements and expressions used in other Jewish meals rather than peculiar distinctions of the meals of Qumran. Thus, this evidence for the connection between the Qumran meal and the eucharist submitted by Kuhn seems to be not enough for decisive proof.[65]

More recently, the theory of Zebah Todah (the thank-offering/sacrificial meal) has been magnified as the source of the eucharist by scholars such as Leon-Dufour,[66] Hartmut Gese[67] and Louis Marie Chauvet.[68] The Zebah Todah traces back to "the sacrifice of peace" (*Zebah Shelamim*) recorded in chapters three and seven of Leviticus. Especially "the sacrifice of peace" in chapter 7 of Leviticus is divided into three sacrifices according to various purposes, including thanksgiving (*Todah*), a votive offering (*Neder*) and a freewill offering (*Nedabah*). Among them, "the sacrifice of peace" for "thanksgiving" is the Zebah Todah. The emphasis on "thanksgiving," the core of Zebah Todah, caused a development of the form of Zebah Todah, that is, the shift "from the animal victim toward the prayers."[69] In the time of Jesus, the Zebah Todah became more spiritualized and symbolized with criticism against the temple sacrifice in Jerusalem. In the first century the Zebah Todah pervaded not only Jerusalem but all regions under Hellenism.

62. Jeremias, *The Eucharistic Words of Jesus*, 31–32.
63. Ibid., 31.
64. Ibid., 32–33.
65. Bradshaw, *The Search for the Origin of Christian Worship*, 64
66. Leon-Dufour, *Sharing the Eucharistic Bread*, 41–57.
67. See Gese, *Essays on Biblical Theology*, 117–40.
68. Chauvet, *Symbol and Sacrament*, 240–44.
69. Ibid., 243.

As evidence, Chauvet introduces the work of R. K. Yerkes. Yerkes, exploring the Hermetic literature,[70] finds that in those sources not the "ritual sacrifice" but the "spiritual sacrifice" (*logike thusia*) with a pure heart and the prayer of "thanksgiving" (*eucharistia*) are emphasized as the only true sacrifice.[71] He finds additional evidence of the Zebah Todah prevailing among the Hellenistic world in the writings of Philo. Philo places "the eucharistic sacrifice" (*tes eucharistias thusia*)[72] at the highest position among sacrifices. Based on this evidence, Chauvet designates "the eucharistic sacrifice" of Philo as the Zebah Todah and finally maintains that the last supper and the eucharist of the early Christian community were obviously the Zebah Todah.[73]

Given that the theological emphasis of Zebah Todah is on "thanksgiving as to the sacrifice of Jesus for deliverance," the focal idea seems to be well described in the interpretation of Paul concerning the eucharist inserted in 1 Corinthians 11. From this point of view, Leon-Dufour asserts that the ritual proclamation of "the Lord's death until he comes" (1 Cor 11:26) corresponds exactly to the Todah.[74] This theory might be useful for an explanation of the reason why the early churches preferred "thanksgiving" of the sacrifice of Christ for deliverance, that is, the *hodayah/eucharistia* form to the "blessing" (*berakah*) form. However, just like other theories, the Todah theory seems to be insufficient because the "thanksgiving" which is believed by Kuhn and other scholars to be the defining characteristic of the Zebah Todah is found in other Jewish meals as well. Plus, the Todah theory fails to explain sufficiently for the anticipation of *Parousia* embedded in the early churches' eucharistic tradition.[75]

From the accounts observed above, all possible attempts to connect the origin of the last supper with a certain type of Jewish meal tradition are plausible but not entirely convincing. Also, an important thing to remember is that most theories explored above are based on the traditional presupposition that the origin of the eucharist is the last supper. Although Lietzmann and some scholars regard the eucharist as being from the meals of Jesus

---

70. The Hermetic literature is "a body of non-Christian texts reflecting a religious statement drawn from Greek philosophy and Near Eastern traditions.... Much of the Hermetic literature is of an occult nature, dealing with ASTROLOGY, alchemy, and MAGIC, but of more importance is an array of writings which purport to teach mysteries concerning God, the universe, human nature and salvation." Mills et al., *Mercer Dictionary of the Bible*, 375.

71. Chauvet, *Symbol and Sacrament*, 241.

72. *De specialibus legibus* (On the Special Laws) I, 285. Ibid., 242.

73. Ibid., 243–44.

74. Leon-Dufour, *Sharing the Eucharistic Bread*, 57.

75. Bradshaw, *The Search for the Origin of Christian Worship*, 65.

shared with his disciples during his public life their theories have not been carefully considered by the PCK.

5 A Scientific Approach to the Origin of the Eucharist

With profound insight concerning the characters of liturgy, Mazza shows how a scientific approach can advance understanding of eucharistic origins. First of all, he raises a question about the suppositions, in which traditional theologians have blind faith, and tries to retain objectivity in his study. He criticizes traditional scholars for having delusions about the Jewish documents of ancient times. For example, he indicates that the texts of the *Birkat ha-Mazon* believed to be the original source of the prayer of the last supper by traditional scholars were actually reconstructed by Finkelstein and thus have never been extant.[76] Furthermore, he differentiates between eucharistic practice which was historically conducted and the eucharistic illustration coloured by theology. Such keen insight is clear from his perception of the relationship between the last supper and the Passover. Mazza accepts that paschal significance is placed in and around the last supper stories but at the same time discerns that paschal theology reflects the perspective of certain early Christian communities. He stresses that the early churches' paschal interpretation must be differentiated from the actual eucharistic event.[77]

In other words, redactors of the New Testament placed the last supper in the context of the Passover with theological intention but historically the last supper was not the Passover meal. Instead, Mazza suggests a Jewish festive meal, Kiddush,[78] as the root of the last supper. He maintains that the Kiddush has three parts: the rite of the cup, the rite of the bread, and the rite of the cup. Then, he pays attention to the eucharistic order, "cup – bread – cup," observed in Luke and the *Didache* which is exactly the same with the Kiddush order. From this point of view, Mazza in turn suggests that the cup – bread – cup order is closer to the primitive eucharist than the bread – cup order which is believed to be the original and proper eucharistic form by the traditional eucharistic understanding.[79]

When considering the traditional scholars from Jeremias downwards who recognize the cup ahead of bread type as not the eucharist proper, one of Mazza's contributions to the traditional eucharist understanding is to

---

76. Mazza, *The Celebration of the Eucharist*, 15–17.

77. Ibid., 25.

78. Mazza prefers "Qiddush" to "Kiddush" as the term for the Jewish festive meal but here for coherence the latter will be used.

79. Ibid., 28–34.

make the fixed concept of the eucharist more flexible. His extensive and careful approach to the eucharist draws on new perceptions of the traditions of the eucharist. Based on literal and linguistic inspection on the institution narratives, Jeremias argued that the account in Mark is closer to the original than the Lukan/Pauline tradition. Mazza, on the other hand, proposed that the complexity of liturgy meant it was not easy to discern between the original and later interpolation through an analysis of linguistic characters. For, the text of the eucharist is not a simply historical record but "the form of the narrative served not only the needs of the *kerygma* but also its liturgical use."[80] Consistently, he maintained that in an appraisal of the historicity of liturgy the focus must be changed from linguistic concern to the structure of the rite. From this point of view, Mazza insists that the account of Luke which retains more liturgical features than Mark is closer to the primitive.[81] Also, regarding the perception of the course of the eucharist, Mazza enlarges the traditional point of view which was confined in the bread – cup type.

However, he is still firmly grounded in the traditional presupposition that the eucharist originated from the last supper of Jesus in the upper room. He believes that the prayers "that Jesus uttered at the supper are the origin and model of the Church's eucharistic prayer, or anaphora."[82] In addition, Mazza's theory does not seem to be established on thoroughly verifiable evidence, depending considerably on his own hypothesis. Mazza's attempt to connect the tripartite presented in the Kiddush with the cup – bread – cup in Luke is praiseworthy but not convincing.

6 Summary and Evaluation

In this chapter, I have focused on the main theories which have supported the PCK's traditional eucharistic understanding. Since the revolutionary discoveries in the middle of 19th century, the origin of the eucharist has been a controversial issue for many decades. Various methodologies have been used for exploring the origin of the eucharist. In the early period of the history of the study on the origin of the eucharist, most scholars used the philological method. They tended to believe naively a name in the title

---

80. Ibid., 23–24.

81. According to Mazza, the course of the eucharist evolved from more liturgical forms to simplifying and combining form. By the tendency of simplification, the order of traditions is: Kiddush – Luke (longer version) – Didache – 1 Cor 10.16–17. By the tendency of Combination, the order is: Luke – 1 Cor 11.23–25 – Mark/Matthew – Luke (Shorter version). For more details, see ibid., 32.

82. Ibid., 19.

of a certain book as the author of the book. Overcoming the limitation of the philological method, Dix studied the origin of the eucharist through his structural approach. Baumstark tried to reconstruct the eucharistic origin with his recognition of liturgy as a living organism. Jeremias and others used an exegetical approach for searching for the origin of the eucharist. Based on these methodologies, some scholars argued that the last supper was a paschal meal. Others have suggested various alternative theories such as the Kiddush, the Chabura and the Zeba Todah, with an attempt to interpret the last supper within the Jewish context.

In the history of the study of the origins of the eucharist, there was a common presupposition shared by the majority of the scholars that the eucharist originated from the last supper. Although the results of the studies were different, this common presupposition made the biggest impact on the PCK's eucharistic theology. Among various eucharistic perspectives, the PCK focused the paschal meaning of the last supper. The eucharistic understanding of the PCK came to have a tendency to adhere to the last supper tradition and theologically interpret the last supper as being closely connected to the death of Jesus. As a result, the PCK came to strengthen its traditional eucharistic regulation which allows only baptized members over the age of fifteen to participate in the eucharist.

However, recent studies of the eucharist challenge the traditional presupposition of the origins of the eucharist. These studies focus on the diversity of the eucharistic theology and practice in the earliest period of Christianity. The more significant finding of these studies is that the eucharist in that period is not based on the last supper tradition. The early church documents do not recognize Jesus in the eucharist as a paschal lamb. Moreover, there is no description of the last supper as the temporal background of the eucharist. These findings raise a question about the reliability of the traditional eucharistic presupposition. At the same time, these findings lead theologians to reconsider not only the origin of the eucharist but the nature of the eucharist. Why was the eucharist, which was held by the early church, different from the last supper tradition? If the actual roots of the eucharist did not derive from the last supper, where can the church seek the origins of the eucharist? If the eucharist was not instituted in the last supper, where can the church seek the theological validity of the eucharist as a sacrament? What do the answers to these questions mention regarding the open table? How can the church embody the theology of the open table in liturgy and an actual practice? These questions lead us to part II.

Part II

The Theology of the Eucharistic Open Table

Chapter 4

The Historical Basis for the Theology of the Open Table (1)

The Eucharist in the First Two Centuries

THERE IS A SCHOLARLY consensus regarding the history of the eucharist that in the earliest two centuries churches celebrated the eucharist with various forms and differences in content. The traditional point of view understands the eucharistic diversity to be the result of the evolution or development from the last supper. Also, traditionalists believe that it is possible to reconstruct the original by extracting common wordings or forms presumed to be the original from the various eucharistic expressions of the early church. However, recent scholars studying the origin of the eucharist challenge the traditional eucharistic understanding which is based on the presupposition that the eucharist originated from the last supper.

Criticizing the traditional presupposition for causing the church to embrace wrong perspectives on the origin of the eucharist, these scholars pursue actual facts in historical documents rather than presupposition. This new approach to the origin of the eucharist recognizes that there are two significant historical facts about the eucharist in the first two centuries. Firstly, the eucharist in the early church was varied in form and content. Secondly, the more important fact is that the eucharist in the early church was quite different from the last supper tradition. These two facts raise fundamental questions regarding the traditional eucharistic understanding adhering to the view that the eucharist originated from the last supper. The first question concerns the notion of one original source. The extant earliest eucharistic sources have too many variants to believe that they are from one original. The second question concerns the notion of the last supper. If the eucharist of the early church originated from the last supper why does it consistently neglect the so-called last supper stories? In order to answer these questions, I will explore the eucharistic practices in the first two centuries which are different from the last supper tradition.

1 The Eucharist of the Fourth Gospel

To define the sacramentalism of the Fourth Gospel has always been a controversial issue. This controversy, especially regarding the eucharist, is amplified by unique eucharistic features in John. Firstly, the institution narrative is absent in the last supper of John 13. Secondly, there is no mention of the breaking of the bread which is recognized as a decisive criterion for the eucharist from a traditional eucharistic perspective. Thirdly, the eucharistic terminology and expressions presented in John 6 undoubtedly reflect the eucharistic sayings of Jesus or at least have a eucharistic overtone. Lastly, the temporal and spatial setting of the eucharist is the feeding of the multitude on a mountain in John 6 and not the last supper in the upper room in John 13. Similarly, such distinctive eucharistic characteristics of John, which are considerably different from the synoptic and Pauline tradition but at the same time clearly eucharistic, provide a space for some to view John as anti-sacramentalist while others view John as pro-sacramentalist.

The Case for John as an Anti-sacramentalist

Among the scholars who support the anti-sacramentalism of John, Bultmann is one of the most influential figures. He argues that the present form of the Fourth Gospel has been completed through several stages. Bultmann names the original author of the Fourth Gospel as the evangelist. The evangelist probably was a member of a Gnostic circle but finally converted into a Christian. The evangelist would have had three sources, the sign source, the revelatory discourse, and the passion and resurrection story.[1] The evangelist completed the proto-gospel of John by using the three sources with his particular theological intention. However, the first edition of the Fourth Gospel had a weakness in chronology. According to Bultmann, the disorder between stories led the second editor, the ecclesiastical redactor, to rearrange it and make interpolations according to his theology. Bultmann believes that during the process the ecclesiastical redactor found a theological weak point, that is, the absence of sacramentalism in the former edition. This could possibly have meant that the Fourth Gospel was recognized by

---

1. For more details on the three sources, see Brown, *The Gospel According to John, Volume 1, I-XII*, xxix-xxx.

the early churches as docetic literature. So, in order to cover the theological weakness, the ecclesiastical redactor interpolated the sacramental source throughout the whole book including in particular the eucharistic concept in John 6.[2] John 6 can be divided into three parts: the feeding of the five thousand (John 6:1–14); Jesus walks on water (John 6:15–21) and dialogue and discourse on the bread of life (John 6:22–71).[3] In dialogue and discourse on the bread of life (John 6:22–71), John 6:51–58 contains evident eucharistic words such as flesh, bread and blood.

Bultmann draws a conclusion that these verses were inserted by an ecclesiastical editor.[4] Similarly, Wahlde suggests that John 6:51–58 interpolated by the third editor echoes obviously the eucharist in the New Testament. According to Wahlde, the second editor of the Fourth Gospel intentionally undermined the material value, so as to emphasize the spiritual dimension of Jesus' existence. After the Johannine community acknowledged the importance of the spiritual phase, the third editor felt the need to recover the significance of the materiality. Thus, the third editor inserted the material concept throughout the Fourth Gospel, including John 6:51–58.[5] Do Bultmann and Wahlde view John as an anti-sacramentalist? With regard to the evangelist, the first writer of the Fourth Gospel, the answer is yes. However, at the same time, it is also true that they never denied the sacramental significance that was spread into the final edition of the Fourth Gospel.

The Case for John as an Anti-ritualist or Pro-sacramentalist

On the other hand, some scholars argue that John was not an anti-sacramentalist but an anti-ritualist. They believe that John objects to the ritual of the sacraments but emphasizes the meanings and theology of baptism and the eucharist much more than other gospel writers. LaVerdiere expresses the view that there exists a broad range of sacramental symbols and meanings throughout John. First of all, LaVerdiere finds indirect sacramental symbols from several discourses.[6] According to LaVerdiere, the sacramental significance emerges from the first part of John. The Word made flesh (John 1:14) which means the incarnation is embodied in the eucharist when

---

2. For more details on his exposition of the bread of life, see Bultmann, *The Gospel of John*, 218–37.
3. O'Day and Hylen, *John*, 71–78.
4. Bultmann, *The Gospel of John*, 219.
5. See Wahlde, *The Gospel and Letters of John*, 331–34.
6. LaVerdiere, *The Eucharist*, 112–13.

Jesus gives his flesh to people in John 6.[7] In a wedding banquet at Cana, the water made wine (John 2:9) and the mention of the passover (John 2:13) are pregnant with the meaning of eucharist. In addition, the water shed on the cross with blood (John 19:34), the water mentioned in the dialogue with Nicodemus (John 3:3-5), and the water told to the Samaritan woman are the symbols of baptism.[8]

With these indirect sacramental references, John also directly mentions the eucharist in three events. Firstly, the miraculous feeding story in chapter 6 is a clear indication of the eucharist. Although there is no mention of the breaking of the bread, John's focus is on the distribution of Jesus not the act of the breaking. Secondly, chapter 13 of John does not record the institution narrative but the setting echoes evidently the eucharist at the last supper. LaVerdiere recognizes the supper illustrated in John 13 as "a homiletic reflection"[9] on the eucharist described in the Synoptic Gospels and 1 Corinthians 11. In other words, John's interest is not in teaching the Johannine community the ritual of the eucharist but in the application of the eucharistic meanings. Lastly, the breakfast after the resurrection in chapter 21 also reflects the eucharist. The act of Jesus' giving bread and fish at the breakfast acts as a reminder of the feeding on the mountain in chapter 6. In addition, after the two eucharistic meals in chapters 6 and 13, a discourse or dialogue always follows them and the same pattern is observed in the chapter 21.[10] Thus, LaVerdiere recognizes the breakfast as the eucharist.

Cullmann further attempts to connect in a sophisticated way all the main miracles and stories recorded in John with baptism and the eucharist. The living water in the conversation with the Samaritan woman (John 4:1-30) and the pool by the sheep gate (John 5:1-19) indicate baptism.[11] In addition, when considering one of the eucharistic emphases of John is

---

7. LaVerdiere assumes that the Gospel of John would have been written between the late 90s and the early part of the second century when the Johannine community was theologically challenged by proto-Gnosticism that undermined the incarnation and humanity of Jesus. According to him, in the process of responding to the docetic tendency the Johannine community developed the theology of the Word made flesh (John 1:14) and the eucharist that is eating the flesh of the Son of Man and drinking his blood (John 6:53). For more details on the relationship between the Johannine community and the docetic challenges, see ibid., 117–18.

8. Ibid., 115.

9. Ibid., 116.

10. After the miraculous feeding (6:1–15), the long discourse of the eucharist (6:22–71) follows it, at the last supper Jesus' farewell discourse (14:1—17:26) is placed after the meal (13:1–38), and at the first breakfast by the Sea of Tiberias Jesus' dialogue with Simon Peter follows it. For more details, see Ibid., 116, 122.

11. Cullmann, *Early Christian Worship*, 80–88.

the nourishment by Christ, the transformation of water into wine at the wedding feast at Cana and the multiplication of the loaves on a mountain are enough to be recognized as the eucharist.[12] Interestingly Cullmann uncovers both eucharistic and baptismal meanings in John 13. He suggests that the last supper is clearly the eucharist and the washing of the feet alludes to baptism. In addition, not only the act of washing but also the conversation between Jesus and Peter concerning bathing imply baptism.[13]

Until now, I have briefly explored diverse understandings on John's position of the sacraments. Some scholars argue that John was an anti-sacramentalist, suggesting that the sacramental features in John were interpolated by later redactors. In contrast, others view that John was a pro-sacramentalist, insisting that the sacramental features should be ascribed to the evangelist. Nevertheless, there is a convergence between the two extremes that the Fourth Gospel, regardless of whether it was written by the evangelist or the ecclesiastical redactor, expresses its intent to claim the significance of the sacraments.

Reasons for John placing the Eucharist in Chapter 6 rather than Chapter 13

The fact that John contains the sacramental features leads us to the next puzzle. While Paul and the Synoptic Gospels describe that Jesus instituted the eucharist at the last supper, the Fourth Gospel places the origin of the eucharist in the miraculous feeding event in chapter 6. In addition, when the Fourth Gospel gives an explanation of the last supper in its chapter 13, there is no mention of the institution narrative. The simple phrase, "during supper," is all the explanation concerning the last supper the Fourth Gospel gives. The focus of the Fourth Gospel in its chapter 13 is Jesus who washed his disciples' feet not the last supper. Many scholars have tried to solve the puzzle. Jeremias argues that John intended to hide the sacred ritual from the heathen by moving the eucharist from the last supper in chapter 13 to chapter 6.[14] From a somewhat different point of view, Morris proposes that John was not an anti-sacramentalist but just concerned about overemphasizing the participation in the eucharist.[15] Carson provides a more plausible answer based on an assumption that at that time superstitious beliefs in the eucharist prevailed

---

12. For more details on Cullmann's exposition as to the miracle at the marriage at Cana, see ibid., 66–71. With regard to the feeding miracle, see ibid., 93–102.

13. Ibid., 108.

14. For more details, see Jeremias, *The Eucharistic Words of Jesus*, 73.

15. Morris, *The Gospel According to John*, 311.

in the Johannine community and also they believed that the eucharistic ritual gave salvation. In such a situation, in order to correct the wrong beliefs and remind them that the centre of the eucharist is Jesus not the ritual, probably John would have removed the eucharist in the chapter 13.[16] Similarly, Leon-Dufour's view is that John highlights the meanings of the eucharist by diminishing ritual characters of the eucharist in chapter 13. The reason why John omits the institution narrative in the chapter 13 is the "fulfillment"[17] of the eucharist presented by the Synoptic Gospels. At that time, the eucharist of the Pauline and synoptic tradition prevailed in the Johannine community. Yet slowly the mystical and magical perception of the eucharist began to permeate into the community. Such a phenomenon was against the true meaning of the eucharist. The main purpose of the eucharist for John was "to intensify in this world that fraternal love which is divine in its origin."[18] While in the eucharist of the Synoptic Gospels participants experienced only the love of God, in John 13 through the washing of feet they not only encounter Jesus but practise love. For this reason, John decided to insert Jesus' washing his disciples' feet not the institution narrative in the last supper.[19] All the attempts are plausible but as Morris concludes quite correctly, "there is no evidence, and all this is conjecture."[20]

A limitation found in the explanations above is that they recognize the eucharist in the Synoptic Gospels as the original style of the eucharist and that of John is an alteration or evolution from the original. There remains still another possibility in understanding the eucharist in John 6. For that to happen, a different perspective is needed. It means that we consider a possibility that John's eucharist based on the miraculous feeding in chapter 6 is not an adaptation from the synoptic tradition to the Johannine community but an independent tradition. Anderson, although he acknowledges a possibility of John as influenced by pre-Markan oral tradition, insists on the independence of the Johannine tradition from the Synoptic Gospels, noting the clear differences between John 6 and Mark 6 and 8.[21]

Brown pays attention to John's use of the eucharistic term σάρξ (flesh) different from the synoptic and Pauline choice of σῶμα (body). Noting that Hebrew or Aramaic language has no terminology corresponding to the word σῶμα, he suggests that the original wording of Jesus at the last supper could

---

16. Carson, *The Gospel According to John*, 458.
17. Leon-Dufour, *Sharing the Eucharistic Bread*, 251.
18. Ibid., 251.
19. Ibid., 252.
20. Morris, *The Gospel According to John*, 311.
21. Anderson, "The Sitz im Leben," 9.

possibly be that "This is my flesh" which is near to Aramaic expression. For this, Brown finds additional evidence from the earliest Christian writers Ignatius of Antioch and Justin Martyr.[22] If it is true that the term σάρξ was derived from the Aramaic linguistic root, the eucharistic tradition of John has two possibilities. One is that it might be older than the synoptic eucharist. Another is that John could have received the eucharistic tradition differently to the synoptic one. From this point of view, Bradshaw further suggests that the eucharistic tradition of John could be an independent tradition which acknowledged only flesh and blood as the eucharistic terminology[23] rather than the "developments or reinterpretations of the classic supper tradition."[24] Stringer, also, says that the Johannine eucharistic tradition had some eucharistic characteristics different from the synoptic and Pauline traditions and possibly was related to the Essene and the Samaritan traditions.[25]

If the Johannine eucharistic features which are different from the synoptic tradition are nowhere to be found except in John, it is quite possible that the Johannine eucharist developed from the synoptic tradition. However, if such features are found in other places, it possibly means that there existed independent eucharistic traditions different from the synoptic tradition. The proof of the independent eucharistic tradition found in the early church literature will be explored in more detail in the later part of this chapter.

The Core of Johannine Eucharistic Theology

One of the most important criteria in interpreting the meals of John 6 and 13 is the significance of time. Paul and the Synoptic Gospels place the eucharist on the night Jesus was betrayed. The temporal setting of the night leads participants to commemorate spontaneously the saving death of Jesus. In contrast, John places the eucharist in chapter 6 which is in the midst of Jesus' "earthly ministry."[26] Here Jesus is still with them, healing them, and providing food for their body and soul.

John M. Perry suggests that the main themes of the Johannine eucharist were the presence of Christ, the joyfulness caused by encountering the risen Lord, and the eschatological expectation. In the earliest Johannine

---

22. Brown, *The Gospel According to John, I–XII*, 285. For the study on the early Christian writers' use of the term σάρξ instead of σῶμα, see also Ignatius of Antioch and Justin Martyr explored later in this chapter.
23. Bradshaw, *Reconstructing Early Christian Worship*, 4.
24. Schwiebert, *Knowledge and the Coming Kingdom*, 49.
25. Stringer, *Rethinking the Origins of the Eucharist*, 76.
26. Kodell, *The Eucharist in the New Testament*, 120.

community's eucharist, "the bread symbolized Jesus' life-giving word and the wine symbolized the joy-causing Spirit mediated to those who received the word with faith."[27] He finds further evidence of the earliest churches' eucharistic features from the *Didache* which has no mention in terms of the last supper.[28] Similarly, Cullmann advocates that the main ideas of the earliest eucharist had nothing to do with the death of Jesus, seeing the *Didache* as an earliest eucharistic form. According to him, before the introduction of the Pauline eucharistic tradition, the eucharist was filled with joy realized by encountering the risen Lord and Maranatha, the eschatological expectation.[29] Perry consistently maintains that in later stage the Johannine community decided to accept the Pauline eucharistic tradition and then the eucharistic bread and wine became slowly the symbols of "the crucified body and blood of Jesus."[30] In that process, Perry assumes that the verses John 6:51–58 were interpolated. However, contrary to Perry's interpretation as to the verses, Cullmann gives a more reasonable exposition of the verses John 6:48–65.[31] According to him, the main emphasis in these verses is on "the material side"[32] so that participants acknowledge that the Word is truly made flesh and that the risen Christ is present in the eucharist.

In the Johannine eucharistic tradition, crucially, the bread is recognized as σάρξ (flesh) of Jesus. The Fourth Gospel starts with a proclamation that λόγος (the Word) became the σάρξ (flesh) of Jesus and lived among us (John 1:14). In chapter 6, Jesus is "the bread of life" (John 6:48) and the bread that "I will give for the life of the world is my flesh" (John 6:51). Thus when considering John's usage of the term "flesh," he seems to use it to emphasize the historicity of the incarnation of Jesus and his real presence as the bread which gives the eternal life in the eucharist.[33] In addition, "flesh" means that Jesus was a true human being.[34] Furthermore, John proceeds

---

27. Perry, *Exploring the Evolution of the Lord's Supper*, 94.
28. Ibid., 41–44, 88.
29. Cullmann, *Early Christian Worship*, 16–20.
30. Perry, *Exploring the Evolution of the Lord's Supper*, 90.
31. Cullmann divides John 6:27–65 into two parts, 27–47 and 48–65 and thinks that both are connected with the eucharist. Cullmann views that, although the first part also says Jesus as the bread of life, the second part reflects more directly the eucharist. Cullmann, *Early Christian Worship*, 95.
32. See Ibid., 99. Cullmann does not at all neglect the significance of the death of Jesus with regard to the sacraments, baptism and the eucharist. However, the focal point of his exposition of these verses is obviously the presence of Christ as σάρξ (flesh). For more details, see ibid., 97–100.
33. Johanny, "Ignatius of Antioch," 53.
34. Barrett, *Essays on John*, 89.

to mention the significance of the blood in the eucharist. Not only the flesh but the blood of Jesus should be taken for the eternal life (John 6:54). When considering the flow of this discourse, the mention of the blood seems unnatural. The main topic of John 6 is the bread. In that chapter, Jesus feeds the multitude with bread and fish. However, as Cullmann suggests, if we approach not just chapter 6 but also the Fourth Gospel as a whole from a eucharistic perspective, it is not unusual that John mentions both bread and blood in the eucharistic sense. The whole book of John is sacramental and so it is not difficult to find the symbols of the eucharistic elements. Moreover, John has already dealt with wine, at the marriage at Cana in John 2, which is identified with the blood in the eucharist. From this point of view, the eucharistic combination of flesh and blood in John 6 seems natural rather than strange.[35]

On the other hand, the term "flesh and blood" was appreciated in terms of the whole human in the Hebraic tradition. Thus the commandment of receiving both the flesh and blood of Jesus in the eucharist might be understood as taking the whole Christ. This perception provided the basis for the Reformers' biblical authority for receiving both eucharistic elements against the medieval church's doctrine of the Holy communion with the bread alone.[36] Moreover, Cullmann views that John employed "flesh" instead of "body" so as to emphasize the material phase of incarnation. He further finds that John intentionally sets special terms in significant places so that participants realize more vividly not only the spiritual but the material presence of Jesus.[37] John uses the verb τρώγω (crunch) in John 6: 54, 56 and 57 which is the climax of Jesus eucharistic instruction instead of ἐσθίω (eat, in John 6: 49, 58).

According to Moloney, ἐσθίω is a term related to the general word "eating" but τρώγω is "a more physical word, describing the process of munching or crunching, and often used for animals."[38] Why did John use this somewhat coarse language instead of ἐσθίω which seems to be more appropriate to explain the eucharist? Cullmann says:

> We understand this only when we consider that the main thing . . . is to stress that the life element which has come down from heaven is the completely incarnate Christ, whose father and mother the Jews know (v. 42). . . . It is a matter of importance for him from the beginning to show that Christ worked in a real

---

35. Cullmann, *Early Christian Worship*, 101.
36. Brown, *The Gospel According to John, I-XII*, 282.
37. Cullmann, *Early Christian Worship*, 99.
38. Moloney, *The Gospel of John*, 381.

body and not in the semblance of a body, that the Logos did really appear in the flesh.[39]

Through this special terminology, the Johannine community would not only recognize but also experience the risen Christ who is present in the eucharist. Thus the eucharist of John is practical rather than liturgical, and an empirical activity rather than one of speculative metaphysics. From this point of view, Bruner says that the sacraments are "simply Jesus' one way of salvation scaled down, physicalized, individualized, simplified, and concretized, from heart to hands, from soul to body, from group to individual."[40]

A Reflection on the Eucharistic Theology of John

As we explored in the previous chapters, generally the traditional eucharistic understanding based on the last supper tradition seems to conform to the following eucharistic statements. The significance of the eucharist is closely connected with the passion and death of Jesus. The eucharistic elements, bread and the cup, spontaneously remind participants of the body which was torn and the blood which was shed on the cross for their salvation. Just as receiving the bread and the cup means participating in the precious body and blood of Christ, so all participants then recognize what they will receive and believe its efficacy before conducting the eucharist. If some receive the eucharistic elements without preparation or acknowledgement, the eucharist is ineffective and leads them to accumulate sins. As a result, the traditional eucharistic regulations allow only baptized people to partake of the eucharist. Sometimes, more strictly, participants' faith and good deeds are recognized as a prerequisite for the eucharist. From this traditional point of view, the eucharist is the commemoration of the sacrifice of Christ and baptism, faith, and good deeds are required to conduct the eucharist properly.

However, as with John's eucharistic understanding, when Jesus' feeding miracle of the multitude occurred on a mountain is recognized as the eucharist, it is possible that our churches would enjoy a deeper eucharistic theology and a much wider eucharistic practice than any eucharist we have experienced. In the eucharist on the mountain, our Lord called not only a small number of the holy baptized but all who want to join, including even sinners. There was no prerequisite and no barrier of sex, age, race, religion or social class. For Jesus, whether or not they knew the meaning

39. Cullmann, *Early Christian Worship*, 99–100.
40. Bruner, *The Gospel of John*, 433.

of the meal was not the most urgent issue. Jesus fed those who hungered with fish and bread and they could eat as much as they wanted. Even so, Jesus did not seem to recognize the eucharist as simply filling their empty stomachs or taking fellowship. After the meal, Jesus taught them the real meaning of the eucharist (John 6:26–58). This eucharistic approach would broaden the passage of grace and enable churches to relish abundantly the feast of the kingdom of God beyond the traditional perspective of the last supper.

2 The Eucharist in the Didache

Interestingly, it is not so hard to find evidence of the eucharist presumed to be ascribed to Jesus' other meals rather than the last supper in a good number of early churches' manuscripts. The most significant example of that is the *Didache*. It is presumed that the *Didache* would have been written between 50 CE and 150 CE in southern Syria or northern Palestine.[41] Since Bryennios published the *Didache* in 1883, there has been a long debate on the eucharistic identity of the prayers in the chapters 9 and 10 of the *Didache*. The main question is whether the text of the *Didache* expresses agape or the eucharist. Betz sorts out the attempts of many scholars from Dix and Jeremias onwards to interpret the meaning of the *Didache* 9–10 in six categories.[42] Then, Betz concludes that "this large number of interpretations shows the uncertainty of the state of the research, the hypothetical character of the explanations and the difficulty of the question."[43] As Betz accurately indicates, a wrong presupposition inevitably leads to distortions of resulting study. For, a wrong presupposition makes for flawed criteria, and then assessing the *Didache* with flawed criteria produces wrong results. As Bradshaw notes, in all the early church manuscripts, "the whole concept of the agape is a very dubious one."[44] Thus it is difficult to make a clear distinction between agape and the eucharist. Moreover, it is not certain that the early churches conducted their eucharists with a clear distinction between agape and the eucharist as recent scholars suggest.

The first eucharistic characteristic of the *Didache* is found in the order of the eucharist of chapter 9. The texts are as follows:

41. Stringer, *Rethinking the Origins of the Eucharist*, 110.
42. Betz, "The Eucharist in the Didache," 247.
43. Ibid., 247.
44. Bradshaw, *Eucharistic Origins*, 29. For more details on the discussion of the agape and the eucharist, see the section "The Eucharist of Ignatius of Antioch" in this chapter.

> 9.1 Regarding the Eucharist, give thanks as follows.
>
> 9.2 First for the cup: "We give you thanks, our Father, for the holy vine of David, your servant, whom you have revealed to us through Jesus, your servant. Glory be to you forever."
>
> 9.3 Then for the broken bread: "We give you thanks, our Father, for the life and the knowledge which you have given us through Jesus, your servant. Glory be to you forever.
>
> 9.4 As this broken bread, scattered over the mountains, was gathered together to be one, so may your Church be gathered together in the same manner from the ends of the earth into your kingdom; for to you are the glory and the power through Jesus Christ forever."[45]

Here, the sequence of the eucharist of the *Didache* is the cup (9:2) and then the bread (9:3) whereas Matthew, Mark and 1 Corinthians 11 show the opposite, the bread first followed by the cup. The cup is presumed to be grape wine rather than water when considering "the holy vine of David" (9:2). Rordorf argues that the wine recalls "the hidden meaning of which has been revealed in the passion of Christ."[46] However, paying attention too much to the association between red wine and the blood which is shed on the cross has the risk of blurring the main themes of the eucharist contained in the *Didache*. The eucharist in the *Didache* emphasizes Jesus of eternal life rather than death.[47]

Clearly, there is no attempt to connect the eucharist with the passion and death of Jesus in the eucharist of the *Didache*. The bread and the cup in the *Didache* are not expressed as the body or flesh and blood of Jesus in the New Testament but simply as "spiritual food and drink" (10:3). This characteristic suggests that the Didache community would possibly inherit an independent different from the last supper tradition held by Pauline and the synoptic communities.

Furthermore, in the eucharist of the *Didache*, God bestows through Jesus "eternal life" (10:3) upon his children. This view of Jesus as a mediator of the eternal life given from God corresponds to one of the John's eucharistic characteristics presented in chapter 6.[48] As a proof of the close relationship between the *Didache* and the Johannine eucharistic tradition, Betz provides a considerable number of eucharistic words that commonly

---

45. Johnson, *Worship in the Early Church*, 37–38.
46. Rordorf, "The Didache," 9.
47. Bradshaw, *Reconstructing Early Christian Worship*, 5.
48. "Do not work for the food that perishes, but for the food that endures for *eternal life*, which the Son of Man will give you" (John 6.27b).

employed in both documents.[49] From the list Betz provides, Bradshaw focuses on the fact that John and the *Didache* together use, as the term for the bread, κλάσμα (broken piece or fragment, John 6:12) instead of ἄρτος (a loaf of bread) which is chosen by the Synoptic Gospels and 1 Corinthians 11, says that the eucharist of the *Didache* would be influenced by the Johannine eucharistic tradition based on the feeding miracle discerned from the last supper origination.[50]

On the contrary, Niederwimmer supports the theory that the *Didache* used the source of Matthean tradition and insists that κλάσμα must be changed into ἄρτος as the former is a later interpolation:

> The problem appears again in 9.4, where H [tradition] gives us *touto klasma*, and the parallels from later liturgies have *artos* in the analogous location. Peterson has pointed out that *klasma* is a technical term in the eucharistic language of Egypt; it refers to the particle of the host. The expression would then have entered the text of the Didache at a secondary stage. According to Vööbus also, *klasma* is secondary. The original text may have had *artou*. This emendation is probably correct. The secondary *klasma* instead of *artos* could also be an indication of the Egyptian character of the H tradition.[51]

If Niederwimmer's argument is true, the passage of 9:4 in the *Didache* should be corrected as follows: As this loaf of bread, scattered over the mountains, was gathered together to be one, so may your Church be gathered together in the same manner from the ends of the earth into your kingdom. However, as Aaron Milavec indicates,[52] to scatter a loaf of bread rather than fragments of bread seems irrational. Moreover, he focuses on the eschatological significance embedded in κλάσμα:

> Above all, the Eucharist of the Didache was profoundly forward looking: Those whose lives were nourished on the broken loaf were earmarked for the final ingathering – for just as the grains forming the loaf were once "scattered over the hills" (9:4) and only later were kneaded and baked into one loaf, so those who

---

49. According to Betz's study, seven words used in chapter 6 in John are found in Didache and the number of words increases when examples of other chapters are counted: *eukaristein* (11), *klasma* (12), *zoe* (35, 48), *emplesthenai* (12), *gnosis kai pistis* (69), *zoe aionios* (54) and *pneumatike trope* (63). For more details, see Betz, "The Eucharist in the Didache," 255.

50. Bradshaw, *Reconstructing Early Christian Worship*, 5.

51. Niederwimmer, *The Didache*, 148.

52. Milavec, *The Didache*, xvi.

ate the fragments of this loaf were also assured that the Father would one day harvest them "from the ends of the earth" so as to gather them into his kingdom. Those who ate, therefore, tasted the future and collective promise the "one loaf" signified.[53]

From this point of view, the term κλάσμα possibly shows the uniqueness of the eucharist conducted by the Didache community, and in turn as a whole the eucharist of the *Didache* is not a modification or development from the tradition of ἄρτος but an independent tradition formed by the Didache community.

The main members of the Didache community are known to have been Jewish Christians. The identity of the Didache community would have had an influence on the development of the eucharistic tradition of the community. On one hand, the Didache community would reflect the Jewish tradition and, on the other hand, inherit the eucharist of Jesus. First of all, regarding the Jewish influence on the eucharist, many scholars from Louis Finkelstein onwards argue that the eucharistic prayer in chapter 10 of the *Didache* is closely connected with a Jewish prayer after the meal, "Birkat ha-Mazon."[54] The chapter 10 of the *Didache* begins with "When your hunger has been satisfied [*emplesthenai*], give thanks thus . . ." (10:1).[55] Here, Mazza, paying attention to the verb *emplesthenai* (to satisfy fully), insists that the word exactly corresponds to the "Birkat ha-Mazon." Furthermore, in structure, both the *Didache* and the "Birkat ha-Mazon" are divided into three strophes, and the themes of the first two strophes are in concordance with each other although there is a little difference in content. For this reason, he views the prayer of the *Didache* as "a sort of Christian *Birkat ha-Mazon*."[56] Meanwhile, the *Didache* contains a description of the works of Jesus and the vision of the kingdom of God which scattered church gathers together into.[57] These ideas are unique Christian characteristics of the *Didache* different from the Jewish tradition.

The eucharistic regulation of the *Didache* needs to be considered in the light of the identity of the Didache community. The *Didache* 9:5 has been one of the most influential eucharistic directions in forming the traditional eucharistic regulations.[58] It is presumed that the eucharistic regulation of

---

53. Ibid., 68–69.

54. For more details on Mazza's study on the relationship between the Didache and the Birkat ha-Mazon, see Mazza, *The Origins of the Eucharistic Prayer*, 16–30.

55. These words are translated by Mazza. See ibid., 16.

56. Ibid., 19.

57. Ibid., 26–27.

58. "Do not give what is holy to dogs" (The *Didache* 9:5). Rordorf, "The Didache," 2.

restricting those who are not baptized from participating in the eucharist would become standard in the Didache community. The *Didache* 9:5 would be a useful clue through which one might imagine the eucharistic theology and regulation of the Didache community. However, it seems unreasonable to identify the *Didache* 9:5 with the eucharistic regulation of Jesus. In contrast to the Jewish meal practice which deliberately made a distinction between Jews and gentiles and between the righteous and sinners, in the meal practices of Jesus such laws of distinction and discrimination were no longer valid.[59] Even at the last supper, Jesus allowed those who were betrayers and sinners to have his meal.[60] In terms of biblical authority regarding the eucharistic regulation of banning the unbaptised from participating in the eucharist, the *Didache* 9:5 seems to depend on Matthew 7:6: "Do not give what is holy to dogs." In this case, Matthew 7:6 is irrelevant to the eucharist of Jesus. Thus it is unreasonable to assume that Jesus would say Matthew 7:6 during his meal practices. Furthermore, Niederwimmer suggests that the *Didache* 9:5 would possibly be a later interpolation of redactor.[61] If Niederwimmer's assumption is considered, it is probable that the eucharistic practice of the Didache community in the early stage would be conducted in a different way from the regulation of the *Didache* 9:5.

Rordorf gives a more reasonable suggestion regarding the question how the Didache community developed its eucharistic regulation depicted in the *Didache* 9:5. His focuses on the Jewish characteristic of the community. Referring to Audet's study of the Didache, Rordorf suggests that the regulation in the *Didache* 9:5 would have been influenced by the Jewish tradition which did not share the meal of the sacrifice with gentiles:

> In Mt. 7.6 this saying occurs without any clear context. In the Didache the situation is quite precise: only the baptized have the right to take part in the eucharistic meal. J.-P. Audet pointed out that in this passage the Didache stands close to the original Jewish context of the temple-offering, which might not be given to dogs, that is, Gentiles.[62]

To sum up, it is presumed that the *sitz im leben* of the Didache community was based on the Jewish culture and religion. The eucharistic tradition which the *Didache* received is evidently different from the last supper tradition. The linguistic similarity found in John and the *Didache* shows a

---

59. As to the meal practice of Jesus in his ministry, see chapter 6.

60. As to the disciples' understanding of the eucharist at the last supper and those who Jesus accepted in his eucharist, see chapter 7.

61. Niederwimmer, *The Didache*, 139.

62. Rordorf, "Does the Didache Contain Jesus Tradition," 422.

possibility that they share the same eucharistic tradition. The *Didache* was probably influenced by John, even if it is true the Didache community did not merely follow the Johannine tradition. For, the *Didache* contains various distinctive eucharistic elements from the eucharist of John. As an example, the *Didache* does not employ the term "flesh" which is a decisive eucharistic feature of John's language. Also, the eucharistic sequence, which is the cup and then the bread, is characteristic. Conversely, there is also the possibility that John was influenced by the *Didache*. However, there is no convincing evidence that one precedes the other. The more probable suggestion would be that the *Didache* received the proto-eucharistic source ascribed to the miraculous feeding which in turn formed the Johannine eucharistic tradition, and the Didache community would develop the eucharist for their own community in their unique *sitz im leben*.

3 The Eucharist of Ignatius of Antioch

According to the early church historian Eusebius, Ignatius of Antioch was famous as the second bishop of Antioch succeeding to the first bishop Peter.[63] It is presumed that he was born a little later than Jesus' death and resurrection and martyred in the reign of Emperor Trajan (98–117).[64] On the way to martyrdom, he wrote seven letters to the churches of Ephesus, Magnesia, Tralles, Rome, Philadelphia and Smyrna, and to the bishop Polycarp.[65] Among the letters, the Greek *eucharist* or *eucharistia* is presented four times in *Ephesians* 13, *Philadelphians* 4, and chapters 7 and 8 of *Smyrnaeans*[66] though in some of them there are still debates on whether the exact meaning of the term is the eucharist or just linguistic thanksgiving.[67] And, the eucharistic terms and meanings are shown in all the letters.[68]

---

63. Maier, *Eusebius*, 108.
64. Raymond Johanny, "Ignatius of Antioch," 48.
65. Ibid., 49.
66. Cummings, *Eucharistic Doctors*, 12.

67. As an example, as to *"eis eucharistian"* (to give thanks) in Ephesians 13 Stringer argues that the term means just thanksgiving prayer. See Stringer, *Rethinking the Origins of the Eucharist*, 133. However, Cummings views it as the eucharist because Ignatius seems to support strongly gathering for the eucharist frequently. See Cummings, *Eucharistic Doctors*, 12.

68. LaVerdiere argues the six letters except the letter to Polycarp contain the source regarding the eucharist. See LaVerdiere, *The Eucharist*, 152. However, even in the letter to Polycarp there is an obviously eucharistic reflection on the Johannine eucharistic tradition. For more details of that, see the section "Bread of God" in this chapter.

HISTORICAL BASIS FOR THE THEOLOGY OF THE OPEN TABLE (1)

The matter of the relationship between the eucharist of Ignatius and the last supper tradition is still debated. Schwiebert argues that Ignatius reflected on the last supper tradition although there is no direct mention of it in the writings of Ignatius. Schwiebert repeatedly insists that especially "ἕνα ἄρτον κλῶντες" (breaking one bread) in the *Ephesians* 20 echoes not only "τὸν ἄρτον ὃν κλῶμεν"(the bread which we break) in 1 Corinthians 10:16 and "ἐκ τοῦ ἑνὸς ἄρτου μετέχομεν" (form on bread we partake) in 1 Corinthians 10:17 but "λαβὼν ἄρτον εὐλογήσας ἔκλασεν" (taking bread, having blessed, he broke it) in Mark 14:22. In addition, the phrase "Take care, therefore, to participate in one Eucharist for there is one flesh of our Lord Jesus Christ, and one cup which leads to unity through his blood; there is one altar, just as there is one bishop" in *Philadelphians* 4 is not reciting but alluding to the last supper tradition as 1 Corinthians 10.16 does.[69] However, as Schwiebert also recognizes, there is no direct account or quotation of the institution narratives based on the last supper in the source related to the eucharist in the letters of Ignatius. Rather, objective linguistic evidence suggests that Ignatius retains the Johannine eucharistic tradition not the last supper.

One of the significant instances of the evidence that the eucharistic tradition of Ignatius was different from the last supper tradition, might be the use of the Greek σάρξ (flesh) in explaining the eucharist:

Ephesians 20
... gather together in the same faith and in Jesus Christ who descended from David according to the flesh, Son of Man and Son of god ...

Magnesians 6
Follow God's ways, all of you; respect one another; do not regard your neighbor according to the flesh; but always love one another in Jesus Christ.

Philadelphians 4
Take care, then, to participate in the one Eucharist, for there is only one flesh of our Lord Jesus Christ, and only one cup to unite us with his blood, and one altar, just as there is one bishop with the presbyterate and the deacons, my fellow servants. And so whatever you do, do in the name of God.

Smyrnians 7
They abstain from the Eucharist and from prayer because they do not confess that the Eucharist is the flesh of our Savior Jesus Christ, the

---

69. Schwiebert, *Knowledge and the Coming Kingdom*, 46.

flesh which suffered for our sins and which the Father in his goodness has raised from the dead.

Polycarp 7

I desire not corruptible food, nor the delights of this life; what I desire is the "bread of God," which is the flesh of Jesus Christ who was of the seed of David; and for drink I desire his blood, which is incorruptible love.[70]

As to the reason why Ignatius uses the term "flesh" rather than "body," Schwiebert gives an answer that Ignatius responds to heretics who deny Jesus' incarnation and his real presence in the eucharist.[71] However, as in the case of John, Schwiebert's interpretation might be effective in understanding the milieu of Ignatius' community but it still does not seem enough to explain why Ignatius does not mention the last supper which is a temporally crucial setting in understanding the eucharist. Agreeing with Schwiebert's suggestion of the historical context of Ignatius's community challenged by docetic heresy, Bradshaw provides a more plausible answer of the puzzle by connecting Ignatius' eucharistic tradition with John:

> The author's choice of the word 'flesh' (*sarx*) here rather than 'body' (*soma*) reveals a greater affinity with the eucharistic thought of the Fourth Gospel than that of the Synoptics or Paul, which he shows no sign of knowing: 'The bread that I shall give for the life of the world is my flesh . . . . Unless you eat of the flesh of the Son of Man and drink his blood, you have no life in you' (John 6.51, 53). Thus Ignatius is stressing both the reality of Christ's incarnation and the reality of that same presence in the Eucharist.[72]

The eucharist as the medicine of immortality is one of the well-known eucharistic understandings of Ignatius.[73] According to Cummings, the term "the medicine of immortality" was a technical term used by physicians in the ancient world. In *Ephesians* 7, Ignatius illustrates Jesus as our one ἰατρός (physician).[74] Although linguistically the term seems to be disconnected with the account of the New Testament, semantically the idea cor-

---

70. Johnson, *Worship in the Early Church*, 48–52.

71. Schwiebert, *Knowledge and the Coming Kingdom*, 47.

72. Bradshaw, *Eucharistic Origins*, 87.

73. ". . . you gather out of obedience to the bishop and to the presbyterate, in perfect unity, breaking the same bread which is the medicine of immortality, an antidote so that one does not die but lives forever in Jesus Christ" (*Ephesians* 20). See Johnson, *Worship in the Early Church*, 49.

74. Cummings, *Eucharistic Doctors*, 16.

responds to the bread of life of John 6. In Ignatius, the participants of the eucharist are offered immortality in Jesus. In John, Jesus says, "Whoever eats of this bread will live forever; and the bread that I will give for the life of the world is my flesh" (John 6:51). This creative imagery of Ignatius as to the everlasting life further develops into "incorruptible love" in the seventh chapter of Romans:[75]

> The Letter to the Romans 7
> I desire not corruptible food nor the delights of this life; what I desire is the bread of God, which is the flesh of Jesus Christ who was of the seed of David; and for drink I desire his blood, which is incorruptible love.[76]

Like the term "the medicine of immortality," this term "incorruptible love" is also related to the idea expressed in John 6. Here, the eucharistic blood is incorruptible love like the bread which is the medicine of immortality. As well as the idea of the eternal life, John and Ignatius share the method of containing the idea within the eucharist. John, explaining the eternal life offered through the eucharist in Jesus, employs various eucharistic phrases such as bread of God, bread of life, flesh of Christ and blood of Christ. Similarly, Ignatius also endeavors to express the incorruptible love in the same way with John and, in the process, Ignatius borrows a considerable number of eucharistic phrases from John.

The term "the bread of God" in the letter to the *Romans* 7 and *Ephesians* 5 is decisive evidence of showing the connection between John and Ignatius. For, the term "the bread of God" employed by Ignatius is found only once in John 6:33 throughout the whole New Testament.[77] Moreover, in the same passage, the term "the seed of David" is recorded in John 7:42 although it is observed in Romans 1:3 of the New Testament as well.[78]

Ignatius believes that the eucharist must be led by the bishop in the Catholic Church. In *Smyrnians* 8, he teaches that if any eucharist is not led by the bishop the eucharist will lose its legitimacy. However, while teaching the eucharist, he uses a special term "agape":

> Smyrnians 8
> All of you are to follow the bishop just as Jesus Christ follows his Father, and you are to follow the presbyterate as you would the apostles; regarding the deacons, respect them as you would God's law.... Without the bishop's permission it is not allowed to baptize or to hold an

---

75. Ibid., 17.
76. Johnson, *Worship in the Early Church*, 52.
77. Hill, *The Johannine Corpus*, 433.
78. Johnson, *Worship in the Early Church*, 52.

agape, but whatever he approves is also pleasing to God. Thus all that you do will be sure and steadfast.[79]

Was the agape the same as the eucharist or a meal practice for fellowship? Dix argues that the agape of Ignatius was a Christian common meal (*Chaburah*) different from the eucharist (*Berakah*).[80] From a sociological perspective, Smith gives his suggestion of the development of the eucharist. According to him, the original meal conducted by Jesus and his disciples was the messianic banquet. As times went, however, when the place of worship was changed from house room to meeting hall to basilica, the meal practice was moved from a meal sharing with symposium discussion to liturgically well-organized rites. In the process, two types of the communal meal which are the agape or love feast and the eucharist came to develop separately. He assumes that the separation of the two communal meals was completed around the end of the first century CE. Thus, Smith views that the agape recorded in the letter to the *Smyrnians* 8 is a different meal from the eucharist.[81]

However, to define what exactly the term "agape" meant is not an easy task. As Bradshaw indicates, there is no clear evidence that the early churches conducted both the eucharist and the agape.[82] Luke Timothy Johnson, questioning the assumption that the agape was different from the eucharist in the early church, says:

> My complaint about the dissections of Lietzmann, Mack, and Chilton is not the premise of a plurality of practice – which makes good sense, given the circumstances of Christianity's expansion – but the pretense that (1) these strands can now adequately be distinguished, and that (2) the diversity represented fundamental disagreement among the parties. There is simply no basis in the sources for either premise.[83]

In the third century CE, it seems likely that the community of Tertullian celebrated both eucharistic meals (*Apology* 39).[84] However even in the case of Tertullian, it is still possible that the agape was one of the synonyms for the eucharist especially held at evening, as Tertullian in his other writings calls the evening eucharistic meal as "the Lord's Supper" in *De spec.*

---

79. Ibid., 51.
80. Dix, *The Shape of the Liturgy: NEW EDITION*, 99.
81. Smith, *From Symposium to Eucharist:*, 285.
82. Bradshaw, *Eucharistic Origins*, 29.
83. Johnson, *Religious Experience in Earliest Christianity*, 171.
84. See the section "The Eucharist of Tertullian" in chapter 5 of this study.

13, "the Lord's banquet" in *Ad uxor.* 2.4 and "God's banquet" in *Ad uxor.* 2.8. Furthermore, the agape included all characteristics of earlier Christian eucharistic meals such as prayer, the singing to God, moderate eating and drinking. Based on this analysis, Bradshaw identifies the agape as an "act of religious duty."[85] Then, he concludes that Ignatius employs the term "agape" in the *Smyrnians* 8 recognizing it as a synonym of the eucharist.[86]

4 The Eucharist of Justin Martyr

Justin, one of the most crucial apologists of the early church, was born in Flavia Neapolis, whose biblical name was Shechem. Before his conversion, he pursued religious and philosophical truth, learning from various teachers such as the Stoics, Peripatetics, Pythagoreans and the Platonists. However, the place where he found the truth was the Old Testament covenant and its fulfillment in Jesus. After his conversion, he endeavored to introduce and vindicate the truth of Christianity.[87] He was a prolific writer but unfortunately only three of his writings survive which are two apologies and *Dialogue with Trypho*. Due to his refusal to sacrifice to the gods, he was tried by Rusticus, the prefect of Rome, and then beheaded with his six disciples probably in 165 CE.[88]

Justin's writings reveal a similar linguistic usage to Ignatius of Antioch which in turn shows a close relationship with John's eucharistic tradition. First of all, in the *First Apology* 66, Justin describes the eucharistic bread as the flesh of Jesus given for the salvation and nourishment of Christians:

> First Apology 66
> We call this food the "Eucharist." No one is permitted to partake of it except those who believe that the things we teach are true and who have been washed in the bath for the forgiveness of sins and unto rebirth and who live as Christ has directed. We do not receive these as if they were ordinary bread and ordinary drink, but just as Jesus our Savior was made of flesh through God's word and assumed flesh and blood for our salvation, so also the food over which the thanksgiving has been said becomes the flesh and blood of Jesus who was made flesh, doing so to nourish and transform our own flesh and blood.[89]

---

85. Ibid., 99.
86. Ibid., 30.
87. Cummings, *Eucharistic Doctors*, 19–21.
88. Johnson, *Worship in the Early Church*, 65.
89. Ibid., 68.

Furthermore, in the *First Apology* 66 and *Dialogue with Trypho*, the additional evidence of the connection with John is found:

> First Apology 66.3
> Jesus took bread and gave thanks and said, "Do this in remembrance of me, this is my Body." Likewise [ὁμοίως] taking the cup and giving thanks, he said, "This is my blood," and gave it to the apostles alone.[90]

> Dialogue with Trypho 41
> . . . that is to say the bread of the eucharist, and likewise (ὁμοίως) the cup of the eucharist.[91]

In the passage above, Justin, in introducing the cup, chooses the term ὁμοίως (likewise) which is recorded in John 6:11 rather than the term ὡσαύτως (likewise) of Paul and Luke echoing the last supper tradition. Richardson, refuting Benoit who argues that the term ὁμοίως of Justin corresponds with the term ὡσαύτως in Luke 22:20 and 1 Corinthians 11:25, correctly maintains that "Justin's ὁμοίως is not ὡσαύτως, and we shall presently suggest that it reflects a source other than Luke or Paul."[92] Richardson repeatedly provides further evidence of Justin's dependence on John that in Justin's institution narrative Jesus takes the bread and gives thanks without the action of the breaking of the bread just as in John 6:11. In the last supper tradition, by contrast, the action of the breaking of bread is treated as crucial.[93] Bradshaw, also, suggests that the eucharistic tradition of Justin echoes that of John which has the feeding of five thousand as the setting for the institution.[94]

If this was so, did Justin never know the last supper tradition? Evidently Justin, according to his works, knew the existence of certain sources called "Gospels" written by apostles and which also followed the eucharistic teachings of the documents. Yet, it is worth noting the wording of Jesus

---

90. Ibid., 68. The Greek "ὁμοίως" in bracket is my interpolation for this study.

91. Richardson, "A Further Inquiry," 243. The Greek "ὁμοίως" in brackets is my interpolation for this study.

92. Richardson, "A Further Inquiry" 238.

93. From Dix's great work, *The Shape of the Liturgy*, onward, many believe that the action of the breaking of the bread was an essential eucharistic order in the sevenfold shape of the last supper and later, also, in the fourfold shape of the early churches. Simon Jones argues that the first clear example of the fourfold shape of the eucharist is Justin Martyr, and after him the four eucharistic actions "can be clearly discerned in the majority of eucharistic rites in east and west." Dix, *The Shape of the Liturgy: NEW EDITION*, xiii. However, there is no reference to the breaking of bread as a eucharistic order in Justin's works.

94. Bradshaw, *Eucharistic Origins*, 90.

which Justin quotes from the Gospels in illustrating the eucharist: "Do this in my remembrance; this is my body" (*First Apology* 66:3). The term "remembrance" from the Gospels which Justin used would probably have been from the Lukan or Pauline tradition. For, there is no mention of the commandment of memorial in Matthew and Mark. On the other hand, regarding the cup Justin seems to reflect Matthew or Mark rather than Luke or Paul due to his direct mention of "blood" instead of the cup of covenant:[95]

An interesting observation is that the eucharistic wording of Jesus in *First Apology* 66:3 is similar to Luke and Paul but not exactly the same as theirs. Uniquely, Justin places first the commandment of remembrance and then "this is my body." In addition, there is no additional theological interpretation of the bread and the cup such as "which is given for you" and "the new covenant" of the Lukan and Pauline traditions.

As an answer to the question of the difference, Justin did not quote the eucharistic source from the Gospels but reconstructed the wording according to his theological intention. Also, it is probable that Justin would depend on his memory of the account of the Gospels rather than written sources. From this point of view, with a strong belief in the close relationship between Justin and the last supper tradition, Schwiebert argues that Justin's account is a finely honed rehearsal of the Last Supper tradition, employing virtually all of the key terms and little else within the structure.[96]

There is still a question, however, as to why there is no mention of the action of the breaking of the bread and a depiction of the night before the death of Jesus which are essentially treated in the synoptic and Pauline eucharistic traditions. In relation to this, Bradshaw assumes that the Gospels from which Justin quoted would have been different from the present form of the Gospels. He further suggests that the Gospels used by Justin would possibly have been a collection of the sayings of Jesus with a simple form before theological meanings and interpretation were added by later communities.[97] Moreover, the phrase, "the suffering of Jesus" explained in *Dialogue with Trypho* 41, which is often referred by scholars who maintain the relationship between Justin and the last supper tradition, seems to mean the suffering due to the incarnation not the death on the cross. In *Dialogue with Trypho* 70, when Justin adds an explanation of the bread and the cup, his interpretation of the eucharistic bread and cup as the incarnation not

---

95. Jourjon, "Justin," 76.

96. Schwiebert, *Knowledge and the Coming Kingdom*, 52.

97. From this point of view, it is presumed that at the time of Justin churches did not have fully completed gospels, and thus the eucharistic practice and theology contained in the earliest gospels would possibly be different from today. For more details, see Bradshaw, *Reconstructing Early Christian Worship*, 6–7.

the suffering from the cross is further clarified. Finally, Richardson gives an exposition of the passage:

> Plainly, it is not the Passion of Christ which is remembered in Justin's eucharist but – if we must use the terms of a developed theology – the Incarnation. The bread is a reminder of his being embodied for our redemption; and in this context the remembrance of "his blood" must refer to blood as belonging to the reality of his body.[98]

Justin's illustration of the eucharistic elements in his work, *First Apology*, shows an additional example that in at least Justin's community the eucharist was conducted in a way that was different from the last supper tradition:

> 65.2 Having ended the prayers, we greet one another with a kiss.
>
> 65.3 Then are brought to the president of the brethren bread and a cup of water and of wine-mixed-with-water, and he, having taken, sends up praise and glory to the Father of all through the name of the Son and of the Holy Spirit, and makes thanksgiving at length for (our) having been deemed worthy of these things from him. When he has finished the prayer and the thanksgiving, all the people present assent, saying, 'Amen.'
>
> 67.5 Then we all stand up together and send up prayers; and as we said before, when we have finished the prayer, bread and wine and water are brought.[99]

Schwiebert, paying attention too much to the terms, "bread" and "cup" (*First Apology* 65:3), argues that Justin follows the Pauline and Markan versions which use "bread" and "cup" as the eucharistic elements.[100] However it should be noted that the eucharistic elements employed by Justin of bread, wine and wine-mixed-with-water are evidently dissimilar from the last supper tradition with bread and wine. In *First Apology* 65:3, the term ὕδατος καὶ κράματος can be literally translated into "water and wine-mixed-with-water."[101] Furthermore, Harnack, paying attention to the fact that the term καὶ κράματος is absent from one of the manuscripts containing the passage above, the *Codex Ottobianus*, suggests that the term καὶ κράματος might be an interpolation of a later editor who thought the wine-less eucharist of Justin as oddity.[102] The eucharistic usage of the wine-mixed-with-water is

---

98. Richardson, "A Further Inquiry," 243.
99. Bradshaw, *Eucharistic Origins*, 61–62.
100. Schwiebert, *Knowledge and the Coming Kingdom*, 50.
101. Bradsahw, *Eucharistic Origins*, 77.
102. Ibid., 76–77.

also found in Cyprian's letter to Bishop Caecilius of Biltha. Here, Cyprian claims that the element to be contained in the cup is neither water nor wine but the wine-mixed-with-water (*The Epistles of Cyprian* 62:13).[103] This record gives information that around the third century at least the churches of Carthage within Cyprian's parish celebrated the eucharist with bread and the wine-mixed-with-water.

Concerning the elements for the cup, why did Justin choose water and the wine-mixed-with-water rather than wine only? Regarding the wine-mixed-with-water, it is probable that at that time mixing wine with water might have been the normal custom in Justin's community. Yet, this assumption cannot solve the more important question of water. Regarding this, Cummings adds a plausible answer that the mixing custom would echo "the desire to counter pagan gossip about drunkenness among Christians."[104] McGowan gives a more reasonable answer for this riddle with concrete proof from early church documents. Going further than merely being conscious of how they tried to look pagan, McGowan tries to seek the answer that the early Christians employed water rather than wine in the eucharist in order to discern their eucharistic elements from the pagan's sacrificial elements, meat and wine, and to practise asceticism with an aversion to drunkenness.[105]

However, the tendency of abstaining from wine due to asceticism or rejection of the pagan sacrifice goes beyond the peculiarity of the churches at the only time of Justin. Much more earlier than Justin, the tendency is observed in the New Testament as well. First of all, Paul's teaching of food is found in the letters to Corinthians[106] and Romans.[107] He believes that in Jesus Christ there is nothing unclean. Yet, the conclusion of his exhortation on food is to refrain from meat and wine. The reason is not because he changes his mind about the nature of food but because the action of having meat and

---

103. "Thus the cup of the Lord is not indeed water alone, nor wine alone, unless each be mingled with the other; just as, on the other hand, the body of the Lord cannot be flour alone or water alone, unless both should be united and joined together and compacted in the mass of one bread; in which very sacrament our people are shown to be made one, so that in like manner as many grains, collected, and ground, and mixed together into one mass, make one bread; so in Christ, who is the heavenly bread, we may know that there is one body, with which our number is joined and united." Roberts et al., *The Ante-Nicene Fathers*, 362.

104. Cummings, *Eucharistic Doctors*, 24.

105. McGowan observes that many early eucharistic sources contain quite different foodstuffs from the general assumption that the early eucharistic elements were bread and wine. For more details, see McGowan, *Ascetic Eucharists*, 95–191.

106. 1 Cor 8:10–13.

107. Rom 14:13–21.

wine would cause the ruin of other weak believers. In the time of Paul, almost all the meats were offered at the pagan's sacrificial ceremony and a libation to gods before drinking wine in meetings or banquets began to occur as a normal custom. Given that Paul's letters were read with an apostolic authority, the recipients would make an effort to abstain from meats and wine in their ordinary life and the discipline would possibly affect the eucharistic elements. In addition, Colossians 2:16–23 and 1 Timothy 5:23 show indirectly the early Christians' attitudes towards wine.[108] This is especially so with the latter: "No longer drink only water, but take a little wine for the sake of your stomach and your frequent ailments" (1 Tim 5:23). This text connotes that not a few Christians at that time practised the abstinence from wine.[109] McGowan, focusing on the eucharistic imageries "living water" in John 4 and "bread of life" in John 6, attempts to find the possibility that Johannine community would have practised the eucharist with bread and water.[110] The cases observed above show that water alone, and sometimes with wine, was recognized as a meaningful eucharistic element by the early churches.

5 The Eucharist of Irenaeus

Irenaeus, Bishop of Lyons, who is presumed to have died at the end of the 2nd century or the beginning of the 3rd century, was also a prolific writer.[111] However, among his writings, most of the information concerning the eucharist he gives is in his main work, *Adversus haereses* (*Against the Heresies*).

Irenaeus seems to own a good number of the books of the New Testament. Although he does not depict in detail a list of books in the Bible, it is possible to infer a quite complete list from his citation. It is presumed that Irenaeus would have used almost all the New Testament except Philemon and 3 John, although James, Jude and 2 Peter are still controversial.[112] For the first time he reports the existence of the four Gospels as follows: "the Word . . . gave us the fourfold Gospel" (*Adv. haer.* 3.11.8),[113] and attacks some groups which disagree with the four (*Adv. haer.* 3.11.9).[114] If this is the case, how much eucharistic theology and content does he borrow from the four Gospels?

---

108. McGowan, *Ascetic Eucharists*, 220.
109. Bradshaw, *Eucharistic Origins*, 51.
110. McGowan, *Ascetic Eucharists*, 236–37.
111. Minns, *Irenaeus*, 1, 15.
112. Irenaeus, *St. Irenaeus of Lyons*, 9.
113. Ibid., 8.
114. Mutschler, "John and his Gospel," 330.

First of all, Irenaeus seems to pay more attention to John than the Synoptic Gospels. For example, Irenaeus mentions John by name approximately 60 times, in contrast to a total of 54 times regarding the synoptic authors.[115] However, he emphasizes the harmony of the four gospels, that is, a single gospel which is "given under four aspects, but bound together by one Spirit" (*Adv. haer.* 3.11.8).[116] *Adv. haer.* 3.11.1–6 contains the core of John's theology which is the incarnation, the Word of God made flesh.[117] One of the most interesting things is that in *Adv. haer.* 3.11.5 Irenaeus enlarges the eucharistic theology of John based on the miraculous feeding (John 6), by interpreting the miracle in Cana (John 2) with a eucharistic perspective:

> This wine was good, which the vine of God produced in accordance with the laws of creation and which the guests drank first at the wedding feast of Cana.... Although the Lord could have served wine and fed the hungry without using any preexistent matter, he did not do so. On the contrary, he took the loaves produced by the earth and gave thanks over them; so too did he change water into wine. Thus he fed those who were eating, and quenched the thirst of the wedding guests (*Adv. haer.* 3.11.5).[118]

It should be noted that Irenaeus evidently echoes John' theology but he never follows the same path of John. Rather, he develops and modifies it to his milieu. As a result, Irenaeus does not employ the term "flesh" which is one of the most significant characteristics of the Johannine eucharistic tradition although he does it in mentioning the flesh of human beings which is nourished by the body of Christ. Regarding the eucharist, was Irenaeus influenced by the synoptic or Pauline tradition more than the Johannine one? Irenaeus employs the term "body" rather than "flesh" in depicting the eucharist and the words, "This is my body" in *Adv. haer.* 4.17.5, seem to echo Matthew 26:26. For, in *Adv. haer.* 5.33.1 Irenaeus seems to cite the passages of Matthew 26:27–29.[119] It would be worth observing the passage containing the term "body" in the works of Irenaeus:

> Adv. haer. 4.17.5
>
> He directed his disciples to offer God the first fruits of his creation, not as if God needed them but so they themselves would not be unfruitful

---

115. Ibid., 320.
116. Ibid., 330.
117. Ibid., 335.
118. Hamman, "Irenaeus of Lyons," 87–88.
119. Bingham, *Irenaeus' Use of Matthew's Gospel*, 294.

or ungrateful. He took the bread, which is created, and gave thanks, saying, "This is my *body*."[120]

Adv. haer. 5.2.3

When the mixed cup and the baked bread receive the word of God and become the Eucharist, namely, the blood and *body* of Christ, . . . Which is eternal life – the flesh nourished by Christ's *body* and blood, and which is his member, as the blessed apostle says in his Letter to the Ephesians, "We are members of his *body*," formed of his flesh and bones? . . . It is this very organism that is nourished by the cup which is Christ's Blood and that is strengthened by the bread that is his *body*. . . . the Eucharist, namely, Christ's *body* and blood.[121]

It seems very clear now that Irenaeus cites the texts of Matthew. However, in treating the eucharist, with regard to the last supper as a temporal background he does not mention the action of "the breaking of bread" and any additional interpretation of the meaning of the body of Jesus. In other words, his focal point of the body and blood of Christ is the nourishment for human flesh and the hope of resurrection to eternal life rather than the sacrifice of Jesus on the cross for human salvation.[122] What is more interesting is found in his illustration of the cup in *Adv. haer.* 5.33.1:

When he had given thanks over the cup, and had drunk of it, and given it to the isciples, he said to them: 'Drink of it, all (of you): this is my blood of the new covenant, which will be poured out for many for forgiveness of sins. But I tell you, I will not drink henceforth of the fruit of this vine until that day when I will drink it new with you in my Father's kingdom.' [123]

Irenaeus seems to closely follow the Matthean tradition. However, the illustration of Jesus' drinking the cup is a unique characteristic of Irenaeus which is different from the account of Matthew. Moreover, treating the eucharistic sources which are presumed to derive from the synoptic or Pauline tradition, Irenaeus does not merely follow it but reinterprets it.

If Irenaeus did not follow exactly the synoptic and Pauline traditions which are based on the last supper context nor the Johannine tradition using the term "flesh," how can the eucharist of Irenaeus be defined? A possible answer would be to suggest an independent eucharistic tradition. Irenaeus'

120. Johnson, *Worship in the Early Church*, 77–78.
121. Ibid., 81.
122. Bradshaw, *Reconstructing Early Christian Worship*, 8.
123. This text has been translated by Paul Bradshaw. See Bradshaw, *Eucharistic Origins*, 17.

community possibly was already conducting their own eucharist relying on the sources they received, although we do not know exactly what it was, even before they owned the whole books of the New Testament. In other words, as was stated in examining Justin, it is presumed that Irenaeus used the proto-Gospels or the composition of Jesus' sayings which would have been different from the completed New Testament today.

6 Summary and Evaluation

We have explored the earliest two centuries' manuscripts which contain information about the eucharist of the Johannine community, the Didache community, Ignatius of Antioch, Justin Martyr and Irenaeus.

Regarding the sacramentalism of the Fourth Gospel, some scholars have argued that John was the anti-sacramentalist. One of the most important reasons for their arguments is that chapter 13 in John replaces the eucharist with the washing of feet of disciples. Moreover, the Fourth Gospel does not contain the typical eucharistic features of the last supper, which are commonly presented in the Synoptic Gospels and 1 Corinthians 11. However, recent scholars suggest that John contains evidently a eucharistic tradition which is different from the last supper tradition. The context of John's eucharist is not the last supper in chapter 13 in John but the miraculous feeding in its chapter 6. Moreover, John uses the term σάρξ (flesh) in indicating the eucharistic bread whereas the synoptic and Pauline traditions choose the term σῶμα (body).

The *Didache* also provides evidence that the eucharist of the Didache community was different from the last supper tradition. The eucharistic sequence of the *Didache* is the cup and then bread whereas bread comes first in the synoptic and Pauline traditions except Luke. In addition, the *Didache* does not connect the eucharist with the passion of Jesus. Furthermore, the Didache does not use the representative eucharistic phrase "this is my body; this is my blood."

One of the second century church fathers, Ignatius of Antioch uses the term σάρξ (flesh) rather than the term σῶμα (body) of the last supper tradition. Ignatius' interpretation of the eucharist as "the medicine of immortality," "incorruptible love" and "the bread of God" is identical with the eucharistic understanding of the Fourth Gospel.

Justin Martyr also shows a close relationship with the Johannine eucharistic tradition rather than the last supper tradition. Justin explains the eucharistic bread as the σάρξ (flesh) of Jesus. In addition, for the adverb connecting the sentences of bread and the cup, Justin uses the term ὁμοίως (likewise) recorded in John 6:11 rather than the term ὡσαύτως (likewise) of Paul and Luke.

There is reasonable evidence to suggest that Irenaeus' eucharistic understanding was influenced by the Johannine eucharistic tradition. Irenaeus attempts to interpret the miracle in Cana (John 2) with a eucharistic perspective. At the same time, Irenaeus knows clearly the last supper tradition. In describing the eucharist, Irenaeus uses the term σῶμα (body). Moreover he cites accurately from much of the text regarding the last supper in Matthew 26. However, Irenaeus does not follow exactly the last supper tradition. There is no account of the action of Jesus' breaking of bread which is regarded as an essential element by the last supper tradition.

If the last supper was the original through which Jesus left certain regulations to be followed by church, why is it hard to find the significant features of the last supper in the eucharistic practices in the first two centuries? Even in the case of Irenaeus who had known the last supper tradition, why did not he follow the last supper tradition? In particular, regarding the temporal background of the eucharist, all the documents previously referred to do not mention the time of the last supper believed to be the original from the traditional view point. In other words, there is no illustration of the time, that is, the night before Jesus was arrested, which is the core element of the last supper tradition expressed in the Synoptic Gospels and 1 Corinthians 11. Also, regarding the style and content of the eucharist, it is difficult to find something common to all the early eucharistic practices.

The evidence that the earliest two century churches' eucharistic traditions were not the same as the last supper tradition raises these questions. What made the early eucharistic diversity disappear in church history? When did churches begin to recognize the last supper tradition as the proper eucharist? These questions lead us to the next chapter.

Chapter 5

The Historical Basis for the Theology of the Open Table (2):

The Eucharist after the Third Century

1 The Emergence of the Last Supper Tradition with Canonization

EVEN THOUGH THE FIRST and second century church fathers seemed to know a considerable number of books of the New Testament, the assumption that they would use these as sources is evidenced by not direct textual citations but almost by allusion. Why is it we can hardly find any biblical citations exactly the same as the present text of the New Testament in the earliest church fathers' works? There is a scholarly consensus that they would have depended on their memory of the sayings of Jesus, and even if they had written sources the texts would possibly be different from the closed-biblical texts of today.[1] This might bring us to the next question, concerning the process of canonization in that period. What was the churches' concept of the canon in the second century?

The scope of the canon for Clement at the last half of the second century seems to have been somewhat flexible. Farmer suggests that, except

---

1. According to Bradshaw, from the earliest period of Christian history, there were the attempts to associate the eucharistic sayings of Jesus with the last supper narrative. He maintains that the sayings of Jesus in the so-called last supper stories are later interpolation. Such an attempt is firstly found in Paul's letter to Corinthians although he would not be the founder of the tradition. Then, the last supper tradition would be introduced to Mark, and he would add the sayings of Jesus into his already existing last supper narrative. However, as Bradshaw observes, this last supper tradition did not have substantial influence on the actual eucharistic practice at least until the early of the third century. For more details, see Bradshaw, *Reconstructing Early Christian Worship*, 19.

for James, 3 John and 2 Peter, Clement possibly recognized and used, as the canon of the New Testament (NT), most of the present books of the NT which are the four gospels, Acts of the Apostles, Fourteen letters of Paul including Hebrews, 1 Peter, 1 and 2 John, and the Revelation of John. In addition, he included in the canon the Gospel of the Hebrews, the Gospel of the Egyptians and the Acts of Mattathias, 1 Clement, Barnabas, the Preaching of Peter, the Revelation of Peter, the *Didache*, and the *Shepherd of Hermas*. Indeed, he referred to more books such as the Protoevangelius of James, the Acts of John and the Acts of Paul, although it is not clear whether he recognized them as canonical.[2] Such a generous view of the canon of the NT in the time of Clement is evidenced by his contemporary Christian writer Irenaeus. According to Theissen, Irenaeus also used most of the books of the present NT, except Philemon, 3 John, Jude and probably 2 Peter.[3] Beyond the present canon, he referred the *Shepherd of Hermas* and 1 Clement. Regarding the four gospels, he seems to have a firm conviction concerning the canon. He probably had almost all the Pauline letters but he never commented on their completeness. In addition, regarding the non-Pauline letters, he seems to have had a somewhat open perspective.[4]

However, from the third century on, the perception of the canon of the churches entered a new phase. Origen of Alexandria (185–254 CE), travelling widely and visiting many churches, acquired information about which books were recognized as constituting canon by those churches. Although he did not make a formal list of the canon, he made profuse comments about the biblical authority of the early Christian literature. In *Ecclesiastical History* (H. E.), Eusebius summarized Origen's research on the churches' views of the canon of the New Testament at that time. Origen divided all the Christian documents used by churches at that time into three groups. The first group included the books which were recognized as canonical by the whole church: the four gospels, the thirteen Pauline letters, 1 Peter, 1 John, Acts, Revelation. The second group contained disputed books: 2 Peter, 2 and 3 John, Hebrews, due to a literary style which seems not to be Paul's (H. E. 6.25.11–14), James and Jude. He clearly rejected the third group: The Gospel of the Egyptians, the Gospel of Thomas, the Gospel of Matthias, the Acts of Paul.[5] In his early period of ministry, he accepted as canonical the Didache, the Shepherd of Hermas, and the Epistle of Barnabas, but he

---

2. Farmer and Farkasfalvy, *The Formation of the New Testament Canon*, 17.

3. Theissen, *The New Testament*, 208. However, Dillon offers the view that James, Jude and 2 Peter are uncertain while Philemon and 3 John are not definitely presented in Irenaeus. See Irenaeus, *St. Irenaeus of Lyons*, 9.

4. Theissen, *The New Testament*, 208.

5. Gamble, *The New Testament Canon*, 50.

changed his thinking in a short space of time. Regarding Hebrews, Origen tried to defend its apostolic character even though he recognized the possibility that Hebrews might be a pseudo-Pauline literature.[6]

Compared with Clement and Irenaeus, Origen's canonical categorization of the canon seems to some extent to have been conservative. What would have influenced Origen to be more conservative in terms of defining the boundary of the canon than his predecessors? Farmer attempts to draw the reason for Origen's conservative tendencies from the fierce persecution of Christian communities and martyrdom at that time.[7] Rowan Greer gives an illustration of the time of Origen in these words: "a list of imperial murders, civil wars, and their disastrous consequences in social and economic life."[8] During the persecution, Origen witnessed the death of many martyrs including his father. This experience and social context would lead Origen to develop more conservative theology and views on the canon.[9]

Hippolytus (170–235) in the west, Origen's near contemporary, shows similar canonical categorization to Origen. He believed the canon to be twenty-two books which are the four Gospels, Paul's thirteen letters, Acts, 1 Peter, 1 and 2 John, and Revelation. The only difference between Origen and Hippolytus is that the latter adds 2 John. Regarding Hebrews, although Hippolytus did not regard it as the Scripture, he made frequent quotations from it. He esteemed James, Jude and 2 Peter and also the first and second century Christian writings such as the Shepherd of Hermas, the Apocalypse of Peter and the Acts of Paul to be valuable.[10] When considering Hippolytus' perceptions of the canon, we cannot neglect the historical situation in which he was placed. Callistus, the theological opponent of Hippolytus, believed in "two-Gods-ism, ditheism."[11] Callistus' belief that "the Father was the name for the divine Spirit indwelling the Son"[12] was never accepted by Hippolytus due to his Trinitarian sense. Moreover, they had different opinions on the qualification of the participants in the eucharist. Callistus gave permission for even sinners to receive the eucharist as long as the sinners sincerely repented of their sins but Hippolytus excommunicated them until they finished completely the whole process of penitence regardless of their

---

6. Farmer and Farkasfalvy, *The Formation of the New Testament Canon*, 18.

7. Ibid., 14.

8. Greer, *Origen*, 1.

9. Regarding the influence of martyrdom on the formation of Origen's theology, see Farmer and Farkasfalvy, *The Formation of the New Testament Canon*, 24–26.

10. Gamble, *The New Testament Canon*, 51.

11. Cummings, *Eucharistic Doctors*, 29.

12. Ibid., 29.

confession or faith.¹³ It seems to be clear that Hippolytus' rigorism found in his writings is not irrelevant at all to the theological conflict with Callistus. This historical context would possibly have affected the whole process of Hippolytus' canonization.

Later, in the fourth century, Eusebius (260–340) divided Christian literature into three groups. His canonical categorization was similar to Origen and Hippolytus. Firstly, in *homologoumena* (recognized books) he included twenty-two books which are the four gospels, Acts, the 14 letters of Paul, 1 John, 1 Peter and possibly Revelation. Secondly, in *antilegomena* (disputed, but accepted as an authentic by the majority, books), he set James, Jude, 2 Peter, 2 and 3 John, and in *notha* (spurious and hardly authentic books) he placed the Acts of Paul, the Shepherd of Hermas, Apocalypse of Peter, the Acts of Barnabas, and the Didache, Gospel of the Hebrews and probably Revelation. Lastly, he considered the Gospels of Peter, the Acts of Thomas, the Acts of Andrew and Matthias, Acts of John, and other Acts of apostles to be heretical writings.¹⁴

The twenty-seven books of the NT were mentioned as canonical for the first time in the thirty-ninth Easter letter of Athanasius, bishop of Alexandria, written in 367. However, region by region, the views on the canon varied. For example, even until the early fifth century the Syrian church accepted only twenty-two books as canonical. In the west, the Council of Hippo (393) and the Council of Carthage (397) both adopted the twenty seven writings as the canon of the NT.¹⁵

To sum up, various Christian documents were cited with a considerable authority in the church fathers' writings until the second century. However, at the turn of the third century, the churches began to fix the number of the New Testament canon from as few as twenty-two books to as many as twenty-seven books which is the same as today. In the process of the canonization, churches faced many changes of situation and it affected the churches' decision in terms of choosing particular books as part of the canon. In the time of Origen when churches suffered from severe persecution, whether the theology of martyrdom was included or not was a crucial criterion as to whether to categorize a book as canonical. In case of Hippolytus, the rigorism formed through theological argument with Callistus would influence his concept of the canon. As we explored in the former chapter, if the eucharistic texts contained in the New Testament existed in the first and second centuries were different from today, the modification of the old

---

13. Easton, *The Apostolic Tradition of Hippolytus*, 23.
14. Theissen, *The New Testament*, 209.
15. Gamble, *The New Testament Canon*, 55–56.

texts would possibly have occurred along with this period of canonization. In this period, a radical change is found in the eucharist. As Stephen Burns notes, the canon, that is, "the Bible was formed in the context of Christian worship,"[16] and after canonization churches' worship began to be formed following the theology and directions of the Bible. During this process, the varied expressions of the eucharist of the early churches would have gradually disappeared and evolved into the canonized style of the eucharist which was authorized by the Synoptic Gospels and the Pauline tradition.

2 The Eucharist of Tertullian

Tertullian (155–220) provides useful but limited information of the eucharist at Carthage.[17] He is the first writer who places the eucharist in the setting of the last supper outside the New Testament.[18] He mentions the last supper narrative in the treatise, *Against Marcion* 4. 40:

> When He so earnestly expressed His desire to eat the passover, He considered it His own feast; for it would have been unworthy of God to desire to partake of what was not His own. Then, having taken the bread and given it to His disciples, He made it His own body, by saying, "This is my body," that is, the figure of my body. . . . He likewise, when mentioning the cup and making the new testament to be sealed "in His blood," affirms the reality of His body. For, no blood can belong to a body which is not a body of flesh. . . . Thus, from the evidence of the flesh, we get a proof of the body and a proof of the flesh from the evidence of the blood.[19]

For Tertullian, the last supper was clearly the passover meal. Tertullian emphasizes the paschal significance by directly connecting Jesus' desire to participate in the passover meal with the action of taking the bread. However, even though it is true that Tertullian's paschal understanding of the eucharist is clearly presented in this passage, the practice of this eucharist is not the same as that of the Synoptic Gospels or Paul. First of all, there is no mention of the breaking of bread and thanksgiving. In addition, the explanation of the bread and cup also does not follow the so-called last supper story. Here, Tertullian's focus is on the incarnation of Jesus or his real

16. Burns, "The Treasures of the Bible," 2.

17. Saxer, "Tertullian," 132.

18. Bradshaw, *Reconstructing Early Christian Worship*, 8–9. See also Mazza, *The Celebration of the Eucharist*, 117.

19. Roberts et al., *The Ante-Nicene Fathers*, 417–18.

presence in the elements rather than the new covenant or salvation through the sacrifice on the cross. From this point of view, it is uncertain whether this passage contains information of the actual eucharistic practice of Tertullian's community or that his exposition of the so-called last supper story recorded in Matthew 26 was in order to refute Marcion.[20] Thus, Bradshaw suggests that the purpose of Tertullian's treating the eucharist in this passage would "more probably be accounted for by his desire to combat the docetism of his opponent than by adherence to an independent catechetical tradition."[21]

Elsewhere, Tertullian attempts to interpret the meaning of bread in the Lord's Prayer from a spiritual and eucharistic perspective. In *De oratione* 6.2 which was probably written between 200 and 206, Tertullian echoes the Fourth Gospel's eucharistic tradition:

> This petition 'Give us today our daily bread' we understand rather in a spiritual sense, for Christ is our bread because he is life and bread of life. 'I am the bread of life,' he says, and, a little earlier, 'The bread is the word of the living God that has come down from heaven.' In addition, his body is a kind of bread: 'This is my body.' Consequently, in asking for daily bread, we are asking to live forever in Christ and never to be separated from his body.[22]

It can be observed that a Christian meal practice is illustrated in his *Apology* 39. Here Tertullian depicts quite different styles of communal meals from the eucharist based on the last supper tradition:

> Our feast explains itself by its name. The Greeks call it *agape*, i.e., affection.... The participants, before reclining, taste first of prayer to God. As much is eaten as satisfies the cravings of hunger; as much is drunk as befits the chaste. They say it is enough, as those who remember that even during the night they have to worship God; they talk as those who know that the Lord is one of their auditors. After manual ablution, and the bringing in of lights, each is asked to stand forth and sing, as he can, a hymn to God, either one from the holy Scriptures or one of his own composing,--a proof of the measure of our drinking. As the feast commenced with prayer, so with prayer it is closed.[23]

---

20. In this passage, Tertullian seems to follow the story line of Matthew 26 including Jesus' prediction of Judas' betrayal and, additionally, he directly mentions the words "as narrated in the Gospel of Matthew" (*Against Marcion* 4.40).

21. Bradshaw, *Eucharistic Origins*, 18.

22. Saxer, "Tertullian," 141.

23. Roberts et al., *The Ante-Nicene Fathers*, 47.

Even today, many scholars reach the conclusion that this passage is not about the eucharist but agape. However, as explored in the previous chapter, in the earliest Christian literature the terms, the eucharist and agape, are employed without distinction. Also it is hard to find evidence that the early church conducted two different types of eucharist.[24] Additionally, Tertullian expresses the eucharist with various names such as "*Cena domini*" (the supper of God) in *De spec.* 13, "*Convivium Dei*" (the banquet of God) in *Ad uxor.* 2.8, or "*Convivium dominicum*" (the banquet of the Lord) in *Ad uxor.* 2.4.[25]

3 The Eucharist of Cyprian, Bishop of Carthage

Cyprian (200–257 CE) demonstrated quite a different perception of the eucharist from his predecessors. Cyprian's eucharist reflected the Pauline and synoptic eucharistic traditions in quite an exact way from the accounts of the last supper. Before exploring in detail his eucharistic theology, it would be worth noting briefly his career. Cyprian was converted about the year 245. After his election as bishop by the people of Carthage in 248 or 249, he underwent unceasing difficulties with intolerable persecution and attacks from heretics. In the period of persecution, Christians responded in two ways, with fidelity and defection, that is, as martyrs and apostates. In this situation, Cyprian had to do something for the churches in Carthage, and all his efforts are contained in his writings.[26] As a response to persecution, following the passion of Christ through martyrdom was recognized as an explicit way to verify true discipleship. As observed in the previous chapter, Ignatius of Antioch also expressed his longing for martyrdom in a similar situation. For the Cyprian community too, to live as a Christian meant an imitation of the passion of Christ. When we consider the significance of the eucharist in Christian life and worship in those times, it is not difficult to imagine the church fathers' belief that "the Eucharist too is an imitation of the passion."[27] Because of the period of persecution, the connection between the passion of Christ and the eucharist came to be stronger. However, there have been persecutions against Christians since the beginning of Christianity. If so, why was the clear connection between the death of Jesus and the eucharist expressed for the first time in the writings of Cyprian in the middle of the third century? The persecution itself is not sufficient for the answer. We need to look further into

---

24. See the section of "The Eucharist of Ignatius of Antioch" in chapter 4 of this study.

25. Saxer, "Tertullian," 133, 152.

26. Johanny, "Cyprian of Carthage," 156–59.

27. Mazza, *The Celebration of the Eucharist*, 135.

the process of canonization. In the middle of the third century, the Pauline letters and the gospels were coming to be recognized as canonical with apostolic authority while other books, containing different eucharistic traditions from the Pauline and synoptic, were excluded from the canon. Spontaneously, eucharistic theology and practice based on the Pauline and Synoptic Gospels became mainstream. Then, the link between the eucharist and the passion of Christ became more robust.

Cyprian's letter to Bishop Caecilius of Biltha probably written in 253 is the most important source containing his eucharistic understanding.[28] This letter titled as "On the Sacrament of the Cup of the Lord" is exclusively focused on the eucharist. In this letter, he cites Matthew 26:28–29, teaching the eucharistic cup with an explanation of the setting of the last supper:

> For, taking the cup on the eve of His passion, He blessed it, and gave it to His disciples, saying, "Drink all of this; for this is my blood of the New Testament, which shall be shed for many, for the remission of sins. I say unto you, I will not drink henceforth of this fruit of the vine, until that day in which I shall drink new wine with you in the kingdom of my Father."[29]

Cyprian constantly provides the eucharistic model that church has to follow, citing 1 Corinthians 11:23–26 with an emphasis on Paul's authority as an apostle:

> Moreover, the blessed Apostle Paul, chosen and sent by the Lord, and appointed a preacher of the Gospel truth, lays down these very things in his epistle, saying, "The Lord Jesus, the same night in which He was betrayed, took bread; and when He had given thanks, He broke it, and said, This is my body, which shall be given for ye: do this in remembrance of me. After the same manner also He took the cup, when he had supped, saying, This cup is the new testament in my blood: this do, as oft as ye drink it, in remembrance of me. For as often as you eat this bread and drink this cup, ye shall show forth the Lord's death until He come."[30]

His letter indicates indirectly the eucharistic practice around the middle of the third century. Cyprian claimed that churches should preserve the tradition delivered from Matthew and Paul, believing firmly that the proper eucharistic practice was to follow what Jesus did at the last supper. The reason why he emphasized the last supper tradition in this letter was

---

28. Ibid., 125.
29. *The Epistles of Cyprian* 62.9. Roberts et al., *The Ante-Nicene Fathers*, 361.
30. *The Epistles of Cyprian* 62.10. Ibid., 361.

that the recipients conducted the eucharist differently from the last supper tradition. In the church, "aquarianism, the practice of using water alone, instead of wine mixed with water, for the celebration of the eucharist"[31] was common. Thus, Cyprian insisted that the wine representing Christ's blood and the water representing baptism are to be mixed for the eucharist. Yet, even though Cyprian tried to conduct the eucharist in the same way as the last supper, full restoration of it was impossible. His community celebrated the eucharist in the morning but not in the evening. He tried to defend the morning eucharist:

> It behooved Christ to offer about the evening of the day, that the very hour of sacrifice might show the setting and the evening of the world; as it is written in Exodus, "And all the people of the synagogue of the children of Israel shall kill it in the evening." Exodus 12:6 And again in the Psalms, "Let the lifting up of my hands be an evening sacrifice." But we celebrate the resurrection of the Lord in the morning.[32]

From Cyprian's eucharistic sources, we might make three assumptions. Firstly, around the third century, Cyprian's community had the Pauline letters and Synoptic Gospels and recognized those books as authoritative and canonical. Secondly, the eucharistic understanding based on the last supper story spontaneously began to influence the development of the eucharistic theology and practice of the community of Cyprian. Thirdly, nevertheless, the Pauline and synoptic eucharistic traditions based on the last supper story were not recognized as an absolute principle for the eucharist. Thus, in practice, Cyprian's community preserved their regional tradition differently from the last supper tradition.

4 The Institution Narrative in the Anaphora since the Fourth Century

With the Edict of Milan in 313, the persecutions against Christians came to an end. In 380, Emperor Theodosius declared Christianity as the only state religion. This caused not only the expansion of converts but also the transformation of Christians' life and worship. The property of church was secured by the imperial administration and bishops came to have more influence on society, having jurisdiction.[33] During this period, a distinctive

---

31. Johanny, "Cyprian of Carthage," 160.
32. *The Epistles of Cyprian* 62.16. Roberts et al., *The Ante-Nicene Fathers*, 363.
33. Metzger, *History of the Liturgy*, 64.

characteristic of eucharistic liturgies was the introduction of the institution narrative into the eucharistic prayers.[34] The institution narrative would lead participants to be reminded of the death of Christ at the moment of taking the body and blood of Jesus. Finally the institution narrative became the centre of the anaphora of Christian liturgy.[35]

In the mid-fourth-century the anaphora of Serapion (or Sarapion), or more accurately Pseudo-Serapion,[36] showed clearly the recognition of the eucharist as doing what Jesus at the last supper foresaw regarding his death on the cross:

> To you have we offered this bread, the likeness of the body of the only-begotten. This bread is the likeness of the holy body. For the Lord Jesus Christ, in the night when he was betrayed, took bread, broke it, and gave it to his disciples, saying, 'Take and eat; this is my body which is broken for you for forgiveness of sins.' . . . We have offered also the cup, the likeness of the blood: for the Lord Jesus Christ, taking a cup after supper, said to his disciples, 'Take, drink; this is the new covenant, which is my blood, which is shed for you for the forgiveness of sins.' Therefore we have offered the cup also, presenting the likeness of the blood.[37]

In the west, in the latter half of the fourth century, Ambrose of Milan employed the institution narrative in his treatise *De Sacramentis*:

> Make for us this offering approved, reasonable, acceptable, because it is the figure of the body and blood of our Lord Jesus Christ; who, the day before he suffered, took bread in his holy hands, looked up to heaven to you, holy Father almighty, eternal God, gave thanks, blessed, and broke it, and handed it to his apostles and disciples, saying, 'Take and eat from this, all of you; for this is my body, which will be broken for many.' Notice this. Likewise also after supper, the day before he suffered, he took the cup, looked up to heaven to you, holy Father, almighty, eternal God, gave thanks, blessed, and handed it to his apostles and disciples, saying, 'Take and drink from this, all of you; for this is my blood.'[38]

---

34. Bradshaw, *Eucharistic Origins*, 140.
35. Mazza, *The Eucharistic Prayers of the Roman Rite*, 22.
36. Mazza, *The Celebration of the Eucharist*, 139.
37. "Prayer of Offering of Bishop Sarapion." See Jasper and Cuming, *Prayers of the Eucharist*, 35.
38. *De Sacramentis* (On the Sacraments) 4.21–22. See ibid., 99.

At the same period, in the east, the liturgy of John Chrysostom which had become the principal rite of the Greek Orthodox Church also placed the institution narrative in the centre of the anaphora:

> When he had come and fulfilled all the dispensation for us, on the night in which he handed himself over, he took bread in his holy and undefiled and blameless hands, gave thanks, blessed, broke and gave it to his holy disciples and apostles, saying, (aloud) 'Take, eat; this is my body, which is [broken] for you [for forgiveness of sins].' People: Amen. Likewise the cup also after supper, saying, (aloud) 'Drink from this, all of you; this is my blood of the new covenant, which is shed for you and for many for the forgiveness of sins.'[39]

From these three cases, all the biblical citations for bread seem to echo the account of Matthew. The phrase "for forgiveness of sins" for "the bread" in the anaphoras of Serapion and Chrysostom was probably an intentional interpolation as there is no biblical account mentioning this phrase for bread. Yet the words for "the cup" seem to be from the account of Luke. Through this combination of Matthew and Luke, they attempted to realize a unified and harmonized eucharist. Here it would be worth observing the composition of the words for the two elements. First of all, the symmetry was found in Jesus' commandment. While biblical accounts of the institution narrative used the word "take" only in the words for the bread, Serapion and Ambrose applied it to the cup in order to parallel both elements. Furthermore, the parallelism completed by inserting the phrase "for forgiveness of sins" in the word of the bread, in the light of a ritual, would provide "a well-balanced audible performance"[40] to participants. An interesting point is that the phrase for the bread "which is broken for you for forgiveness of sins" had been absent in the Roman Canon manuscripts since the eighth century.[41] This phenomenon seemed to echo the churches' efforts to follow the text of the Scripture.[42]

However, the institution narrative which was emerging as the essential part of the anaphora around the late of the fourth century did not rule over the whole church at that time. Evidence of this is found in the anaphora of *Addai and Mari*, representing the east Syrian eucharistic tradition. This liturgy is presumed to have been written from as early as the second century and the fourth century as it retains the Semitic character and the Syrian

---

39. "The Anaphora" in the liturgy of St John Chrysostom. See ibid., 80.
40. Jungmann, *The Mass of the Roman Rite*, 195.
41. Byars, *Lift Your Hearts on High*, 16.
42. Jungmann, *The Mass of the Roman Rite*, 195.

churches were comparatively isolated from other churches.[43] According to Jones, although his assumption is open to question, the liturgy of *Addai and Mari* dates from the seventh century.[44] Yet, interestingly, this liturgy does not contain an institution narrative.[45] Among various extant manuscripts from the twelfth century to the twentieth century, there are only three extant versions which contain an institution narrative, but they were published in 1890, 1901 and 1936 for the editors' liturgical or theological purposes.[46] This means that the institution narrative is the editor's interpolation. From this point of view, this liturgy possibly echoes the eucharistic practice of the east Syrian churches not only in the fourth century when canonization was nearly completed but much more lately. The original part of the anaphora of *Addai and Mari* in which several editors attempt to insert an institution narrative is as follows:

> And the priest recites quietly: And with these heavenly powers we give thanks to you, O Lord, even we, your lowly, weak and miserable servants, because you have effected in us a great grace which cannot be repaid, in that you put on our humanity so as to quicken us by your divinity. And you lifted up our poor estate, and righted our fall. And you raised up our mortality. And you forgave our debts. You justified our sinfulness and you enlightened our understanding. And you, our Lord and our God, vanquished our enemies and made triumphant the lowliness of our weak nature through the abounding compassion of your grace. *Qanona* (Doxology). And for all. And they reply: Amen. And the deacon says: In your minds. And the priest recites quietly: You, O Lord, in your unspeakable mercies make a gracious remembrance for all the upright and just fathers who have been pleasing before you in the commemoration of the body and blood of your Christ which we offer to you upon the pure and holy altar as you have taught us. And grant us your tranquility and your peace all the days of the world. Repeat. And they reply: Amen.[47]

During the Middle Age, the role of the institution narrative became much more crucial and essential in the anaphora even though this phenomenon was not universal as seen in the case of *Addai and Mari*. Spontaneously,

---

43. Bradshaw, *The Search for the Origins of Christian Worship*, 111.
44. Jones, "The History of the Nestorian Liturgies," 174.
45. See Spinks, *Addai and Mari*, 3.
46. Ibid., 5.
47. Ibid., 16, 18.

the institution narrative, that is, what Jesus did at the last supper became the sole ground to judge the authenticity of the eucharist of the church. After fixation concerning the eucharistic origins of the last supper, eucharistic theology developed with discussions of the operation and efficacy of the eucharist. In the medieval controversies around this, the core was the presence of Christ in the eucharist. There were two theologians who provided theoretical foundations for later controversies of the presence of Christ: Ambrose and Augustine. Although these two theologians might not expect that their names were connected to these two extremes, the realists who supported the real presence of Christ in the eucharist found the evidence for their argument in the former, and the symbolists who supported the spiritual or symbolic presence of Christ regarded the latter as the representative of the symbolists.[48]

Ambrose believed the real presence of Christ to be in the eucharist. After consecration, the ordinary bread is changed into the body of Christ although the appearance is still bread. Ambrose believed that what changed was not a matter of appearance but substance. Similarly, the substance of wine is changed into the blood of Christ after the consecration. Thus, the consecration which changes the elements into the body and blood of Christ by divine power is crucial in the eucharistic understanding of Ambrose.[49]

Augustine viewed the eucharist as a communal event. Christ is the head of the church and the church is the body of Christ. In the eucharist Christ bestows the bread which is his body upon the church which is also his body. Therefore, if someone who does not belong to the body of Christ receives the eucharistic elements, the bread and wine are no longer the body and blood of Christ.[50] Augustine, in his *Treatise on the Gospel of St. John*, XXVI, notes the communal significance of the eucharist:

> He explains how it is that what He speaks of happens, and the meaning of eating His Body and drinking His blood. "He that eateth My flesh and drinketh My blood abideth in Me, and I in Him" [John 6:56]. This then is to eat that food and to drink that drink, to abide in Christ, and to have Him abiding in oneself. And in this way he who does not abide in Christ, and in whom Christ does not abide, without doubt neither eats His flesh nor drinks His blood, but rather to His own judgement eats and drinks the Sacrament of so great a thing.[51]

48. Wawrykow, "The Heritage of the Late Empire," 74.
49. Ibid., 67.
50. Mazza, *The Celebration of the Eucharist*, 155–56.
51. Johnson, *Sacraments and Worship*, 209–10.

As to the presence of Christ in the eucharist, Augustine was in agreement with Ambrose. Also, he believed that even after the consecration, there is no change in the appearance of the elements which was the same as the position of Ambrose. In explaining the change of the eucharistic elements, he used the concepts of *signum* (sign) and *res* (reality). For him, the eucharistic elements are the visible *signum* (sign) and the body and blood of Christ are the invisible *res* (reality). During the eucharist, it is the reality that is changed not the sign.[52] However, regarding the interpretation of their understanding the presence of Christ in the eucharist, there is a difference between them. While Ambrose believed that the consecrated elements are the real body and blood of Christ, the focus of Augustine was on the spiritual meaning of the presence of Christ and the faith of partakers. Augustine developed his appreciation of the eucharistic presence of Christ in the exposition of John 12:8: "You always have the poor with you, but you do not always have me." In this verse, Augustine focuses on the fact that church cannot have Jesus' physical body because he will ascend into heaven after the resurrection. Therefore, the presence of Christ in the eucharist can be experienced spiritually through the participants' faith:

> It may be also understood in this way: "The poor ye will have always with you, but me ye will not have always. . . . And why? Because in respect of His bodily presence He associated for forty days with His disciples, and then, having brought them forth for the purpose of beholding and not of following Him, He ascended into heaven, and is no longer here. . . . In this respect the Church enjoyed His presence only for a few days: now it possesses Him by faith, without seeing Him with the eyes. In whichever way, then, it was said, "But me ye will not have always," it can no longer, I suppose, after this twofold solution, remain as a subject of doubt.[53]

In the ninth century, an important debate of the presence of Christ in the eucharist was led by Radbertus and his pupil Ratramnus. Both of them confirmed that Jesus is present in the eucharist. Yet, Radbertus identified the eucharistic elements with the body and blood of the historical Jesus in the same way as Ambrose, whereas Ratramnus, echoing Augustine, discerned the sacramental body of Christ as different from the historical body of Christ which was crucified and buried.[54]

---

52. Jones, *Christ's Eucharistic Presence*, 38–39.
53. Augustine, *St. Augustin*, 282–83.
54. Jones, *Christ's Eucharistic Presence*, 72–78.

By the eleventh century, the controversy of the eucharistic presence intensified more. For Berengar, the change of substance was not reasonable. First of all, philosophically, it was impossible that the flesh of Christ could be changed into bread in terms of the laws of nature. In addition, Berengar used the biblical foundation to verify the substantial difference between Christ's real body and the eucharistic bread. Christ has already overcome the power of death, now sits at the right hand of God and in the future will come again. Berengar thought that it was unimaginable that the glorified body of Christ became the bread which was broken by the hands of priests and eaten by human beings.[55] However, his idea of interpreting spiritually the presence of Christ in turn was judged as heretical by the mainline church. Lanfranc, an orthodox opponent of Berengar, refuted all thoughts of Berengar, and emphasized the substantial presence of Christ in the eucharistic elements. For Lanfranc, if the bread and wine were not changed into the body and blood of Christ, the eucharist could no longer be effective.[56] The term "transubstantiation," which echoed the idea of Lanfranc, came into fashion from the early thirteenth century onwards.[57] There are still debates on who first used the exact term "transubstantiation" (Latin = *transubstantiatis*).[58] However, more important is the fact that the concept of "transubstantiation" already prevailed at that time. In 1215, the fourth Lateran Council affirmed that the process of transubstantiation was the orthodox churches' official position concerning the issue of the presence of Christ in the eucharist.[59]

After the fourth Lateran Council's affirmation of the doctrine of the transubstantiation, the idea of the substantial presence of Christ in the elements received much more robust and sophisticated expression by Thomas Aquinas. His ideas are well described in Questions 75–77 of *Summa Theologica*, Part III.[60] He believed that after consecration the substance of bread and wine is changed into the real body and blood of Christ (Question 75:

---

55. Ibid., 80–83.

56. Ibid., 83–84.

57. Jeffrey, *Dictionary of Biblical Tradition in English Literature*, 775.

58. According to Cummings, Robert Pullen (1080–1146) first used the term *transubstantio* although it was not the term *transubstantiates*. See Cummings, *Eucharistic Doctors*, 117. On the other hand, Osborne argues that "the first usage of the term transubstantiation itself can be found about a half century later in the writings of Magister Roland (c. 1150), Stephen of Tournai (c. 1160), and Peter Comestor (c. 1170)." See Osborne, *The Christian Sacraments of Initiation*, 191.

59. Johnson, *Sacraments and Worship*, 225–26.

60. Jones, *Christ's Eucharistic Presence*, 93.

Article 2). The substantial conversion does not follow the laws of nature but is completed by the power of God in mystery (Question 75: Article. 4).[61]

At the same time, Aquinas tried to make harmony with the Augustinian eucharistic approach from which later scholars attained their theoretical foundations for the spiritual understanding of the Christ's eucharistic presence. As Augustine explained, the eucharistic presence of Christ was described through the terms *signum* (sign) and *res* (reality). Aquinas also employed the terms "accidents" and "substance," which were borrowed from Aristotelian philosophy.[62] The "accidents," that is, the appearance of bread and wine, are not changed even after consecration, but the "substance" of the elements is entirely transformed into the body and blood of Christ when the word "institution" is mentioned by a priest (Question 76: Article 1).[63] He further explained that participants could understand the eucharistic bread and wine as the true flesh and blood of Christ not through our human senses but only through faith (Questions 75: Article 1).[64]

The emphasis on the transubstantiation spontaneously underscores the meaning of the passion and sacrifice of Christ in the eucharist. Is Christ sacrificed in every eucharist? Regarding this question, Aquinas gives two answers in respect of the sacrifice and passion of Christ. Firstly, the sacrifice of Christ was once offered on the cross and the same sacrifice is repeatedly offered in the eucharist. Secondly, the passion of Christ is connected with the salvation of sinners. Receiving the eucharist means participation in the passion of Christ and, as a result, the partakers experience the enactment of salvation in the eucharist. However, such understanding of the eucharist includes two conflicting ideas. The sacrifice for the salvation was historically once offered by Jesus on the cross, but the saving sacrifice is equally offered in every eucharist. In order to harmonize these two conflicting ideas, Aquinas employs a decisive image. How is the coexistence of the two extremes possible? Aquinas' answer is expressed in this way: "the celebration of this sacrament is an image representing Christ' Passion, which is His true sacrifice" (Questions 83: Article 1).[65]

While Aquinas led the medieval church's eucharistic theology with his elaborate and astute perception of transubstantiation, various other theologians, recognizing the weak points of the doctrine of the transubstantiation, opened the door to the reformation. Among them, John Duns

---

61. Johnson, *Sacraments and Worship*, 226.
62. Jones, *Christ's Eucharistic Presence*, 93.
63. Ibid., 94.
64. Ibid., 93.
65. Aquinas, *Summa Theologica*, 2506.

Scotus (1265/66–1308) and William of Occam, or Ockham, (1288–1348) put forward the view that consubstantiation was more logical than transubstantiation. While Aquinas insisted that the substance of bread is changed into the body of Christ, they deemed that the substance of the body of Christ coexists with the substance of the bread. They believed that God's divine power enables two substances to exist in one place.[66] John Wyclif (1330–1384) more directly attacks the doctrine of the transubstantiation. His critical point was that transubstantiation has little scriptural and rational base.[67] Wyclif insists that physically the body of Christ is in heaven but sacramentally and symbolically the body and blood of Christ are in the eucharistic elements. Scotus' perspective was reflected later by Martin Luther and Wyclif's idea was found in the theological ideas of Zwingli and Calvin.[68] The Czech theologian Jan Hus (1369–1415) was partly influenced by Wyclif's view that after consecration the substance of bread and wine remains with the substance of the body of Christ. Moreover, he proposed that lay Christians should receive not only bread but the cup contrasting at that time with the medieval church tradition that only bread is delivered to the laity. However, the medieval church accused him of propagating a heretical idea of the eucharist and subsequently burnt him at the stake.[69]

5 The Dominant Position of the Institution Narrative in the Reformers' Eucharistic Understanding

After the death of Hus, the doctrine of transubstantiation dominated the medieval churches for nearly one hundred years until the advent of one of the most influential protestant reformers, Martin Luther. With regard to the real presence of Christ in the eucharist, Luther agreed with the medieval doctrine. However, Luther rejected the idea of transubstantiation. Luther suggested that Christ is ubiquitous in the eucharist.[70] The belief about transubstantiation focused on substance of the eucharistic elements being totally changed into the body and blood of Christ, whereas Luther's view was that the two substances, the bread and the body of Christ are mingled and coexist. Just as Jesus is God and a human, the body of Christ is seated at the right hand of God and at the same time is present in the eucharistic elements. For Luther, to understand the real presence of Christ in the eucharist was not a matter of human reason.

66. Jones, *Christ's Eucharistic Presence*, 98–100.
67. Schreiner and Crawford, *The Lord's Supper*, 171.
68. Jones, *Christ's Eucharistic Presence*, 102.
69. Byfield, *Renaissance*, 77.
70. Stookey, *Eucharist*, 52.

Thus he proposed, "Even though philosophy cannot grasp this, faith grasps it nonetheless."[71] Luther insists that both eucharistic elements must be given to the laity, criticizing the medieval eucharistic system of withholding the cup from the laity as "the tyranny of Rome."[72] In addition, Luther suggested that the word of institution of the eucharist is more important than the external eucharistic factors such as vestments and ornaments. "For in that word, and in that word alone, reside the power, the nature, and the whole substance of the mass."[73] Luther's emphasis on the word in the eucharist made the position of the institution narrative, based on 1 Corinthians 11 and the Synoptic Gospels, absolute. He maintained that John 6 is irrelevant to the eucharist as Jesus instituted the eucharist at the last supper (John 13) not on the mountain (John 6). He suggested that the theme of John 6 is the word made flesh rather than the eucharist.[74]

Zwingli proposed a symbolical interpretation of the presence of Christ in the eucharist, refusing both the ideas of medieval transubstantiation and Luther's idea of consubstantiation. Zwingli suggested that Christ is in heaven and it is impossible that his physical body is present in the eucharist. Therefore, the body of Christ which is present in the eucharist is not his physical body but the Holy Spirit. At this point, when he commented on the text "this is my body" he suggested that the verb "is" should be understood symbolically not literally. According to Zwingli, the eucharist reminds participants of the body and blood of Christ which were once sacrificed on the cross. Eating and drinking the eucharistic elements are symbolic acts through which they commemorate Jesus who offered his body for them. From this point of view, Jesus says, "Do this in remembrance of me" in the word of institution.[75] In addition, differently from Luther's dissociation of John 6 and the eucharist, Zwingli found the eucharistic meaning in John 6. However, the texts in which he found the meaning of the eucharist were not the miraculous feeding of Jesus (John 6:3–13) but the teaching of Jesus regarding the bread of life (John 6:26–63). Zwingli did not recognize Jesus' feeding on the mountain as signifying the eucharist.[76] Zwingli's focus was on John 6:63: "It is the spirit that gives life; the flesh is useless." This verse effectively contrasts the spirit with the flesh, downplaying the meaning of

---

71. *The Babylonian Captivity of the Church* 2.36. See Luther, *Three Treatises*, 151.
72. *The Babylonian Captivity of the Church* 2.21. Ibid., 142.
73. *The Babylonian Captivity of the Church* 2.39. Ibid., 153.
74. *The Babylonian Captivity of the Church* 2.3. Ibid., 133.
75. Wandel, *The Eucharist*, 72.
76. Bagchi and Steinmetz, *The Cambridge Companion to Reformation Theology*, 87.

the latter. Zwingli employs this verse as a scriptural root for his eucharistic thought that Christ is present spiritually not physically in the eucharist.[77]

However, Zwingli emphasizes the symbolic meaning of the eucharist too much. He treats the eucharist as a means of support to affirm the participants' faith and devotion. In other words, the eucharist does not have an independent role as a means of grace.[78] Such perceptions of the eucharist led to the practice of infrequent eucharists, "four yearly celebrations of the eucharist,"[79] and affected the later protestant churches' decision as to how often they conducted the eucharist.

As a second generation of the reformation, Calvin tried to establish a harmonized eucharistic theology arbitrating between Luther and Zwingli. Calvin, following Zwingli, suggested that the whole universe is full of the divinity of Christ but his human body is in heaven. Physically, Jesus was born through the Virgin Mary. He suffered, was dead, rose again, and then ascended to heaven. His physical body is not here but he is seated at the right hand of God (*Institutes of Christian Religion*, IV, 17. 26).[80] Therefore, Christ cannot be present physically in the eucharist. However, it is true that Christ is always with his children. In the eucharist, the body of Christ is taken by participants and his blood is absorbed in their body and spirit. At this point, Calvin agrees with Luther. In understanding Calvin's eucharistic theology, the key is the role of the Holy Spirit in the eucharist. By the secret power of the Holy Spirit, the body of Christ in heaven is given to the partakers in the eucharist (*Institutes of the Christian Religion*, IV, 17.10).[81]

Like Zwingli, Calvin finds some eucharistic undertones in John 6 rather than a direct relationship with the eucharist. In John 6, Calvin, in interpreting "bread" as "the spiritual food" and "eating" as "faith," corroborates the motto of the reformation, "justification by faith."[82] In addition, Calvin uses the texts of John 6 in explaining that Christ is present in the eucharist beyond the limitation of time and space by the divine power of the Holy Spirit (*Institutes of the Christian Religion*, IV, 17.7; 17.32).[83]

---

77. Cummings, *Eucharistic Doctors*, 165.

78. Stookey, *Eucharist*, 82.

79. White, *The Sacraments in Protestant Practice and Faith*, 85.

80. Calvin, *Institutes of the Christian Religion*, Vol. 2, 1393–1395. See also White, *Documents of Christian Worship*, 205.

81. Calvin, *Institutes of the Christian Religion*, Vol. 2, 1370–1371. See also Johnson, *Sacraments and Worship*, 236.

82. Hylen, *Allusion and Meaning in John 6*, 19.

83. Calvin, *Institutes of the Christian Religion*, Vol. 2, 1366–1367. See also White, *Documents of Christian Worship*, 204–5.

The reformers are thought of as having contributed to the recovery of the eucharist from the medieval abuses in terms of a spiritual approach towards the presence of Christ, with the emphasis on communal significance rather than rite by a priest, and the balance between the word of God and the sacrament. In spite of the difference between the reformers and the medieval church, as observed above, they agreed with the view that the eucharist was instituted by Jesus at the last supper. Like the teachings of the medieval church, the reformers use basically the institution narrative in their eucharistic theology and practice.[84] Especially, the temporal significance of the "last" supper led the reformers to focus on Calvary in the whole life of Jesus.[85] Obviously, the reformers discovered the meaning of the eucharist as a feast and thanksgiving moving away from the medieval doctrine, the repeated sacrifice. Yet, they failed to prevent the eucharist from being ruled by "the tone of melancholy, penitence, and humiliation."[86] The main reason for this might be found in the reformers' persistent belief in the origin of the eucharist, the last supper. A good example of this is shown in Calvin's thought. Criticizing the view that the meanings of the eucharist are undermined by the medieval sacrificial understanding of the eucharist, Calvin viewed the essential meaning of the eucharist to be centered on Christ's passion, death and benefit which partakers can experience through pondering the saving death on the cross (*Institutes of the Christian Religion*, IV, 18.5–6).[87]

The reformers' recovery of the eucharist enabled the churches to rethink the medieval eucharistic system which paid too much attention to external actions and elements. Instead, in emphasizing the faith and preparation for the eucharist, the churches were immersed in keeping the eucharist holy. As an illustration, Calvin focused on the worthy celebration of the eucharist through the "self-examination"[88] of participants. As seen in chapter 3 of this study, this self-examination included repentance and faith.[89] In that eucharistic understanding, the most important aspect is the preservation of the holiness in conducting the eucharist rather than the experience of the grace of God. To achieve that goal, churches have developed

---

84. McMichael, *Eucharist*, 29.

85. Byars, *Lift Your Hearts on High*, 24.

86. Ibid., 25.

87. Calvin, *Institutes of the Christian Religion*, Vol. 2, 1433–35.

88. Moore-Keish, *Do This in Remembrance of Me*, 34.

89. For more details on how Calvin and his descendents developed their eucharistic principles, see the section "John Calvin (1509–1564) and the Westminster Confession of Faith and Catechisms (1647)" in chapter 2 of this study.

their eucharistic theology and practice, reinforcing the prerequisites for the eucharist such as baptism, faith, morality and age.

6 The Eucharistic Understanding of John and Charles Wesley

In the eighteenth century a new approach to the eucharist was found in the Wesley brothers' ideas. Their eucharistic emphasis was on the grace of God through the eucharist rather than in keeping the eucharist holy by the inspection of partakers' qualifications. In 1747, Charles Wesley showed the crucial value of Methodist teachings concerning the eucharist in the first stanza of a hymn, *The Gospel Feast*. "Come, sinners, to the Gospel feast; Let every soul be Jesus' guest."[90] Literally, this hymn teaches that there is no restriction or prerequisite for anyone to come to the table. "Whether they have been properly churched or not, whether baptized or not,"[91] all are welcome to participate in the eucharist. While it is true that John Wesley did not conduct an open table on the same level as that of his heirs today, we can observe the foundational principles of the open table in the eucharist of Wesley.[92] Wesley recognized the eucharist as a means of grace in his sermon, *The Means of Grace*, in 1746. The means of grace was "the ordinary channels"[93] through which human receives the grace of justification and sanctification of God. His concept of the means of grace came to be clear in debates with the Moravians. They argued that only those who experienced justification were able to receive the means of grace like the eucharist. However, Wesley believed that through the means of grace sinners could reach the true faith.[94] For Wesley, the eucharist is not only the "confirming ordinance" in which believers can participate but the "converting ordinance" through which weak believers can be stronger and even non-believers can experience the grace of God.[95] At this point, Wesley says:

> The falsehood of the other assertion appears both from Scripture precept and example. Our Lord commanded those very men who were then unconverted, who had not yet "received the Holy Ghost," who (in the full sense of the word) were not

90. This hymn was written by Charles Wesley and first published in 1747. See Stamm, *Let Every Soul be Jesus' Guest*, ix.
91. Ibid., xiii.
92. Ibid., 63.
93. Chilcote, *John & Charles Wesley*, 183.
94. Stamm, *Let Every Soul be Jesus' Guest*, 64.
95. Crockett, *Eucharist*, 205.

believers, to "do this in remembrance of him." Here the precept is clear. And to these he delivered the elements with his own hands.... [T]he Lord's Supper was ordained by God to be "a means" of conveying to men either preventing or justifying or sanctifying grace, according to their several necessities.[96]

However, even in Wesley brothers' eucharistic understanding, the last supper still played a crucial role just like the reformers and the medieval church. For them, the eucharist was instituted at the last supper. The sacrificial languages and meanings contained in Jesus' sayings at the last supper came to be essential materials for their eucharistic theology. Such a eucharistic focus on the passion and death of Jesus is consistently expressed in their hymns:

Hymn 761
... Our hearts we open wide,
To make the Savior room;
An lo! The Lamb, the Crucified,
The sinner's Friend, is come.

Hymn 765
Come, Thou everlasting Spirit,
Bring to every thankful mind
All the Saviour's dying merit
All His sufferings for mankind
True Recorder of His passion
Now the living faith impart,
Now reveal His great salvation
Preach His gospel to our heart.

Hymn 771
Victim divine, Thy grace we claim.
While thus Thy precious death we show
Once offered up, a spotless Lamb.[97]

With regard to the issue of the sacrifice of Jesus in the eucharist, they followed the reformers not the medieval church's position. While the medieval church viewed the eucharist as "a repetition of the unique sacrifice of

---

96. Outler, *John Wesley*, 365.
97. Methodist Conference Office, *The Methodist Hymn-Book*, 291–93.

Christ on the cross,"[98] the reformers taught that in the eucharist participants commemorated Christ who once suffered for the salvation of sinners and experienced his real presence. Nevertheless, although the Wesley brothers did not recognize the eucharist as a repetition of the sacrifice, the passion of Christ was the central theme of their eucharistic theology because their eucharistic understanding was firmly based on the last supper tradition.

7 Summary and Evaluation

In the course of the third century, eucharistic theology and practice took a new turn. Eucharistic teachings based on the last supper tradition and direct quotations from the institution narratives began to appear more frequently in Christian literature. Among the early church fathers, Tertullian, in the third century, described first the eucharist in the setting of the last supper. In his view, the eucharist was the passover meal. Around the middle of the third century, Cyprian of Carthage argued that church had to follow the eucharistic model described in 1 Corinthians 11:23–26 because the eucharistic teaching was from Paul, an apostle of Jesus. After the fourth century, the institution narrative began to play an essential role in the eucharistic prayers although that phenomenon was not universal. By the late fourth century when the canonization was completed, the last supper tradition engrafted in the institution narratives of 1 Corinthians 11 and the Synoptic Gospels came to be recognized as the proper eucharist and prevail in churches. Spontaneously, the style of the eucharist evolved from the early churches' diversity to unity affirmed by the canon. When we consider the reciprocal relationship between the Bible and worship, these phenomena were a natural consequence.

During the middle ages, the eucharistic theology developed with the controversies of the presence of Christ in the eucharist. The medieval church's excessive emphasis on the transubstantiation caused several problems in conducting the eucharist. The reformers made an effort to rectify the medieval eucharistic abuses and a contribution to recovering the eucharist. The Wesley brothers broadened the eucharistic understanding with their new insight for the eucharist, that is, the means of grace. However, from the medieval church through the reformers to the Wesley brothers, although there were various eucharistic theologies and practices, there was always a solid common ground that Jesus instituted the eucharist at the last supper. The passion and death of Christ was always at the heart of their eucharistic perception. As a result, today most mainline churches have the

---

98. Cummings, *Eucharistic Doctors*, 221.

traditional eucharistic understanding based on the last supper tradition, following their ancestors.

The result of the study of the history of the eucharist leads us to rethink the traditional eucharistic presupposition that the last supper was the origin of the eucharist, and to focus on the eucharistic significance of the meals of Jesus. In the next chapter I will explore the meals of Jesus in the light of the eucharist, seeking the biblical base for the open table.

Chapter 6

The Biblical Basis for the Theology of the Open Table

So far, in the preceding two chapters, this study has explored the development of the eucharist from the early churches through the medieval era to the reformers and the Wesley brothers which altogether provide the foundations of eucharistic practice and theology for their heirs. In the history of the eucharist, there was a turning point between the second and third centuries. At the turn of the third century, the last supper tradition supported by most modern mainline churches began to be clearly observed. Around that time, with the process of the canonization, the early varied eucharistic theologies and practices came to dissipate and be unified into the last supper tradition attested to by the Synoptic Gospels and the Pauline tradition. In contrast, during the first two centuries the eucharist was celebrated in various ways by regional Christian communities without any mention of the last supper. The diversity was caused by the unique eucharistic perspectives formed by the distinctive features of each local community. The features of a community would be described with questions such as the following: who were the main members of the church?, were they Jews, gentiles or multiracial?, where did they live, Jerusalem, Rome or Syria?, what was their historical, cultural, and social context?, were their religious traits conservative, radical, or moderate?, more importantly, which eucharistic tradition did they inherit?, and what kind of memory of the eucharist of Jesus did they have? Each community would have its own answers to these questions, and the uniqueness of the answers would reflect the identity of the community which in turn would form and develop its own eucharistic tradition. This led to a rich diversity of the early church eucharistic practice.

These findings in the history of the eucharist have caused us to rethink the traditional eucharistic understanding that the eucharist was instituted by Jesus "at the last supper." Did Jesus institute the eucharist at the last supper? Did Jesus command churches to do, in the same way, what he did at the last supper? From an analysis of the eucharists of the first two centuries, the answer is likely to be cautious one. Furthermore, the results of the analysis indicate clearly that the origin of the eucharist is not the last supper but the meals of Jesus. Thus, in this chapter I will explore the role of the meals of Jesus in his ministry in terms of the kingdom of God and attempt to derive the eucharistic significance from the meals of Jesus.

1 The Meals of Jesus and the Kingdom of God

Mark and Matthew begin the public life of Jesus with the proclamation: "The kingdom of God has come near" (Mark 1:15; cf. Matt 4:17). Luke connects the kingdom of God with the life of Jesus, quoting a messianic prophesy from Isaiah 61. In the kingdom of God, Jesus will preach good news to the poor, proclaim freedom to the captivities, heal the blind, and do justice to the oppressed (Luke 4:18). The kingdom of God is the central message of the public life of Jesus.[1] According to Wright, the principal motive of the ministry of Jesus was the embodiment of the kingdom of God. For Jesus, the miracles of healing were not just a manifestation of his mercy but a way to teach the kingdom of God. His sermons and parables were not to reveal a mysterious wisdom of heaven but to proclaim the kingdom of God.[2] The fulfillment of the kingdom of God was the ultimate goal of the whole ministry of Jesus.

According to the gospels, Jesus performed a large number of miracles including seventeen healings and six exorcisms. He healed the blind, the deaf and the lame. He healed those who suffered from an infectious skin disease, bleeding, and palsy. Children, women and men were freed from demonic possession by Jesus' exorcism. Why did Jesus perform those miracles? Jesus did not do it as a physician or magician. Wealth or fame was not the goal of his ministry. His actions contained a transformational message, that is, the coming of the kingdom of God.

On the one hand, the transformational message is that the kingdom of God will be fulfilled in the future. On the other hand, the transformational message is also that the kingdom has already come in the ministry of Jesus. When we consider the latter perspective, the kingdom of God which has arrived with Jesus is closely connected with the existence of this earthly world. Dominic Crossan tries to interpret the kingdom of God envisaged by Jesus from a socio-political perspective. According to Crossan, to be in Palestine at that time, and to be possessed by a demon was not a simple mental or

---

1. Bond, *The Historical Jesus*, 89.
2. Wright, *The Challenge of Jesus*, 39.

spiritual problem. He views that being possessed by a demon was closely related to a socio-political dimension not a psychological one. In the first century, people who lived in Palestine were oppressed both economically and politically by the Roman Empire and the Jewish authorities. In this situation, some revolutionaries attempted to overthrow the government, insisting that they were the messiah. However, the only thing almost all ordinary people were able to do was to endure the oppression and to wait for the messiah. The harsh reality of life led some people to lose their minds. In this way, they were thought to be possessed by a demon. For Crossan, the identity of the demon driving people insane was in fact due to the rule of the Roman imperialism. Those who were possessed with the imperialistic demon came to lose the power to resist their oppressors and so stopped criticizing their rulers. In such a social context, the exorcism of Jesus has a special meaning beyond a mental dimension. Freedom from being possessed by demons would have enabled them to face again the reality of being oppressed by their colonial rulers. It seems to be true that exorcism itself has a much lesser political effect than a physical revolution. However, when we consider that those who were freed from the control of imperialism had the potential to join in an actual revolution in the future, the rulers would possibly have recognized Jesus' repetitive actions of exorcism as a prelude to a political revolution.[3]

Crossan observes, also, the healing miracle of Jesus from a socio-political perspective. At the time of Jesus, generally most diseases occurred due to insanitary surroundings which were closely related to economic conditions. The poor lived in poor living conditions. In addition, they would have had a weak immune system due to starvation and malnutrition. As a result, the poor would have been exposed to the risk of diseases more than the rich. Although the poor tried to emerge from poverty, imposing heavy taxes made the poor poorer. In such a social system, the main reason for disease was the rulers' oppression and heavy taxes. However, the ruling class and religious leaders were sympathetic to the imperialist view that the poor's diseases were caused by their own sin.[4] Even if sick people were healed by spending a lot of time and money, they were still isolated and recognized as sinners in Jewish society. In order to rejoin in society, they had to see the temple authorities and receive confirmation that they were clean and forgiven. For that process, they had to pay additional costs to the temple. In such a situation, Jesus again healed sick people and proclaimed the forgiveness of sins in the street for nothing. Indeed, he did not expect any reward

3. See Crossan, *The Historical Jesus*, 313–18.
4. Crossan, *The Historical Jesus*, 324.

from them. Such transformational and radical acts of Jesus would have scandalized the Jewish authorities and especially the temple priests who derived the most benefits from the temple system. Perrin gives an explanation of the meaning of Jesus' healing in the Jewish society which was operated by the temple system:[5]

> That the itinerant Jesus attained his fame primarily through his therapeutic abilities, together with the fact that the temple was the primary venue for healing within Judaism, makes it altogether plausible that Jesus' healing ministry, which he apparently shared with his disciples (Matt. 10.1; Mark 3.15), was meant to mark off the movement as the mobile embodiment of the temple.[6]

As Crossan asserts, the miracles of Jesus' healing "challenged not the medical monopoly of the doctors but the religious monopoly of the priests."[7] In light of that point, it seems to be natural that the chief priests were looking for some ways to kill Jesus (John 5:18; Mark 11:18; Mark 14:11; Luke 22:2; Mark 3:6; Matt 12:14).

The place and time that Jesus lived were not somewhere apart from this world. If we try to remove social and political meanings and effects from the ministry of Jesus, it becomes an act of distorting the life of Jesus. However, in order to understand the ultimate destination of the ministry of Jesus, something beyond a socio-political perspective is needed. The reason for this is in order to observe the ministry of Jesus from the perspective of the kingdom of God. Clearly, Jesus, attested by the gospels, was not an ordinary political revolutionary, magician or philanthropist. He did everything with the self-consciousness of a messiah. As the messiah he anticipated the kingdom of God which was still to come. However, he did not simply wait for the kingdom. He showed the kingdom in this world through his teachings, healing and exorcisms. When the disciples of John the Baptist asked Jesus whether he was the messiah or not, Jesus responded to them with a quotation from Isaiah's prophesy about the messiah: "the blind receive their sight, the lame walk, the lepers are cleansed, the deaf hear, the dead are raised, the poor have good news brought to them" (Luke 7:22).[8] Another prophet proclaimed that when the kingdom of God would come, the messiah would remove the unclean spirit from the land (Zech 13:2). The

---

5. As to the role of the temple system in the Jewish society, see the section, "The cleansing of the temple" in this chapter.

6. Perrin, *Jesus the Temple*, 154.

7. Crossan, *The Historical Jesus*, 324.

8. Bond, *The Historical Jesus*, 108.

kingdom of God which was prophesized in the Old Testament had been established in the exorcisms of Jesus. The kingdom of God embodied by Jesus was an eschatological and already realized kingdom. The healing of diseases, the freedom of souls from demonic possession and the recovery of social relationships were the evident fruits of the kingdom of God. These miracles were the "manifestations of God's power"[9] in the kingdom of God which had already come with Jesus, the messiah.

For Jesus, meals were "the privileged place"[10] for the teaching of the kingdom of God. In the gospels, the act of eating is frequently described in the ministry of Jesus. In his parables, meals played an instrumental role in explaining the kingdom of God. In his actual life, Jesus shared many meals with various kinds of people. Jesus went into the houses of sinners and tax collectors such as Zacchaeus and Levi and ate with them (Matt 9:9–13; Mark 2:13–17; Luke 5:27–32; Luke 19:1–9). Jesus stayed in the home of Simon the leper (Matt 26:6; Mark 14:3; cf. Luke 7:36) and possibly ate a meal with him. Jesus did not keep away from the Pharisees who were against him, and shared meals with them (Luke 11:37–54, 14:1–24). Jesus fed thousands of his followers who were hungry. Among them, there would be women, children and gentiles (Matt 14:13–21; Mark 6:30–44; Luke 9:10–17; John 6:1–14; Matt 15:32–39; Mark 8:1–10). The Fourth Gospel provides more clearly evidence of Jesus eating with gentiles. Jesus was invited by the Samaritans and must have eaten with them (John 4:39–42).[11]

Were there any prerequisite conditions for the meals of Jesus? The primary principle found in the meals of Jesus is that of "unconditionality."[12] Jesus shared his meals with sinners and outcasts. Did Jesus allow them to participate in his table because they believed in Jesus Christ and made a commitment to dedicate themselves to the kingdom of God? Jesus did not offer his meals to them as a reward for their beliefs and dedication. Rather, through the fellowship of the meal Jesus led them to the mission for the kingdom of God. "This dynamic of God's prevenient outreach"[13] evoked a hope for the kingdom of God from the sinners.

---

9. Ibid., 109.

10. LaVerdiere, *Dining in the Kingdom of God*, 14.

11. Foley views that not only John 4 but also Mark 8:1–9 contain the meal of Jesus with gentiles. He presumes that the large crowd fed by Jesus in Mark 8:1–9 was the gentiles who lived in a town on the east side of the Sea of Galilee. Foley, "Eucharist," 61.

12. Tanner, "In Praise of Open Communion," 476.

13. Edmondson, "Opening the Table," 218.

2 The Meals of Jesus as the Messianic Banquet

Some Jews' criticism of Jesus as being "a glutton and a drunkard" (Matt 11:19; Luke 7:34) hints how importantly Jesus treated meals in his ministry. It would be an excessive inference that Jesus regarded all his ordinary meals as the eucharist. However, the gospels attest that a good number of meals of Jesus were not simply an act of eating but "a prophetic sign."[14] Chilton suggests that Jesus attempted to symbolically connect his table fellowship with the banquet in the kingdom of God.[15] The teaching of Jesus through a practice of a meal would effectively lead participants to foretaste the feast of the kingdom of God more than any other parables and sermons through speeches. Chilton writes:

> To join in his meals consciously was, in effect, to anticipate the kingdom in a certain manner, the manner delineated by Jesus. Each meal was a proleptic celebration of God's kingdom; the promise of the next was also an assurance of the kingdom. . . . Within Jesus' movement, the bread which sustains us and the wine which rejoices us are taken as a foretaste and a warrant of the kingdom which transform us.[16]

What was the banquet of the kingdom of God which Jesus embodied in his meal practices? The eschatological expectancy of the messianic banquet had often appeared through the Jewish literature since the period of exile. Although Israel had returned from the Babylonian exile to the land God promised, they still lived under pagan rule. The eschatological restoration of Israel which they had anticipated was "liberation from slavery to oppressive pagan rule as well as return from exile."[17] God transmitted the message of the salvation and restoration through the prophets to Israel who was in despair. Israel longed for the kingdom established by the messiah and dreamed of the eschatological banquet which would be held on the last day of salvation.[18] An interesting point is that the main guest of the banquet is not only Israel. In the banquet prepared by God, all nations and people along with Israel will be nourished and consoled. This is how the scene of the messianic banquet is described vividly in Isaiah:

---

14. Fabian, "The Scandalous Table," 143.
15. Chilton, *A Feast of Meanings*, 38–39.
16. Ibid., 39.
17. Bauckham, "The Restoration of Israel in Luke-Acts," 437.
18. Stutzman, *Recovering the Love Feast*, 27.

> On this mountain the Lord of hosts will make for all peoples a feast of rich food, a feast of well-matured wines, of rich food filled with marrow, of well-matured wines strained clear. And he will destroy on this mountain the shroud that is cast over all peoples, the sheet that is spread over all nations; he will swallow up death for ever. Then the Lord God will wipe away the tears from all faces, and the disgrace of his people he will take away from all the earth, for the Lord has spoken.[19]

Echoing the eschatological banquet, Jesus said that "many will come from east and west and will eat with Abraham and Isaac and Jacob in the kingdom of heaven" (Matt 8:11, cf. Luke 13:29). Furthermore, he practised the messianic banquet through the meals shared with sinners and gentiles who were excluded by Jews.

The openness of the banquet of the kingdom is a crucial theme in the parables of Jesus. In Luke 14:15–24, Christ, the host, invites many people to his great banquet. However, those who are invited make excuses and refuse the invitation. Then, the host becomes angry and orders his servant: "Go out at once into the streets and lanes of the town and bring in the poor, the crippled, the blind, and the lame" (Luke 14:21). There is still room and the host orders again the servant: "Go out into the roads and lanes, and compel people to come in, so that my house may be filled" (Luke 14:23). There are no boundaries for the banquet. Here, Jesus "aggressively gathers a table full of guests, none of whom seems to belong."[20] Crossan compares three texts (Luke 14:15–24; Matt 22:1–14; *The Gospel of Thomas* 64) containing the parable of the great banquet and insists that all three communities interpreted and altered the original parable according to their own theology and situation. In spite of the differences between the three perspectives, Crossan discovers the common and main theme shared by the three communities, which is "the random and open commensality."[21] Similarly, Hultgren explores the three texts and suggests four structures in common:

> 1. Each has a banquet setting to which persons have been invited previously (according to typical Near Eastern custom). 2. The host sends a slave/slaves to announce to the guests that the banquet is ready (again, according to typical Near Eastern custom). 3. The invited guests reject the invitation. 4. The slave/slaves are sent by

---

19. Isa 25:6–8.
20. Stamm, *Let Every Soul Be Jesus' Guest*, 43.
21. Crossan, *The Historical Jesus*, 262.

the host to bring in replacements from the streets without regard for their social, economic, and religious standing.[22]

Here, also, the openness of the banquet of the kingdom is observed. Especially in section four above, Hultgren provides a more concrete description of the guests who will ultimately participate in the banquet. The final participants go far beyond the expectations of the old Israel. Fabian notes:

> The presence of genuinely wrong and *unacceptable* people at the table was essential for Jesus' sign. It fits his teaching perfectly. The outstanding heroes of his authentic parables are criminals and pushy women. Jesus' criminals are real criminals: not to be rehabilitated by our 'understanding' how they grew up oppressed or in dysfunctional families; not to be welcomed into our company in hopes they will change their ways. In Jesus' parables they never change their ways.[23]

Also, Luke 15:11–32, which is generally known for the story of the prodigal son, implies the banquet of the kingdom of God. The epitome of the parable is as follows: The younger son leaves his father with his inheritance. Not long after that, he wastes his wealth with prostitutes. He has to live as the bottom abandoned by everyone. He decides to return to his father. At last, the prodigal son is embraced by his gracious father who has been looking forward to the return of his son. The father holds a grand banquet with a fattened calf although the banquet causes the elder son to complain. This is the last parable among three parables presented in Luke 15. The classical title, the prodigal son, seems to be insufficient to cover the whole story. Vinson, trying not to lose all the three main characters, the father and the two sons, suggests the title "The Man and His Two Sons."[24] However, the more we reflect on this set of three parables regarding a lost sheep, coin and son, the clearer it becomes that the main character of the third parable is not the prodigal son or his elder brother but their father. More exactly, the third parable focuses on the father's love and forgiveness of sinners rather than the two sons' sin and repentance. Bock gives us a plausible commentary on the three parables:

> Jesus' commitment to the lost, like tax collectors and sinners, is pictured in the parables of the lost sheep, the lost coin, and the prodigal son. Heaven rejoices and welcomes all sinners who return, so Jesus is taking the initiative to find them. Unlike the older

---

22. Hultgren, *The Parables of Jesus*, 333.
23. Fabian, "The Scandalous Table," 144–45.
24. Vinson, *Luke*, 507.

brother of the prodigal who complains when his lost brother is restored, we should welcome all who were lost but are now found.[25]

Jesus who loves sinners and waits their return is the host of the banquet of the kingdom of God. For those, supporting the closed table, a principle can be derived from the story that the person who participated in the feast was not an outsider but a son of the host despite his profligacy. For, the sonship might be interpreted as symbolic of baptism and church membership. However, as Stamm properly notes, "the parable is theological poetry and not a church order filled with rubrics."[26] Thus, from the parable, what we can expect to gain is not a dogmatic regulation but the knowledge of who God is. When we ponder over Jesus' motive for the third parable, it is possible that the true message Jesus wanted to transmit through the parable might be more clearly revealed. In Luke 15:1–2, the Pharisees and the scribes blamed Jesus for welcoming and sharing meals with tax collectors and sinners. Then Jesus began to give the three parables to them in response to their criticism. Penetrating the main theme of the third parable, Wright states:

> From the moment he generously gives the younger son what he wanted, through to the wonderful homecoming welcome, we have as vivid a picture as anywhere in Jesus' teaching of what God's love is like, and of what Jesus himself took as the model for his own ministry of welcome to the outcast and the sinner.[27]

The openness of the banquet to the kingdom of God and the nature of the host of the banquet, that is, God's love forgiving even sinners, are revealed in the parables. Jesus taught the essence of the banquet in the kingdom of God through the parables which in turn was realized in his table fellowship.

However, it should be noted that the passages relating to the banquet do not simply describe God as the host full of love and grace. The eschatological banquet is not a joyful celebration for all human beings. The banquet is not the place where God forgives his opponents unconditionally. The sound of the trumpet announcing the beginning of the banquet will be good news for the righteous but a prelude to punishment for the unrighteous. On the day, the unrighteous will be doomed to slaughter (Isa 34:1–6). The day will be the day of punishment for the foes of God (Jer 46:10). On the day the Lord will punish all who wear foreign attire except his consecrated guests (Zeph 1:7–9).[28]

---

25. Bock, *A Theology of Luke and Acts*, 74.
26. Stamm, *Let Every Soul Be Jesus' Guest*, 44.
27. Wright, *Luke for Everyone*, 189.
28. Davies, *Bread of Life and Cup of Joy*, 88.

Nevertheless, these three passages of the prophets are not to be used as providing biblical reasons for refuting the open table. We need to remember who the host of the banquet is. A human cannot be the host but just a guest. Who does decide who can come to the feast? The sole right to judge whether a guest is righteous or unrighteous is held in the hands of God not in the laws and tradition of church. The Pharisees and the scribes believed that those who were able to come to the feast of God were the righteous in terms of the law. In contrast, Jesus had the table fellowship with sinners and gentiles who were far from the righteous as understood in the Jewish tradition. Through the table fellowship, Jesus recovered the righteousness in the kingdom of God, demolishing all the boundaries which made judgments between the righteous and the sinner under Jewish law. The Jews would have viewed Jesus as a lawbreaker. For Jesus, however, following the word of God was more important than keeping the Jewish tradition. As Fabian notes, Jesus is "loyal to biblical tradition" but "his opponents are the wrongheaded innovators."[29] The church's responsibility is to invite all people to the feast of God. That is the purpose of the God's calling toward church. Indeed, God is inviting all the people who thirst and hunger (cf. Isa 55:1–5). God wants to transmit the invitation through the church to the world. Anyone who hears the voice of God's invitation can come to the table and all participants deserve to relish the rich food prepared by God. The only one who can close the door of the banquet is God. Here, it would be worth hearing Fabian's insightful comment on the church's hesitation in conducting the open table:

> How remarkable, then, that later Jewish usage followed Jesus' example better than his Church did! Rabbis soon shifted their focus from the purity of the diners, to the purity of their dinner foods – and the kosher kitchen was born. Today all but ultra-orthodox Jews welcome non-Jews to their tables, while Christians cannot agree formally to eat with each other; instead, we mimic Jesus' opponents, with their various *chaburoth* for diners variously purified.[30]

3 The Cleansing of the Temple

The Synoptic Gospels place the cleansing of the temple in the passion narratives (Matt 21; Mark 11; Luke 19) but according to John the incident occurs in the early period of Jesus' public life (John 2). Although the time of

---

29. Fabian, "The Scandalous Table," 146.
30. Ibid., 147.

the cleansing of the temple is different, the four gospels agree that Jesus entered the temple area and overturned the tables of the money changers and the chairs of the merchants. He expelled them and obstructed anyone carrying merchandise through the temple. What was Jesus' intention in this action? In order to solve this question, it is necessary to explore the role of the temple system in the Jewish society.

Jewish society was ruled by the purity laws grounded on the Torah. Leviticus expresses the demand that Israel live under the purity system: "You shall be holy, for I am holy" (Lev 11:45; 19:2; 20:7). In the Jewish purity system, everything in life was classified into "clean" and "unclean." The purity system controlled Jewish society, categorizing all human acts, regulations, races, sects and even foods into those of purity and impurity.[31] The pursuit of the purity laws ended in religious and social sectarianism with strict boundaries.[32]

A crucial way that Israel came to be holy was to keep purity with the commitment to eat what was clean (cf. Lev 11:46, 47).[33] In Jews' ordinary life, a meal was the place where they had to keep the purity laws and where their identity as the chosen people was able to be confirmed. In other words, the matter of what they ate and whom they ate with is a statement of who they are. Indeed, for the Jews, "deciding who could eat with whom was a life-and-death matter."[34] Jewish sectarians showed their identity and doctrine through the meal practice. The Pharisees, the Sadducees and the Essenes all had their own dietary regulations. The Pharisees seemed to have more strictly kept the purity laws in the meal practice than others. They were reluctant to eat food with other Jewish sectarians and, needless to say, declined to eat with gentiles.[35]

The core of the purity system in the Jewish society was the temple sacrifice. For Jews, the temple was the place where God dwelt. Jews offered God sacrifices in the temple and their sins were forgiven.[36] All the offerings were to be without defect and all worshippers also were to be clean. The pursuit of cleanliness in the Temple sacrifice was extended into the ordinary life of Jews. Thus, everything within Israel related not only to sacrifice but every person and every action had to be pure.[37] Indeed, the temple

31. Countryman, *Dirt, Greed and Sex*, 20–22.
32. Ibid., 64–65.
33. Chilton, *Jesus' Prayer and Jesus' Eucharist*, 16.
34. Joncas, "Tasting the Kingdom of God," 341.
35. Feeley-Harnik, *The Lord's Table*, 97.
36. Wright, *The Challenge of Jesus*, 63.
37. Chilton, *Jesus' Prayer and Jesus' Eucharist*, 16.

was the heart of the religion and the life of Jews. In addition, the temple played an important role as a political symbol. Historically, many kings of Israel and political leaders sought the validity of their leadership through cleansing the temple or rebuilding it. In the first century, Menahem, Simon bar-Giora, Bar-Kochba and others used the temple for claiming themselves that each was a messiah and a new king of Israel.[38] In other words, for the present ruling powers, the temple was used for reinforcing their regime but the challengers to the leadership insisted that they were the true kings through cleansing the temple. In the temple, Jesus acted quite aggressively with overturning tables of merchants and hindering commercial activities.

What was the aim of the actions of Jesus? According to Wright, the cleansing of the temple was Jesus' symbolic action that the temple sacrifice would be ended. When Jesus stopped people carrying merchandise necessary for the sacrifice in the temple, spontaneously, the temple sacrifice stopped.[39] Similarly, Crossan views that the incident of Jesus in the temple was "a symbolic destruction"[40] of the temple system. Crossan focuses on Mark's intentional positioning of Jesus' curse on a fig tree between his visitation in the temple and the cleansing of the temple in Mark 11. In Mark 11:11, Jesus enters the temple and observes everything that happens there and goes out to Bethany. The next day, on the way from Bethany to the temple, Jesus curses a fig tree which has no fruit but leaves: "May no one ever eat fruit from you again" (Mark 11:14). Then Jesus enters the temple again and cleanses it. The next morning, Jesus and his disciples see the fig tree withered from the roots (Mark 11:20). When considering the plot of these episodes, Mark understands the cleansing of the temple as Jesus' symbolic action to announce that the temple system has already been destroyed or at least would be soon.[41]

On the other hand, Chilton insists that Jesus' occupation of the temple means not the fulfillment of the prophecy of the destruction of the temple system but a cleansing for the recovery of true temple sacrifice.[42] According to Chilton, the target of Jesus' critique was not the temple sacrifice but the distorted temple sacrifice by Caiaphas' innovation of introducing traders into the temple.[43] Also, Bond views that Jesus' occupation of the temple was

---

38. Wright, *The Challenge of Jesus*, 63.
39. Ibid., 67.
40. Crossan, *The Historical Jesus*, 357.
41. Ibid., 357–358.
42. Chilton, *The Temple of Jesus*, 100.
43. Originally, the market for the sacrificial animals was located on the Mount of Olives not in the temple. However, Caiaphas installed vendors in the porticos of the temple and expelled the Pharisees and teachers who taught the laws and supervised the

not against the temple sacrifice or the temple itself. However, in different way from Chilton, Bond insists that the purpose of the action of Jesus in the temple was not against the commercialism or corruption of the temple. She relates the actions of Jesus in the temple to the teachings of prophets in the Old Testament.[44]

Was the purpose of Jesus' occupation of the temple a prophetic action related to the destruction of the temple and its sacrificial system? Was the occupation intended for the recovery of the temple sacrifice through criticizing commercialism and the corruption of the priests? Or, was his action in the temple intended for teaching that worship pleasing God is not concerned with burnt offerings but with the moral life of worshippers? Discovering the purpose of Jesus' occupation of the temple is not a simple problem. Information about the historical Jesus is limited and, further, even the little information might be interpreted in various ways as observed above. However, despite a sharp contrast between these opinions, there is common ground that Jesus was not satisfied with the temple at this time. We observe Jesus and his disciples kept meeting, teaching and praying in the temple (Mark 12:35; 14:49; Acts 2:46; 3:1; 5:42; 22:17), and this implies that Jesus would probably have regarded the temple as a means of grace. At least, he does not seem to insist that the temple and sacrifice should be immediately demolished. Nevertheless, for Jesus, the temple was not the best place to meet God and the temple sacrifice was not the best way to be forgiven. Jesus disclosed in his messages and actions that the final day of the temple was coming and after that day people would worship God in a new way in a new temple (John 4:21; Matt 27:51; Mark 15:38; Luke 23:45).

Moreover, the day of the new temple is not only about the future but also embraces the past and the present. Jesus had already shown through his ministry what worshippers had to do in this form of worship in the era of the new temple. Wright finds the meaning of the kingdom of God which has already come in Jesus' explanation of the time of a fast in Mark 2:18–22.[45] Some people asked Jesus why his disciples did not fast but the Pharisees and the disciples of John the Baptist did so. Jesus said to them that guests cannot fast while the bridegroom is with them. That is to say, there is no reason for a fast because the bridegroom Jesus is in the banquet. According to Wright, for Jews, a fast was not a simple religious discipline. Since the period of exile, Jews had fasted in waiting for the restoration of the temple.

---

temple sacrifice from that place. For more detail, see Chilton, *Jesus' Prayer and Jesus' Eucharist*, 59–70.

44. Bond, *The Historical Jesus*, 142.

45. Wright, *The Challenge of Jesus*, 70.

They would stop fasting when Yahweh recovered the temple. Zechariah prophesized that the days of the fast would be seasons of joy and gladness and happy festivals (Zech 8:19). About five hundred years after the prophecy of Zechariah, Jews were still living the period of exile. Geographically they returned to their ancestors' land and temporally the Babylonian exile period was over. However, they were still ruled by the laws of the Roman Empire. Pious Jews continuously conducted fasts, anticipating the day that God would rebuild the new temple.[46] In contrast to the belief of the Jews, Jesus said that now was not the time to fast. In Jesus' words, the wedding banquet has been already held and the bridegroom is here with us. The new temple promised by God has been recovered. Now is the time to enjoy the great banquet with Jesus the messiah.

The cleansing of the temple of Jesus was part of Jesus' movement towards the kingdom of God. In the light of the kingdom of God, Jesus' action in the temple was not an accidental incident. The kingdom of God was the essence of the ministry of Jesus which was proclaimed by preaching, taught in the parables, experienced in miracles and embodied in table fellowship. The temple envisaged by Jesus in the light of the kingdom of God was the place where the feast promised by the prophet Isaiah (25:6–8) for all nations and peoples was to be held. However, temple sacrifice at that time was hindering the banquet of the kingdom of God. The temple which had to be a house of prayer for all nations was used as a den of robbers (Matt 21:13; Mark 11:17; Luke 19:46). The temple was no longer the house that God dwelt in and the holy place that God met with his people. The temple was just a building which had lost its function and meaning. According to Wright, Jesus recognized clearly the limitation of the old temple system and believed that the new temple had to be restored.[47] Jesus says to a Samaritan woman that in the time of the new temple people will worship God in a new way with a new concept of worship place not the old temple (John 4:21). If not in the temple, where will be the place YHWH dwells in? Where can we worship God and meet him? If we cannot be forgiven through temple sacrifice any longer, where and how can we receive the forgiveness of sins? These questions lead us to focus Jesus who is the new temple.

---

46. Ibid., 71.

47. Borg and Wright, *The Meaning of Jesus*, 45.

4 Jesus is the New Temple

In the New Testament, both views of anti-temple and pro-temple coexist. First of all, the pro-temple perspective is clearly present in Luke-Acts. Perrin provides the following evidence:

> It is in the temple that John's birth is announced (Luke 1.5–25) and that Jesus is circumcised (2.21–40); it is to the temple the young boy Jesus returns, insisting on his need to be at his 'Father's house' (2.49). Later, Jesus sends those he heals to the temple priests (17.14), enjoins temple prayer (18.9–14), and commends temple giving (21.1–4). In Acts, following Pentecost, the Christians continue to meet in the temple (Acts 2.46; 3.11; 5.12), while the leaders of the movement maintain established hours of temple prayer (3.1). In this context, the temple grounds serve as the primary venue for the Jerusalemite Christians' proclamation (5.17–42). Further on in the narrative, Paul shaves his head as part of a vow that can only be discharged through the temple (18.18); he also pays for the offering of his four companions, as the culmination of purification rites (21.17–26).[48]

Also, in other gospels we can find a description of Jesus who does not seem to argue that the temple sacrifice should end immediately. Nevertheless, all four gospels agree that Jesus prophesized that the old temple would be destroyed and the new temple would be rebuilt. According to Walker, the focus of Mark is not the Jerusalem temple but Jesus who will recover the new temple made without hands after the destruction of the old temple (Mark 14:58).[49] Similarly Watts, finding a crucial role for the four Davidic Psalms (2, 118, 110, and 22) which are used by Mark in his understanding of the relationship between Jesus and the temple, notes:

> [Mark] presents Jesus as both Israel's Davidic Messiah (Pss. 2, 118) and the temple's Lord (Ps. 110) who, coming to purge Jerusalem but rejected by the temple authorities, announces the present structure's destruction and, through his death and vindication (Ps. 22), its replacement with a new people-temple centered on himself.[50]

Matthew recognizes Jesus as "something greater than the temple" (Matt 12:6). The presence of God is experienced not in the temple but when two or

---

48. Perrin, *Jesus the Temple*, 61–62.
49. Walker, *Jesus and the Holy City*, 302.
50. Watts, "The Lord's House and David's Lord," 307.

three people pray Jesus is with them (Matt 18:19–20).[51] It is unclear whether Luke understands Jesus as the new temple or not. However, it is obvious that Luke illustrates Jesus as the new high priest. For this, Perrin provides as evidence: "Jesus' touching a leper without incurring uncleanness (Luke 5:12–16), his forgiving sins (Luke 5:17–26), [and] his assumption of Davidic priestly status (Luke 6:1–10)."[52] In addition, Luke records that Jesus prophesized the destruction of the temple (Luke 21:5–6); at the moment of the death of Jesus the veil of the temple was torn in two from top to bottom (Luke 23:45); not in Jerusalem where the temple stood but in Bethany, Jesus blessed his people and they worshipped him before his ascension (Luke 24:50–52).[53] These texts can be interpreted as Luke's anti-temple perspective, and, at the very least, as Luke's expectation of the new temple.

While Luke views Jesus as the high priest and Matthew and Mark allude to the understanding of Jesus as the new temple, John declares clearly that Jesus is the new temple. Kerr finds from the account of John that "Jesus replaces and fulfils the Jerusalem Temple and its cultic activity."[54] Carson, also, analyzing John 2:19–21,[55] remarks that Jesus is "the fulfillment of all the temple meant, and the centre of all true worship."[56]

Further, the conversation between Jesus and a Samaritan woman by a well in Sychar demonstrates that Jesus embodies not only the new temple but also the new place of worship. The woman asks Jesus regarding the place of worship, as her ancestors worshipped on the mountain in Samaria but Jews adhered to worshipping in Jerusalem. In a contrasting way to her interest in the place of worship, Jesus answers that what pleases God is not the holiness of the place of worship but those who worship in spirit and truth.[57]

In the time of the Old Testament, the place of sacrifice, that is, the temple was considered to be crucial. However, the Fourth Gospel gives a new approach to worship that what is important in the worship of the kingdom of God is not a matter of place. For, the only place of worship is Jesus.

---

51. Walker, *Jesus and the Holy City*, 302.

52. Perrin, *Jesus the Temple*, 62.

53. Ibid., 62–63.

54. Kerr, *The Temple of Jesus' Body*, 2.

55. "Jesus answered them, 'Destroy this temple, and in three days I will raise it up.' The Jews then said, 'This temple has been under construction for forty-six years, and will you raise it up in three days?' But he was speaking of the temple of his body" (John 2:19–21).

56. Carson, *The Gospel According to John*, 182.

57. "Jesus said to her, 'Woman, believe me, the hour is coming when you will worship the Father neither on this mountain nor in Jerusalem. You worship what you do not know; we worship what we know, for salvation is from the Jews'" (John 4:21–22).

Jesus is the new temple, the new place of worship in the kingdom of God.[58] Carson connects the new concept of worship presented in John 4 and the new Jerusalem in Revelation 21, and suggests that John has a clear understanding of Jesus as the object and the place of worship in new Jerusalem, the kingdom of God.[59] John sees the new Jerusalem in a vision that "I saw no temple in the city, for its temple is the Lord God the Almighty and the Lamb" (Rev 21:22). In the worship of the kingdom of God, a single sanctuary, that is, the temple and sacrificial offerings are no longer necessary. Jesus is the holiest temple and the eternal lamb. In addition, John 7 shows the recognition of Jesus as the eschatological new temple. Walker suggests that the verses in John 7:37–38 echo the image of the eschatological temple prophesized in Ezekiel 47:9.[60] Here, Ezekiel prophesizes that wherever the water is from the temple, the salt water will become fresh and everything will live. Likewise, John proclaims: "[Jesus] cried out, 'Let anyone who is thirsty come to me, and let the one who believes in me drink. As the scripture has said, Out of the believer's heart shall flow rivers of living water'" (John 7:37–38).

In John, the time of the new worship is also a crucial theme. When will the kingdom of God, the new Jerusalem, which brings about a genuine transformation in worship come? In John 4, Jesus has a clear recognition of the eschatological time to worship God in an entirely different way. For Jesus, the time of the new worship is the future which is "coming" and at the same time the present which is "now here" (John 4:21–22). The distinctive nature of eschatological time, "already and not yet," is a crucial theme consistently found in John (John 5:25). It is not certain whether Jesus said that the temple worship must be ended immediately. However, there is no doubt that Jesus had said that the kingdom of God had already come with him and now was the time to worship in a new way. The eschatological time of the new worship definitely embraces the present.[61]

When considering Jesus who had an innovative concept of worship and the temple, Jesus' attempt to cleanse the temple would have become a sufficient reason for the Jewish authorities to execute him (Matt 21:15, 46; Mark 21:18; Luke 20:47). For, the temple system had played an important role in Jewish society and for Rome's effective rule over that region as well. Despite his opponents' threats, Jesus went about his ministry unceasingly for the kingdom of God through teaching and meal practices. Jewish

58. Kerr, *The Temple of Jesus' Body*, 167.
59. Carson, *The Gospel According to John*, 226.
60. Walker, *Jesus and the Holy City*, 302.
61. O'Day and Hylen, *John*, 54.

authorities began to plan more thoroughly to execute Jesus. About that time, Jesus knew that the time of his death was near.[62]

5 Researching the Last Supper

Jesus shared the last supper with his disciples before the death on the cross. The Synoptic Gospels and 1 Corinthians 11 attest that Jesus instituted the first eucharist at the last supper. However, the Fourth Gospel and the history of the eucharistic liturgy proposes that it is more likely that the origin of the eucharist is Jesus' meal practices reflecting the anticipation of the kingdom of God rather than the last supper. In other words, the last supper can be regarded as part of the eucharist not the origin of eucharist.

In order to understand more exactly what the last supper was, we need to observe the meal from the perspective of the kingdom of God. According to Smith, the meals of Jesus including the last supper reflect the Greco-Roman banquet or symposium tradition.[63] On the other hand, Chilton finds various features of Jewish meals such as Haburah, Kiddush and Todah from the last supper.[64] However, defining the type of the meal is important but does not seem to be a decisive factor in understanding the nature of the eucharist. For, the type of the meal is just an instrumental tool used by Jesus to embody the kingdom of God which is the essence of his meal practices. As Chilton correctly recognizes, in the expectation of the banquet of the kingdom of God, Jesus was not at all limited to a fixed type of meal.[65] In the massive eucharistic banquets of the feedings of the five thousand and the four thousand and the meals shared with sinners, tax collectors and gentiles, Jesus opened a new paradigm of the meal fellowship of the kingdom of God beyond the boundaries strictly drawn by the Jewish laws. Thus Chilton reckons the distinctive feature of the new meal fellowship in the kingdom to be one of "inclusiveness."[66]

If the last supper was part of Jesus' meal practice of the kingdom of God, did the last supper reflect inclusiveness? Rather, did not the synoptic accounts regarding the last supper imply a symbol of exclusiveness? For, the Synoptic Gospels suggested that the last supper was the meal of Jesus which

---

62. Regarding Jesus' recognition of his death, see Matt 16:21; Mark 8:31; Luke 9:22; John 6:70; Matt 17:22–23; Mark 9:31; Luke 9:44; Matt 20:18–19; Mark 10:33–34; Luke 18:31–33; Matt 26:2, 21–23; Mark 14:18–20; Luke 22:21–22; John 13:21.

63. See, Smith, *From Symposium to Eucharist*, 222–23.

64. Chilton, *Jesus' Prayer and Jesus' Eucharist*, 56–57.

65. Ibid., 57.

66. Ibid., 58.

was shared with his twelve male disciples.[67] Even though the Fourth Gospel does not specify the number and sex of the disciples participating in the last supper, when we consider the nature of the "last" supper of Jesus with his disciples before death, it is presumable that Jesus would have eaten the last meal with his twelve disciples. Yet, the problem is that the membership of the disciples at the last supper is used for the argument that the eucharist should be open to only baptized members. Farwell, for example, regards that there were two different meal practices of Jesus, the meals before the last supper and the last supper. Each meal practice had its own purpose, form and audience. In the former Jesus opened his table to all, but in the latter, that is the eucharist, only disciples who had already committed themselves to the vision of Jesus participated. Thus, he insists that only those who dedicate themselves to the kingdom of God can participate in the eucharist.[68]

However, even if the twelve disciples participated in the last supper, the significance of the inclusiveness of the eucharist cannot be diminished when we raise these questions: Were the twelve disciples "truly" the disciples of Jesus? Did they "truly" believe and "fully" understand who Jesus was? The four gospels seem to agree that all the twelve disciples are not of perfect character. According to John (1:35–51) and Mark (1:16–20), when Jesus called the disciples, they seem to have followed Jesus instantly but in Luke (5:1–11) they followed Jesus after experiencing the miracle of the catching of fish.[69] The actions of James and John, the two sons of Zebedee who claimed a glorious seat beside Jesus (Mark 10:37), in following Jesus seem to be largely political rather than arising from a pure heart. At a certain moment, they express their strong belief in Jesus but suddenly change their minds. Peter, who pledged his loyalty to Jesus, denied him three times (Matt 26:69–75; Mark 14:66–72; Luke 22:56–62; John 18:17, 25–27). Other disciples, also, deserted Jesus when they faced the threat of personal safety (Matt 26:56; Mark 14:50). Most of all, it is remarkable that the disciples showed a lack of understanding about what they were doing at the last supper (Luke 22:24). When Jesus washes his disciples' feet at the last supper, Peter's question reveals the mind of other disciples: "Lord, are you going to wash my feet?" (John 13:6). Jesus responds: "You do not know now what I am doing, but later you will understand" (John 13:7). Jesus' answer connotes that the disciples will understand what they are doing in the future but currently they do not know it.[70] Decisively, Jesus did not prohibit even Judas

---

67. Matt 26:20; Mark 14:17; cf "apostles" in Luke 22:14.
68. Farwell, "Baptism, Eucharist, and the Hospitality of Jesus," 222.
69. Trumbower, *Born from Above*, 129–30.
70. Hylen, *Imperfect Believers*, 65–66.

who was possessed with Satan (John 13:27) from sitting at the table of the kingdom of God. Although it is considerably unlikely that his seat in the kingdom would be eternal, Jesus, apparently, allowed the betrayer to participate in the last supper. The vulnerability of the disciples did not change even after the resurrection of Jesus. Thomas did not believe in the resurrection of Jesus until the risen Lord appeared before him (John 20:24–25). The two disciples going to Emmaus did not recognize the risen Lord even after they spent a considerable time with him (Luke 24:16). These stories reveal who the disciples really were. Nevertheless, Jesus invited them to the banquet of the kingdom of God. Jesus accepted them as they were. The banquet of the kingdom of God was controlled under the laws of grace and inclusiveness that it is indeed hard for human beings to imagine. If we have to draw a eucharistic principle from the last supper, the focus needs to be on "Jesus' practices of eating with sinners and filling the bellies of all comers"[71] rather than membership.

One of the difficult issues in understanding the last supper is the interpretation of the sayings of Jesus: "This is my body; this is my blood." According to the synoptic accounts, Jesus mentioned these words first at the last supper. If the words were exclusively connected to the last supper, it seems to be natural that the focus of the words is on the broken body and the blood shed on the cross as is the traditional eucharistic understanding. For, the last supper was the last and most crucial event to occur before the death on the cross.

Recently, however, Chilton has given a convincing interpretation of the words that is different from the traditional one. While Chilton recognizes the words as being firstly instituted at the last supper, at the same time he does not directly connect the bread and the cup with the death of Jesus on the cross.[72] Here, he attempts to interpret the words in relation to Jesus' cleansing of the temple rather than the death of Jesus. He suggests that when considering Jesus' attempts to reform the temple sacrifice, the most natural meaning of the terms blood and body would be the replacement of the blood and flesh of an animal sacrificed in the temple.[73] Chilton writes:

> As he shared wine, he referred to it as the equivalent of the blood of an animal, shed in sacrifice; When he shared bread, he claimed its value was as that of sacrificial flesh. Such offerings

---

71. Tanner, "In Praise of Open Communion," 476.
72. Chilton, *Jesus' Prayer and Jesus' Eucharist*, 72.
73. Ibid., 73, 75.

were purer, more readily accepted by God, than what was sacrificed in a Temple which had become corrupt.[74]

Chilton's interpretation of the sayings of Jesus at the last supper is plausible in terms of the separation of the eucharistic elements from a direct connection with Jesus' death. He views that the wine and bread were not Jesus' personal blood and body,[75] which would be shed and broken on the cross as a sacrifice, but new sacrificial offerings replacing the temple sacrifices. The new sacrificial offerings pleasing God were in the form of ordinary food such as bread and wine which were offered and owned by ordinary people not by the temple priests.[76] Jesus' meals with bread and wine were "a better sacrifice than what was offered in the Temple."[77]

Furthermore, the Fourth Gospel records that right after the miraculous feeding of the five thousand Jesus mentioned the words in teaching Jews in the synagogue in Capernaum (John 6:59). As we observed in chapter 4 of this study, not only the Fourth Gospel but also the early church documents attest that the sayings of Jesus in the eucharist originated in his other meal practices not the last supper. When considering Jesus who consistently embodied the kingdom of God and the words "my body and blood" in his whole ministry, the real meanings of the words cannot be restricted to the theology of Good Friday.

Jesus was flogged, crucified, and killed. This was a reality. The crucifixion is a decisive event in the redemptive ministry of Christ. Nevertheless, when we focus too much on the death of Christ on the cross, other precious eucharistic themes which must be tasted in the feast of the kingdom of God disappear into the darkness. During the eucharist which is immersed in the death of Christ, the words "my body and blood" remind participants of Jesus who was sacrificed on the cross. Yet, in the experience of the eucharist as a banquet of the kingdom of God the focus of the words is entirely changed. Jesus who was killed in the past is now present in the eucharist. The consciousness of the presence of Jesus induces a shift in interpretation regarding "my body and blood." If Jesus is already present in the eucharist, the eucharistic elements of bread and cup do not necessarily mean the personal body and blood of Jesus.

---

74. Chilton, *A Feast of Meaning*, 148.

75. He views that the connection between the wine and bread and Jesus' personal body and blood is a theological development of later church. See Chilton, *Jesus' Prayer and Jesus' Eucharist*, 72–73.

76. Chilton, *A Feast of Meaning*, 66–68.

77. Chilton, *Jesus' Prayer and Jesus' Eucharist*, 73.

In this new perspective of the eucharist as the banquet of the kingdom, the words "my body and blood" become the food of life provided by Jesus who is the host of the banquet.[78] With the bread and wine, the food of life, Jesus feeds the bodies and souls of his guests. To have eternal life by taking sacred foods was an important motif of the Jewish messianic banquet at the time of Jesus.[79] This motif is found in much Jewish literature. Smith writes of the motif of sacred foods as a feature of the messianic banquet. In *Joseph and Aseneth*, all who eat a honeycomb, which is the food of angels, gain "immortality" (16:8–9). In *Odes of Solomon*, "the living water" of eternity delivers the souls from the death (6:8–18).[80] Jesus would have understood undoubtedly the motif of the messianic banquet in the Old Testament (Lev 23:1–2; Isa 25:6–8).

The presence of the Lord and his feeding of his followers with the food of life becomes the core of the eucharist of both the Old and New testaments.[81] With the vision of the messianic banquet, Jesus shared his meals with his people. The motif of the sacred food of the messianic banquet found in the Jewish tradition is clearly observed in John's illustration of Jesus. Jesus is ὁ ἄρτος τῆς ζωῆς (the bread of life, John 6:48). Whoever eats of the bread of life will have ζωὴν αἰώνιον (eternal life, John 6:54). Whoever drinks of the water given by Jesus will never be thirsty, as the water is ὕδωρ ζῶν (the living water, John 4:10).[82]

The consciousness of the presence of Jesus in the eucharist, also, influences the mood of the eucharist. At the last supper, Jesus says: "Truly I tell you, I will never again drink of the fruit of the vine . . ." (Mark 14:25). "[A] prophetic symbol of his imminent death"[83] is clearly expressed in this passage. However, the allusion to the death was not the end of the sayings of Jesus. The gloomy atmosphere is rapidly changed into a positive expectation involving a desire for the feast of the kingdom of God: ". . . until that day when I drink it new in the kingdom of God."[84] In this passage, Jesus expressed his "hope for the messianic meal."[85]

---

78. The bread and wine as the food of life or spiritual food were a crucial theme in the eucharistic understandings of the Fourth Gospel, the *Didache*, Ignatius of Antioch, Justin Martyr and Irenaeus. For more details, see chapter 4.

79. Smith, *From Symposium to Eucharist*, 166.

80. Ibid., 167.

81. Wainwright, *Eucharist and Eschatology*, 106.

82. Smith, *From Symposium to Eucharist*, 167.

83. Donahue and Harrington, *The Gospel of Mark*, 397.

84. Mark 14:25; cf. Matt 26:29; Luke 22:16; ". . . until he comes" in 1 Cor 11:26.

85. Bieler and Schottroff, *The Eucharist*, 53.

THE BIBLICAL BASIS FOR THE THEOLOGY OF THE OPEN TABLE   159

The kingdom of God as the present event was consistently pursued in the ministry of Jesus, and also was found in the last supper. Although the death of Jesus was at hand, the disciples were participating in the supper with Jesus the bridegroom. It should be noted that the mention of a fast was a vow of Jesus, not a command which was given to his disciples. At the last supper, where the feast of the kingdom of God was held, the bridegroom was with his guests. Thus, what the guests had to do was not a fast but the enjoyment of the feast of the kingdom of God. The eucharist is a mysterious event that the future becomes the present when the church eats the bread and drinks the cup in anticipation of the kingdom of God.[86]

In this sense, the last supper and other meals of Jesus have both discontinuity and continuity. There is a discontinuity between them in that the last supper has a unique temporal setting, that is, the night he was betrayed. At the last supper Jesus foretold his passion and death for the salvation of human beings. However, there is an essential continuity between them in that Jesus invited freely people to his table with the vision of the kingdom of God in his compassionate and self-sacrificing love. All meals of Jesus were a generous and inclusive eucharist.

6 The Meals of Jesus after the Resurrection

According to Luke, the last meal of Jesus on the earth was not the last supper. The risen Jesus visited the two disciples, Cleopas and his companion who were on the road to Emmaus in a state of despair. The two disciples seem to have been surprised by Jesus' marvelous explanation of all the scriptures. They urged Jesus to stay with them. Jesus accepted their request and shared a meal with them. Here, Luke describes the scene using special language: "When he was at the table with them, he took bread, blessed and broke it, and gave it to them" (Luke 24:30). The four-fold action[87] used in this verse is also observed in the illustrations of the eucharist of Luke 9, 22 and Acts 27. Through the use of technical language indicating the eucharist, Luke reveals that the meal in Emmaus was the eucharist not an ordinary meal.[88] Furthermore, focusing on the languages of the four-fold action found in the main Lukan accounts of the eucharist, LaVerdiere suggests that the meal at

---

86. Jenson, *Systematic Theology*, 216.

87. Taking – blessing – breaking – giving. According to Dix, these four actions are essential elements of every eucharistic rite. Dix, *The Shape of the Liturgy*, 48.

88. Luke uses the term "bless" in Luke 9:16 and 24:30 and the term "give thanks" in Luke 22:17, 19 and Acts 27:35. For more details, see LaVerdiere, *The Eucharist*, 87, 91, 109–110.

Emmaus echoes liturgically the actual eucharist, which would have been conducted by the Lukan community, better than other eucharistic texts.[89]

The Emmaus story affirms that Jesus is the host of the banquet of the kingdom of God. At first, the two disciples provided hospitality to Jesus with a dwelling place and food. However, the situation was radically changed when the eucharist began. The two disciples became guests and the former guest, Jesus, became the host.[90] It was not the disciples but Jesus who took the bread and gave it to them (Luke 24:30). The true meaning of the hospitality which has to be given in the eucharist can be more exactly apprehended when we ponder the time that the two disciples recognized Jesus. Not before, but during or after, they received the bread from Jesus, they recognized him (Luke 24:31). The two disciples did not understand the meaning of the bread and did not even recognize Jesus. In a sense, they were passive betrayers of Jesus. When Jesus was arrested and suffered all the disciples deserted him and fled (Matt 26:56; Mark 14:50). They were still foolish and unbelievers (Luke 24:25). When they heard the news of Jesus' resurrection from a woman, they regarded it as nonsense (Luke 24:11). Nevertheless, Jesus did not hesitate to give them the bread. After the hospitality of Jesus was given to the unenlightened disciples, an important change happened in them. Their eyes were opened and they were able to recognize Jesus, the risen Lord. The eucharist at Emmaus was a means of grace which enabled the betrayers and unbelievers to be transformed into true disciples and the faithful.

The meal at Emmaus was not the only meal after the resurrection. Jesus presented himself before his disciples in Jerusalem when they shared a meal (Luke 24:36; cf Mark 16:14). On the shore of the Sea of Tiberius, the risen Lord prepared bread and fish for his disciples (John 21:1–13). As Joncas notes, after the resurrection, Jesus seems to have shared his meals with only his disciples.[91] However, when we observe those meals in the light of the kingdom of God we can realize that the purpose of the stories is not to give a regulation regarding eucharistic boundaries. The main theme of the meals after the resurrection is that "[t]he risen, living Lord eats and drinks with his disciples."[92] The eucharist after the resurrection was not a remembrance of the death of Jesus but a vivid experience of the presence of the living Lord. In addition, when we ponder over the spiritual condition of the disciples it becomes obvious that these texts related to the meals after the resurrection

---

89. LaVerdiere, *Dining in the Kingdom of God*, 170.
90. Karris, *Eating Your Way Through Luke's Gospel*, 49.
91. Joncas, "Tasting the Kingdom of God," 351.
92. Small, "A Church of The Word and Sacrament," 321.

cannot be used as a biblical proof for supporting the closed table. The participants in the eucharist are rebuked by the risen Lord due to their unbelief and doubtfulness (Mark 16:14; cf. Luke 24:37–38). Although it was early in the morning, the seven disciples did not realize it was Jesus who stood on the shore (John 21:4). In addition, even after they had a conversation with Jesus, they did not realize it was him (John 21:5–7). Nevertheless, for such disciples, the risen Lord prepared food (John 21:12). If the meals after the resurrection were indeed the eucharist, which eucharistic principles can we draw from those meals? Obviously, Jesus' hospitality, forgiveness and inclusiveness are to be included in the answer.

7 Summary and Evaluation

The meals of Jesus went beyond ordinary food which filled those who hungered. The meals of Jesus were the most powerful symbol of the banquet of the kingdom of God. Through the meals Jesus showed to the world what the banquet of the kingdom of God really is.

The act of eating in the meals of Jesus was not only a foretaste of the banquet of the kingdom of God, but also an effective way to teach the laws of the kingdom. At the time of Jesus, Jewish society was ruled by the purity laws which had been secured and retained by the temple system. The distinctive character of the temple system was exclusiveness. However, the exclusiveness was challenged by the inclusiveness of Jesus' meal practices shared with tax collectors and sinners who were excluded by the purity laws. More exactly, as Joncas states: "It wasn't simply that Jesus ate with objectionable persons—outcasts and sinners—but that he ate with anyone, indiscriminately!"[93] Jesus shared unceasingly inclusive meals with anyone who wanted to come to his table.

The traditional eucharistic understanding can be used to draw the biblical authority from the last supper stories in order to support its eucharistic regulation, that is, the so-called closed table. For, the Synoptic Gospels describe that Jesus shared the last supper with only his twelve male disciples. However, even in the last supper the inclusiveness of Jesus' meal practice is not diminished. All four Gospels describe the participants in the last supper as those who have a vulnerable faith in Jesus and a lack of understanding of the eucharist. Moreover, among the participants, there was Judas the betrayer. Nevertheless, Jesus did not prohibit them from participating in the eucharist.

---

93. Joncas, "Tasting the Kingdom of God," 350

The supreme laws in Jesus' meal practice were generosity and hospitality. In the banquet of the kingdom of God ruled by these laws, the exclusiveness dividing between the people of God became obsolete. There was no boundary, nor discrimination in participating in the meals of Jesus. Chilton says:

> A sufficient condition for eating in his company and for entry into the kingdom [was] a readiness to accept the hospitality, . . . [and] a willingness to provide for the meals, . . . to join in the fellowship . . . [and] to forgive and to be forgiven.[94]

---

94. Chilton, *A Feast of Meanings*, 146. Brackets are added by this author.

Chapter 7

The Theological Basis for the Theology of the Open Table

SINCE THE THIRD CENTURY, mainline churches have developed their eucharistic practices on the basis of traditional eucharistic theology adhering to the last supper tradition. Traditional eucharistic theology has been embodied in the churches' eucharistic regulations. In the case of the PCK, traditional eucharistic theology has led the church to develop its eucharistic regulation which allows only baptized people who are the age of fifteen and over to participate in the eucharist. However, around the end of the twentieth century, the open table began to be introduced to the church. Those who upheld the eucharistic regulation of "baptism before the eucharist" were probably concerned when they heard about the open table. They considered the open table to be a serious challenge to the church tradition which had been preserved since the early church. At the same time, the introduction of the open table caused theological controversy in the PCK. I will explore the main theological issues raised by scholars supporting traditional eucharistic understanding and suggest the theological basis for the open table.

1 Reconsideration of Discerning the Body

In the early period of the church in Korea, the traditional eucharistic regulations were strictly observed. The church allowed only those who were baptized adult members to partake in the eucharist. In order to be baptized, people needed to complete the catechumenate. However, even an admission to the catechumenate was not easy. The candidate for the catechumenate had to attend regularly all formal services for at least three months. The final gateway to the catechumenate was to pass a catechetical examination:

> Why do you want to become a Christian? What were some of the sins you needed to have forgiven? Have you been forgiven, and what proof have you that you have been forgiven? Through

whom? Who is Jesus? Where was He born? Who was His mother? Who was His father? (Ans. "God" is required.) Who is Jesus in His relation to you? How did He become your Savior? Was He a sinner? Why did He die as one guilty? Did He absolutely perish? Where is He now? Will He return to the world? When, and for what? Where does the Christian go at death? Where does the non-Christian go at death? If you were to die to-night, where would you go and why? Can you recite the ten commandments and the Lord's Prayer? Do you pray daily? How often each day? In whose name do you pray? Have you given up all worship of spirits? Do you read your Bible daily? How much have you read consecutively? Have you done any personal work, told anyone about Jesus?[1]

After completing this course, candidates began the life of a catechumen for six months. In this period, catechumens would prepare not only for catechetical but also for ascetical examinations. They had to refrain from all immoral acts and pagan customs. The contents of "Baptismal Examination" in the early of 20th century show the early Korean Christians' thinking about being a Christian through baptism:

Since you became a catechumen, have you found joy in believing? Why? Have you kept the Sabbath? Tell how you have observed it. Do you have family worship? Do you drink sool (beer) and have it in the home? Do you give it to the day laborers who work for you? Is it right for a man to have two wives? Is it right to marry an unbeliever? Are you a sinner? Can anything sinful enter Heaven? Then how do you expect to get there? Is there any other way than by the Cross of Christ? Are the spirits to be feared? Why not? What are the ordinances of the church? What is the meaning of baptism? Who administers it and in whose name? With what does he administer it? Is baptism necessary for salvation? Then why do you seek baptism? What is the purpose of the Lord's Supper? What does the bread signify? The wine? Who should partake of the sacrament? In what spirit should one partake of the Lord's Supper? Have you led anyone to Christ?[2]

The eucharist of which only those who passed such a strict discipline process were able to partake, was recognized as something holier than normal services by the early Korean Christians. The church gave notice for several weeks before the eucharist in order that church members

---

1. Nisbet, *Day In and Day Out in Korea*, 67–68.
2. Ibid., 68–69.

could prepare themselves for it. If there was a baptized member who acted wrongly, morally or socially, the church banned that person from receiving the eucharistic elements. In a sense, the eucharist was a privilege given to those who were baptized and lived morally, and a kind of compensation for their devotion and loyalty to God. Recently, however, the article regarding excommunication in the constitution[3] has become virtually an anachronism, but there is a consensus in the PCK that baptism and a moral life are appropriate preconditions for the eucharist. Traditionally, the PCK finds biblical authority for such eucharistic regulations from Paul's teaching of the Lord's supper in 1 Corinthians 11:28–29. In these verses, Paul writes of an attitude that the participants in the eucharist should maintain. The PCK interprets these verses to suggest that all participants should examine their individual acts and beliefs before partaking in the eucharist.

However, we need to ponder on what these verses actually mean. Do these verses teach us that self-examination is a prerequisite for the eucharist? Is it an appropriate interpretation that the terms "discerning the body" mean an examination of personal spirituality and morality? For a more correct understanding of the texts, it would be worth exploring the context of the Corinthian church at that time. It is presumed that the Corinthian church consisted of a few rich people and a great number of the poor. Socially, people from various levels would gather together at the Corinthian church. A rough outline of the social composition of the Corinthian church can be observed in 1 Corinthians 1:26. Here, Paul describes three categories of class: σοφοί (wise), δυνατοί (powerful), and εὐγενεῖς (noble birth). According to Theissen, such language should be understood in a sociological sense.[4] In the Corinthian church, although there were not many who were wise, powerful and of noble birth, the minority from the upper class was "the most active and important members of the congregation."[5] As observed in descriptions of early church worship (cf. Acts 1:13; 2:1; Romans 16:5, 23), the place of worship and the eucharist of the Corinthian church would be a private house provided by one of the wealthiest members.[6] The eucharist would be conducted with worship on Sunday evening (1 Cor 16:2). Yet, in the first century CE, Sunday was not a holiday in every region of the Roman Empire. Thus, the majority of church members who were poor would work on Sunday and some of them

---

3. The "Rules of Discipline" (1.5.1) in the constitution of the PCK records that the church might punish those who break church laws by censure, excommunication and expulsion from the church. The General Assembly of The Presbyterian Church of Korea, *Constitution*, 204.

4. See Theissen, "Social Stratification in the Corinthian Community," 97–105.

5. Ibid., 105.

6. Fisk, *First Corinthians*, 65.

who had to work until late that afternoon would be often late for the eucharist.[7] According to Murphy-O'Connor, the private house in which the Corinthian church gathered had a triclinium (a dining room with couches) and an atrium. The house owner and the rich who had plenty of free time would come early and recline on couches in the triclinium, but late comers who were generally poor, because there was no vacancy in the triclinium, spontaneously would be guided to the atrium and sit there.[8]

Paul's criticism of the Corinthian church was based on the fact that there was immoral discrimination in the eucharist rather than simply a physical division according to small gathering spaces. In 1 Corinthians 11:17–34, Paul was concerned about a small number of people who were excluded from having a eucharistic meal. For the occasion of the eucharist, each member would bring food and offer it. However, when the eucharist began, those who offered food did not hesitate to go ahead and enjoy it but the poor who were not able to bring food had to wait until somebody shared food with them. Some members got drunk but others remained hungry (1 Cor 11: 21). According to Winter, a series of events which had occurred in the eucharist of the Corinthian church demonstrates that they followed a typical type of dinner in the secular world at that time.[9] The dinner was called *Asumbolon deipnon* (a private dinner) where participants brought their own food and ate it themselves.[10] Moreover, one of the hallmarks of *Asumbolon deipnon* was drunkenness which Paul mentions in 1 Corinthians 11:21.[11] In this situation, it was natural that Paul chastised the Corinthian church for their indulgence and humiliating the poor in the eucharist (1 Cor 11:22). For, such behavior was identified with *Asumbolon deipnon* and contrasted with what Jesus taught through his dinner.[12]

Paul would give them this teaching arising out of the eucharist: "Whoever, therefore, eats the bread or drinks the cup of the Lord in an unworthy manner will be answerable for the body and blood of the Lord" (1 Cor 11:27). When considering the whole situation, we can get a clearer meaning of the phrase "discerning the body." Traditionally, the church has interpreted these terms to mean that participants should examine their personal self or have a clear knowledge of the eucharistic body distributed to them. Yet, what Paul

---

7. Fitzmyer, *First Corinthians*, 428.

8. Murphy-O'Connor, *St. Paul's Corinth*, 183–84.

9. For more details on a range of dinners in the ancient world, see Winter, *After Paul Left Corinth*, 154–55.

10. Ibid., 155.

11. Ibid., 158.

12. Winter, *After Paul Left Corinth*, 154.

wants to say through these texts is not about a eucharistic regulation, the last supper as the origin of the eucharist, or theological interpretation of the eucharistic elements, but about how to eat the eucharist with others without discrimination and humiliation. Paul's main idea in these texts is that the eucharist is not an individual but a communal act.[13]

In 1 Corinthians 11: 29, the body, which the Corinthian church should have discerned, is the body of Christ, the whole people gathering for the eucharist. Thus, if the Corinthian church discerned the body, they would wait until all members come and eat the eucharist together.[14] At this point, in 1 Corinthians 11:28, Paul's instruction, "examine yourselves," cannot be simply interpreted as a self-examination of a personal dimension. Why should participants examine themselves? For Paul, the ultimate goal of the examination is not to be personally justified by God but to recognize all church members, regardless of social class and whether they are rich or poor, as people who are united with God in "the new covenant established by Christ's body and blood."[15]

Paul's emphasis on the communality of the eucharist leads us to reconsider the traditional approach which tries to draw eucharistic regulations based on self-examination from 1 Corinthians 11:28–29.[16] Through 1 Corinthians 10 and 11, Paul stresses that the eucharist should be the place that the unity of a community becomes realized. The unity in the eucharist involves overcoming "divisions caused by social and economic disparity in the community."[17] In the eucharist, all participants are holy in Christ and are people of God. They have an equal opportunity to take bread and the cup from the Lord's table. If there is an instruction regarding the eucharist to be gained from 1 Corinthians 11:28–29, it would be not as a regulation that discerns the personal body and excludes those who are disqualified but as an encouragement that discerns the body of Christ, members of the whole church, so that all can eat together the eucharist.

---

13. Garland, *First Corinthians*, 533.
14. Stookey, *Eucharist*, 33.
15. Ciampa and Rosner, *The First Letter to the Corinthians*, 555.
16. Paul's recognition of the eucharist as a communal act is exactly identical with the eucharistic perspective of the early Christian communities. See Smith and Taussig, *Many Tables*, 21–69.
17. Hays, *First Corinthians: Interpretation*, 204.

2 Reconsideration of Baptism and Confirmation

One of the problems with the traditional understanding of the eucharist is that the open table which welcomes untested people without baptism and confirmation could damage the meaning and holiness of the eucharist. Thus, generally, the traditional eucharistic understanding believes that church should have two safeguards for keeping the eucharist holy: baptism and confirmation.

First of all, let us explore the relationship between baptism and the eucharist. For the PCK, based on the eucharistic theology of Calvin,[18] baptism is the first official gateway to Christian life and through baptism outsiders can obtain membership of the church. The eucharist is the food to nourish only those who have already begun the journey of Christian life and have membership.[19] Thus, the PCK does not allow those who are not baptized to receive the eucharistic elements because they are not members of the church.

What is the meaning and efficacy of baptism which the PCK confesses as a doctrine? The Westminster Confession of Faith, which is edited by the PCK and contained in the PCK's constitution, gives the following definition of baptism:

> Baptism is a sacrament of the New Testament, instituted by Jesus Christ (Matthew 28:19). It is not only for the solemn admission of the party baptized into the visible Church (1 Corinthians 12:13), but also to be unto him a sign and seal of the covenant of grace (Romans 4:11; Colossians 2:11–12), or his ingrafting into Christ (Galatians 3:27; Romans 6:5), of regeneration (Titus 3:5), of remission of sins (Mark 1:4), and of his giving up unto God, through Jesus Christ, to walk in newness of life (Romans 6:3–4): which sacrament is, by Christ's own appointment, to be continued in his church until the end of the world (Matthew 28:19–20).[20]

Here, it is worth focusing on the words "sign" and "seal" which indicate baptism. The PCK recognizes baptism as a sign and seal of becoming a Christian. Within the PCK's theology regarding sacraments, baptism is crucial and meaningful as a rite of initiation into Christian life but does not

---

18. Calvin, in his *Catechism of the Church of Geneva*, says: "Baptism is for us a kind of entry into the Church." See Reid, *Calvin*, 133.

19. The General Assembly of The Presbyterian Church of Korea, *Constitution*, (2001), 124–25.

20. "Of Baptism" 28:1. See Ibid., 123.

have the actual power of forgiveness or salvation. It is expressed in this way in the Westminster Confession of Faith:

> Although it be a great sin to contemn or neglect this ordinance (Luke 7:30; Exodus 4:24–26), yet grace and salvation are not so inseparably annexed unto it as that no person can be regenerated or saved without it (Romans 4:11; Acts 10:2, 4, 22, 31, 45, 47), or that all that are baptized are undoubtedly regenerated (Acts 8:13, 23).[21]

Furthermore, the PCK supports the statement of BEM regarding the role of the Holy Spirit in the life of believers that "the Holy Spirit is at work in the lives of people before, in and after their baptism" (Baptism II.C.5).[22] If the PCK confesses that through the eucharist the people of God are spiritually nourished and grow in Christ,[23] there is no reason to oppose the idea that the recipient of the eucharistic grace should be the whole people of God including those who are not baptized.

Secondly, along with baptism, confirmation is emphasized by the PCK as a prerequisite for the eucharist. Confirmation involves an intellectual capacity to confess sins and to appreciate what the eucharist means. For this, the PCK defines the age of fifteen as a precondition for participation in the eucharist. Regarding cognitive ability as a precondition of the eucharist, it is important to turn our eyes from doctrinal instruction to the eucharist of Jesus. Who were those invited by Jesus into his table? Did they understand fully what they ate? The gospel accounts suggest that participants in the eucharistic meals of Jesus did not have to be the kind of people who passed a difficult catechetical examination. At the last supper, the disciples did not know what they were doing. The two disciples on the road to Emmaus did not realize that the man who had spent quite a lot of time with them was in fact Jesus until they received the eucharistic bread. Although the disciples swore loyalty to Jesus, what happened at the last supper was the disciples' drastic betrayal of the hospitality of Jesus. In all cases, a clear lesson of the eucharist for the participants was that "their lives depended on God's fidelity to them rather than on the inadequacies of their commitment to God."[24] In the light of the traditional eucharistic regulation, they were all unworthy

21. "Of Baptism" 28:5. Ibid., 125.

22. Thurian and Wainwright, *Baptism and Eucharist Ecumenical Convergence in Celebration*, 2. For more details on the PCK's response to BEM, see Thurian, *Churches Respond to BEM*, 160–64.

23. See the section "Of the Lord's Supper" 29:1 in The Presbyterian Church of Korea, *Constitution*, (2001), 125.

24. Loades, "Table," 74.

to come to the table of Jesus. Nevertheless, Jesus, the host, invited them to his gracious table.[25] The table of Jesus calls the church to have a humble mind. This humbleness helps us realize that "we" who are baptized and confirmed are not different from "them" who are excluded by the eucharistic regulations. It would be worth noting Fabian's insight into human beings standing before the table of Christ:

> Today when we watch people whom we think unworthy join our eucharistic gathering, instead of our telling ourselves we were mistaken about these folks, and should reconsider how they deserve inclusion – we had rather think: these are real, nasty, active sinners, and God sees no difference between them and me. I am just like them. So I hereby abandon my desire to be separate from them.[26]

3 Pastoral and Missiological Requests for the Open Table

Our modern pluralistic social and religious context ceaselessly challenges the church to rethink the traditional eucharistic regulation which recognizes baptism and confession of faith as essential preconditions for the eucharist. Today, church leaders face various pastoral and missiological challenges when they conduct the eucharist.[27] The biggest challenge is linked to the question of the inclusion of children, people from other denominations, people living with mental disabilities and seekers from non-Christian backgrounds in the eucharist. It is possible that these situations in the eucharist might cause pastors and missionaries who are under the influence of the traditional eucharistic theology uneasy feelings. It is easy to simply follow the traditional eucharistic regulation. Yet, the reason why they are embarrassed is that they know that blindly following church laws does not guarantee the best result in all situations of ministry.

What is the best way to keep church tradition regardless of individual ministry situations? This question leads us to look again at the eucharist of Jesus and his attitudes towards human beings. In the light of the eucharist

---

25. Mick says: "Before we come to the table, we acknowledge our unworthiness ('Lord, I am not worthy . . .') and rejoice in the fact that God does not require us to be worthy but heals us by the divine word. This Jesus who gives himself to us is the same Jesus who scandalized the religious leaders of his time by sharing meals with sinners. He continues to do the same today. None of us are worthy of this meal; we share in it by God's gracious invitation." See Mick, *Eucharist*, 20.

26. Fabian, *The Scandalous Table*, 150.

27. Stamm, "Open Communion as a United Methodist Exception," 262.

of Jesus, the church is requested to bear a moral responsibility for humanity beyond denominational doctrines and church traditions. For, Jesus' moral sense was embodied in welcoming sinners who were consistently excluded in Jewish society and in providing them hospitality at his eucharistic table.[28] A special eucharist which Galbraith shared with an Alzheimer patient is a good example of how a pastoral response to a human being can be a better way to experience the kingdom of God in the eucharist than to attempt to observe the dogmatic eucharistic regulation:

> On a recent visit to an Alzheimer patient, we wondered if this individual would understand or even participate in the sharing of the Communion elements. The patient was wandering the halls of the nursing home, but we were eventually able to gather this individual, [his] spouse, and a friend. As we said the prayer and gave the bread and juice, the individual's blank eyes began to focus on the elements. This person, who moments before had seemed totally unaware of the surroundings, seemed to participate actively in the Sacrament. As he received the body and blood of Christ, without prompting, the patient's eyes began to twinkle.[29]

4 The Open Table as a Means of Grace

The main focus of the eucharist of Jesus was not on the righteousness of the participants but on the grace of God through inclusion and hospitality. In the eucharist, the place of grace, sinners met Jesus and renounced their old pattern of life. If we come closer to the nature of the eucharist of Jesus, we might divert our attention from an attempt to preserve the holiness of the eucharist by keeping strictly to the eucharistic regulation concerning the immensity of God's grace and its power of transforming human beings. The understanding of the eucharist as a means of grace is prominent in the theology of the Wesley brothers. They recognized that among church's sacramental ways the eucharist is "the chief means of grace"[30] as follows:

> Of these blessings CHRIST from above is pleased to bestow sometimes more, sometimes less, in the several ordinances of His Church, which, as the stars in heaven, differ from each other in glory. Fasting, prayer, hearing His word, are all good vessels

---

28. Breidenthal, "The Festal Gathering: Reflections on Open Communion," 143–44.

29. This is part of a letter from April Galbraith belonging to Trinity United Methodist Church in Roaring Spring, Pennsylvania. See Stamm, *Extending the Table*, 90.

30. Khoo, *Wesleyan Eucharistic Spirituality*, 181.

to draw water from this well of salvation; but they are not all equal. The Holy Communion, when well used, exceeds as much in blessing as it exceeds in danger of a curse, when wickedly and irreverently taken (IV:6).[31]

Although the PCK does not recognize the eucharist as the chief means of grace, it holds the view that through the eucharist Christians can see and experience the grace of God.[32] It is true that the PCK still holds the eucharistic regulation that baptism and confirmation are the preconditions of the eucharist. However, if the PCK is fully aware that the eucharist is completed by God's acceptance of sinners and hospitality based on the immensity of the divine grace not by human effort and preparation, that awareness will mature the PCK's eucharistic theology and lead to the heart of the eucharist.

In the eucharist, the grace of God urges sinners to turn from evil and live as the people of God. Jesus' embracing sinners in his table does not mean that he allows sin. The purpose of Jesus' inclusivity was the transformation of the life of sinners.[33] Bretherton notes:

> Jesus relates hospitality and holiness by inverting their relations: hospitality becomes the means of holiness. Instead of having to be set apart from or exclude pagans in order to maintain holiness, it is in Jesus' hospitality of pagans, the unclean, and sinners that his own holiness is shown forth. Instead of sin and impurity infecting him, it seems Jesus' purity and righteousness somehow 'infects' the impure, sinners and the Gentiles.[34]

It is a misunderstanding that the open table theology is not concerned with conversion or spiritual growth. The only thing that is different between the traditional eucharistic understanding and the open table is the position of conversion in the journey of Christian life. While the former places the conversion of participants before the eucharist as a prerequisite, the latter recognizes the eucharist as a converting ordinance.[35] In other words, the

---

31. See Wesley and Wesley, *Hymns on the Lord's Supper*, para. For more details on the Wesley brothers eucharistic understanding, see chapter 5 of this study.

32. See Committee on the Book of Common Worship, *The Book of Common Worship*, (2008), 52; The General Assembly of the Presbyterian Church of Korea, *Constitution*, (2001), 55.

33. Newman, *Untamed Hospitality*, 31.

34. Bretherton, *Hospitality as Holiness*, 130.

35. Opposing the open table theology, Farwell insists that in the last supper stories and 1 Corinthians 11 all participants were committed and informed and emphasizes the significance of the preparation of the participants in the eucharist. For more details, see Farwell, "Baptism, Eucharist, and the Hospitality of Jesus," 221–22.

open table, like Wesley's eucharistic understanding, focuses on a possibility that in the eucharist a sinner experiences the grace of salvation, that is the eucharist as a means of grace for conversion.[36]

An example from the practice of the open table as it occurred at in a Uniting Church in Sydney in Australia is helpful to illustrate some points. Bexley Uniting Church (BUC) was preparing the 111th Anniversary Sunday Service.[37] Jeffrey Liu, who was a High School student and not a Christian, inquired of his school teacher Jane, who was a church member of BUC, whether he could sing "The Prayer" in the service of BUC as a rehearsal for his HSC examination. Jane gave him advice about how to contact a church leader of BUC. Jeffrey sent an e-mail to Jim, Chairman of the Congregation:

> Hello Jim,
>
> I am Jane's student Jeffrey and I was asked by her to make a brief introduction about myself to you. First of all I would like to say that I am really honoured to perform at the Church on Sunday. Although I am not Christian, I am agnostic and open minded so I will gladly sing as a prayer to the lord. I am currently a Year 12 student, about to graduate soon and attending North Sydney Boys High School. This year I played the lead Chris in the school musical "Miss Saigon." I also do music as a subject at school and am singing The Prayer as one of my songs for my HSC examination, so hopefully I will learn a lot from this experience. Are there any formalities I should know about a church Sunday service? As I am not very experienced.
>
> Sincerely,
> Jeffrey Liu[38]

Church leaders had a meeting regarding Jeffrey's singing in worship and his participation in the eucharist. Their decision was to welcome the non-Christian stranger and give him an opportunity to not only sing a solo but also take part in the eucharist. Jim sent him good news with a careful description of what they would do on Sunday:

> Dear Jeffrey,
>
> Thank you for contacting me and thank you for your honesty. I am sure you will honour the words you are singing. I imagine you will be sitting with Jane. Our Minister is Rev Dr Sang Taek Lee, who will be leading this Service for our 111th

---

36. See Kennedy, *Eucharistic Sacramentality in an Ecumenical Context*, 61.

37. Bexley Uniting Church (BUC) is located in 29 Gladstone Street, Bexley NSW 2207, Australia.

38. Jeffrey Liu, e-mail message to Chairman of BUC, August 7, 2013.

Anniversary. Our speaker is Rev Dr Dean Drayton, who has been the President of the Uniting church in Australia – the Church's most senior position.

Attached is the Order of Service and other material which the people will be singing and saying. At the time of your contribution you will be invited to move to the front behind the Communion Rail where the people kneel later to receive the elements of bread and wine (actually grape juice) Holy Communion is one of the church's two sacraments in which we remember and relate to the death of Jesus Christ and His resurrection (the bread – His body broken on the Cross; the juice – His blood shed on the Cross – the price Jesus, the Son of God, paid for humanity's redemption. (The other sacrament is Baptism which is the 'doorway' to becoming a member of the Christian Church, which is the 'Body of Christ' on earth.) The Uniting Church has an 'open communion table' which means all who genuinely wish to acknowledge the death and resurrection of Jesus are welcome. No one, however, should feel s/he must move forward, out of courtesy, or embarrassment. It is a personal decision, Jeffrey, which will be accepted. Unless otherwise stated, we stand for the congregational singing and sit otherwise.

Every element of the Service is a part of worshipping God, including your solo. It is not a concert where one might acknowledge the pianist and bow. The people may clap your contribution. If so, just pause a moment and return to your seat. I understand you are providing your own recorded music. We will arrange that at 9am, the time Jane said you would be arriving. We look forward to it very much, Jeffrey.

Blessings, (Dr) JN Pendlebury OAM
Chairman of the Congregation[39]

On that Sunday, Jeffrey participated in the eucharist. After the service he expressed how amazing it was to have the eucharistic elements for the first time and his decision to believe in Christ Jesus. Jeffrey's family also participated in worship and the eucharist. Although their main goal was to encourage Jeffrey, after the service they said that they were moved by the hospitality of church and their recognition of Christianity had changed. The 111th Anniversary of BUC could have been a party for members only but through the open table it became a joyful banquet which the grace of God opened and touched all participants' hearts.[40] In the eucharist, the divine grace not only gives devoted disciples a power to embody their beliefs in their ministry but

---

39. Jim Pendlebury, e-mail message to Jeffrey Liu, August 8, 2013.
40. Sang Taek Lee, Interview by author, Concord, NSW, August 22, 2013.

also leads those, who are not prepared to be a Christian, to meet the risen Christ and begin a new journey as a disciple. The grace of God, the justification and the sanctification of the participants are woven together in the eucharist. Can only those who are perfectly prepared with baptism, the confession of faith and the knowledge of the eucharist participate in the eucharist? When we realize the immensity of God's grace, we cannot ignore the transforming grace of God which may mean that through the eucharist sinners can be led to baptism, a strong belief in Jesus Christ and a deeper knowledge of the eucharist.[41] Before, during and after the eucharist, all participants receive the grace of justification and sanctification from God.

5 Reconsideration of the Traditional Understanding of Sacramentality

One of the problems of traditional churches regarding the open table is a perception that opening the eucharist to all undercuts the meaning of the sacraments. For thousands of years of church history, the number of the sacraments has been a crucial issue. As a result, the Roman Catholic Church has seven sacraments,[42] and the PCK following the reformers recognizes that baptism and the eucharist are the sacraments. Recently, however, the focus of discussions regarding the sacraments has moved from determining the number of the sacraments to a new understanding of sacramentality through reconsidering the meaning of the sacraments.

Traditionally, the meaning of the sacraments has been closely related to ritual actions such as baptism and the eucharist. Based on that perception, churches have believed that human beings can receive divine grace through certain ritual actions. A challenge of the traditional understanding of the sacraments began with modern Christians' empirical recognition of various ways through which they experience the sacramentality not only in the sacraments but also in other elements of worship and even in their ordinary life. As Irwin notes, the sacraments are "signs of the way the divine is manifested in the human, of the sacred in our secular world."[43] God shows his love and reveals his will through the way which humans can perceive

---

41. Edmondson points out that "baptism is seen not as a requirement for access to the grace of fellowship, but as a movement toward the blossoming of this grace in the lives of those who have experienced it." See Edmondson, "Opening the Table," 219.

42. The seven sacraments of The Roman Catholic Church: baptism, confirmation, the eucharist, matrimony, penance, holy orders and extreme unction. See Park, *The Roman Catholic Church*, 296.

43. Irwin, "A Sacramental World," 198.

in history. If there is some means through which humans meet God and receive the divine grace, it is the sacrament. Thus, sacramentality cannot be confined in several ritual ceremonies.[44]

This raises a question: if anything in the world can be a sacrament, is there any reason why we have to conduct the sacraments? This radical approach to the sacraments could cause a vague understanding of the sacraments and perhaps even lead to an abuse of the term "sacrament." From this point of view, churches need to listen to Macquarrie's warning: "If we stretch any term, including the term 'sacrament,' too far and apply it to a great number of rather diverse things, that term begins to lose definition."[45] However, on the other hand, the shift of the understanding of the sacramentality enables churches to ponder on the essence of the sacraments. Why do churches need the sacraments? What can churches gain from conducting the sacraments? What must the church recognize through the sacraments? These questions lead us to the sole answer, that is, we must focus through the sacraments, on Jesus Christ. According to Schillebeeckx, Christ is "the one and only saving primordial sacrament."[46] Jesus Christ is the source and content of the sacraments.[47]

Regarding sacramentality in the eucharist, another important point is that Christ is present when the church gathers for the communion. The meeting of these two points, which are the sacramental perception that Christ is the primordial sacrament and the Christian belief in the presence of Christ, provides a new perspective on the eucharist. When bread and the cup are distributed, Christ, who is risen, is present in the eucharist and with his people. Christ is the host of the banquet and provides his people with spiritual and physical food. While traditional eucharistic theology has been concerned about the eucharistic regulations focusing on human conduct, the open table emphasizes Christ who is present in the eucharist. It is true that bread and the cup and the eucharistic liturgy itself can be a sacrament through which humans receive the divine grace. However, if participants experience directly the risen Christ who is the primordial sacrament, any further medium is unnecessary.[48]

When practising the open table in a church based on the traditional eucharistic theology, we should be careful about theological conflict. For example, traditional eucharistic theology proponents might think that the

---

44. Cooke, *Sacraments & Sacramentality*, 2.
45. Macquarrie, *A Guide to the Sacraments*, 36.
46. Schillebeeckx, *Christ the Sacrament of the Encounter with God*, 40.
47. Macquarrie, *A Guide to the Sacraments*, 38.
48. Ann Loades, "Table," 79.

open table threatens church tradition. This sense of crisis can lead to a dispute and division between church members. That is by no means a desirable consequence. The goal of the open table is not to make a distinction between right and wrong but to bind different eucharistic traditions with a rope of the banquet of the kingdom of God.[49] Proponents of traditional eucharistic understanding have easy access to authority through church tradition and doctrine. However, in order to practise the open table in a traditional church and minimize destructive debates, not only strong biblical and theological foundations but also profound understanding of human beings and the contexts of ministry and mission are essential. Thus, in order to conduct the open table in a church, enough time to study and share the open table theology with all church members is needed. In this process, we should make sure that the study of the eucharist will not turn into debates about the doctrine of the eucharist. For, the open table is the place of unity and joyful banquet.

6 Summary and Evaluation

The focus of the eucharist of Jesus was on inclusivity and hospitality. Regarding the forms of the eucharist, the early church enjoyed their communal meals in various ways. However, the traditional eucharistic understanding has developed its eucharistic regulations, emphasizing membership and individual preparation for keeping the eucharist holy. In that process, Paul's teaching on the eucharist regarding "discerning the body" in 1 Corinthians 11:28–29 has been used as the biblical evidence for the validity of the traditional eucharistic regulation. However, the focus of Paul's teaching in the text is not on self-examination but the eucharist as a communal act.

The traditional eucharistic understanding has believed that the open table practice would weaken the relationship between baptism and the eucharist and finally undermine the meaning of the sacraments. It is true that the traditional order of the sacraments of "baptism before the eucharist" is challenged when a church practises the open table. However, the alteration of the order of the sacraments does not necessarily mean the destruction of the sacraments. The open table theology does not argue that baptism is useless. Rather, the open table theology seeks a way of strengthening the sacraments by focusing on the significance of the sacraments rather than the order of the sacraments.

The open table theology can be an effective response to various missional questions raised in our modern complex and pluralistic society. In

---

49. Edmondson, "Opening the Table," 217

the past, when church leaders faced difficult situations in the eucharist, following church laws was the best answer. Today, however, they recognize the complexity of the situations and the limitations of church laws. In the past church drew eucharistic regulations from the last supper but now the open table theology leads the church to focus on Jesus' love towards a human being and his respect for "little children" (Luke 18:16) in his ministry. The generosity of Jesus makes the eucharist a place of grace and transformation. When people experience the immensity of the grace of God in the eucharist, their sinful and corrupted natures are transformed into the people of God. In this sense, the eucharist is a means of grace. In the open table theology, the church finds the primordial sacrament, Jesus Christ. This new recognition of sacramentality leads church to focus on Jesus who is present in the eucharist not the eucharistic elements or regulations.

The open table theology helps us to reassess the value of the eucharist preserved in the non-mainstream church. As both Jagessar and Burns note, including the eucharistic theology and practice of the non-mainstream church is not at all about undermining church tradition but rather "the rediscovery of varied richness"[50] of Christian traditions. Furthermore, the open table leads church to the heart of the eucharist of Jesus, and its inclusivity and hospitality. The purpose of the open table is not to persuade church to renounce traditional eucharistic practice but to rediscover significant values of the eucharist which traditional eucharistic understanding has lost or neglected so that the church might enjoy theologically and practically the richness of eucharistic diversity.

These theological perspectives based on the meals of Jesus have been accepted and embodied in some modern churches' eucharistic theology and practice. In the next chapter I will research the eucharist of the Uniting Church in Australia which is one of the most representative denominations to have an open table policy.

---

50. Jagessar and Burns, *Christian Worship*, 136.

Part III

A Model of Application of the Open Table Theology in the Uniting Church in Australia (UCA)

Chapter 8

The Way of the Open Table
The Eucharist of the Uniting Church in Australia (UCA) as a Model

IN RECENT DECADES, THE number of mainstream churches having an open table policy has kept increasing. This situation is conspicuous in Protestant churches. In particular, when considering the relationship with the PCK, there were four main denominations which had a significant influence in its formation and development: the Presbyterian Church in USA, the Presbyterian Church in US, the Presbyterian Church of Australia (PCA)[1] and the Canadian Presbyterian Church (CPC). An interesting fact is that today all of the three (four in the past)[2] denominations which contributed to the PCK's worship and theology have an open table policy whereas the PCK keeps conducting a closed table. Although the PCUSA, the UCA and the CPC neither promote the open table as an official doctrine nor practise it universally they recognize the open table as the way to celebrate the eucharist.[3]

1. Some Presbyterian churches along with Methodist and Congregational Churches joined the Uniting Church when it was formed; there is still a Presbyterian Church in Australia independent of the UCA.

2. In the early period of the history of the PCK, there were four denominations which had an influence in the formation of the PCK. However, among the four denominations, in 1983 the Presbyterian Church in USA and the Presbyterian Church in US were united into the PCUSA. Thus, from now on this study will write "three" instead of "four." See Brackenridge, *The Presbyterian Church (U.S.A.) Foundation*, xii.

3. For more details on the open table policy of the PCUSA, see Presbyterian Church (U.S.A.), *Invitation to Christ*. Also, see the section "The Influence of Confucianism on the Eucharist" in chapter 1 of this study. Regarding the UCA's open table policy, see the section "Basis of Union and the Eucharist" in this chapter. While the PCUSA and the UCA have an open table policy which allows those who are not baptised in the eucharist, the focus of the PCC regarding the open table is on the inclusion of children in the eucharist. In 1987, the General Assembly of the PCC recognized that "Children are capable of the same childlike faith that Jesus required of adults; the faith of children

I have explored a theoretical basis of the open table through the previous chapters. In this chapter, I will investigate the practical implications of how the open table theology might be embodied in liturgy and worship. Out of the three denominations, the eucharist of the UCA will be the focus of this chapter. There are several reasons why I have selected the eucharist of the UCA. Firstly, the UCA has had a good relationship with the PCK since the very early period of the history of the PCK. The relationship between the UCA and the PCK commenced in 1889 when J. H. Davis, the first Australian missionary from the Presbyterian Church of Victoria, began his mission in Korea. In 1977, when the PCA united with Congregational Union of Australia and the Methodist Church of Australasia about one third of the PCA did not join the union.[4] However, all the international and Aboriginal mission programs were handed over to the UCA. Thus, the mission partnership of the former PCA with the PCK was spontaneously transferred to the UCA.[5] Since 1889, over 120 missionaries from the UCA (the PCA between 1901 and 1976) have devoted their lives to mission in Korea.[6] Recently, the partnership between the UCA and the PCK has deepened not only through theological exchanges but also through cooperation in mission in Ra Son region in North Korea.[7] Furthermore, the UCA is a union of three denominations. In other words, the open table of the UCA means a theological agreement has been reached by three different denominations with different theological perspectives. At this point, especially in terms of ecumenism, the open table of the UCA is expected to make a contribution to the PCK's study of the open table.

The UCA, a union of three denominations, was inaugurated in 1977. In the process of union, basic and important issues which the three denominations had agreed upon were formulated in the Basis of Union. Since then, the Basis of Union has been recognized as "a document enabling three churches to unite but also a document with continuing authority for the faith and order"[8] of the UCA. In the Basis of Union the UCA expresses the view that the eucharist is the sacrament of baptised people.[9] However,

---

may be nurtured by participation in the Lord's Supper; the participation of children affirms their place in the fellowship we share as a spiritual family at the Lord's Table." The Presbyterian Church in Canada, "Worship and the Sacraments."

4. Among 1437 Presbyterian churches, 521 churches (about 36%) decided to remain Presbyterian. See Harrison, *Baptism of Fire*, 20–21.

5. Brown, "The Australian Mission in Korea since 1977," 89.

6. Lee, "The Presbyterian Church of Australia and Korean Church," 31–33.

7. Barr, "PCK-UCA Partnership from A Uniting Church Perspective," 108–10.

8. Dutney, "It Was Like They'd Had A Vision," 10.

9. See paragraph 8 "Holy Communion" in The Basis of Union of the Uniting

at the same time in actual practice the UCA has an open table policy which allows unbaptised people to participate in the eucharist. How can these two extremes coexist in the one church? An answer might be found in the history of discussion of the open table in the UCA. There are various sources which show the UCA's journey to the open table. First of all, the Basis of Union and historical documents related to this issue will be explored in this chapter. In addition, the results of these discussions are reflected in the UCA's worship resources and embodied in local churches' practice of the eucharist. By analysing these worship resources and investigating the actual eucharistic practice of several congregations in the UCA, I will examine how the open table theology might be embodied in a Christian community. After then, I will try to evaluate the open table of the UCA.

1 Basis of Union and the Eucharist

The Relationship between Baptism and the Eucharist in the Basis of Union

Regarding the relationship between baptism and the eucharist, the Basis of Union of the UCA declares that in the eucharist "the risen Lord feeds his baptized people on their way to the final inheritance of the Kingdom."[10] This statement expresses a strong connection between baptism and the eucharist. As Bos and Thompson recognize, one possible interpretation is that this statement does not necessarily mean that "the unbaptised are to be barred from the sacrament."[11] However, given that the framers of the Basis of Union intended to preserve the Reformed and Methodist traditions and to reflect ecumenical perspectives,[12] this statement would have meant that the eucharist is a sacrament in which baptised people participate. Furthermore, in a strict sense, the open table which allows the unbaptised to participate in the eucharist was not an issue at the time of the formation of the UCA. According to Davis McCaughey, there were discussions of the relationship between baptism and the eucharist when the Basis of Union was drafted.

Church in Australia (1992 edition). The Uniting Church in Australia, *Constitution and Regulations: 2008 Edition*, 23.

10. Ibid., 23.

11. Bos and Thompson, *Theology for Pilgrims*, 500.

12. The Basis of Union is a confessional document which three denominations agreed on. Furthermore, the UCA has been in dialogue with the Roman Catholic, Lutheran, Greek Orthodox, Churches of Christ and Anglican since its inauguration. Dialogue with the Baptists, the Churches of Christ, the Salvation Army, and the Religious Society of Friends are also in progress. Boyd, "Twenty Years, 85–86.

However, the main issue did not consider the open table but whether the baptised children might participate in the eucharist before confirmation or not. Although the framers of the Basis of Union recognized the benefit of confirmation, regarding the eucharist, their emphasis was more on the significance of baptism than confirmation.[13] The strong relationship between baptism and the eucharist which is expressed in paragraph 8 of the Basis of Union is reemphasized in the last sentence of paragraph 12:

> To this end the Uniting Church commits itself to undertake, with other Christians, to explore and develop the relation of baptism to confirmation and to participation in the Holy Communion.[14]

For several years after union, the UCA was involved in several social justice issues including Aboriginal land rights, racism and the acknowledgement and place of homosexual people in the church. Around the early 1980s, the UCA began to focus on the internal issues of the UCA.[15] Concerning the debate regarding infant baptism and adult baptism which already existed at the time of the inauguration of the UCA, the issue of including baptised children in the eucharist was officially raised in 1982.

Admission of Baptised Children to the Eucharist

In a broader sense, the open table policy of the UCA might be considered in two respects: inclusion of baptised children and those who are not baptised. In the early stage, the open table of the UCA was mainly related to the issue of whether to include baptised children in the eucharist. It is worth observing the context in which the issue was raised. In the UCA there were different views on the minimum age considered appropriate to participate in the eucharist. Some churches included baptised children in the eucharist but others excluded them. In 1982, the Third Assembly requested the Standing Committee to study the issue and provide a direction to bridge the disparity within the UCA.[16] After the resolution of the Third Assembly,

---

13. McCaughey, *Commentary on the Basis of Union of the Uniting Church in Australia*, 62.

14. See paragraph 12 "Members" of the Basis of Union. The Uniting Church in Australia, *Constitution and Regulations: 2008 Edition*, 24.

15. Emilsen and Emilsen, *The Uniting Church in Australia*, 2–3.

16. "It was resolved that the Assembly . . . request the Standing Committee, on the advice of the Doctrine Commission, to provide guidance to the Uniting Church with respect to the participation of children in celebrations of Holy Communion." See Assembly Minutes 82.53.16.b.

three agencies[17] in the Assembly began to explore the issue and then completed a remarkable report, "Children and Holy Communion." The decision of the Fourth Assembly 1985, which has guided the UCA's present open table policy, was deeply influenced by the report.

At this point, it seems worth exploring part of the report containing the issue of including baptised children in the eucharist. First of all, the strong relationship of baptism with membership and also with the eucharist which is specified in paragraphs 8 and 12 of the Basis of Union is reaffirmed by the report: "To deny the baptised a place at the Lord's table calls into question the validity and meaning of their Baptism."[18]

This recognition helps the church interpret that regardless of age, if children are baptised, baptism gives them a divine authority to participate in the eucharist. This baptismal understanding of the UCA is not based on a superstitious belief in the baptismal rite. The focus of the UCA's theology of baptism is not on the baptismal rite but the grace of God manifested through the rite:

> When we baptise a child we commit ourselves to provide the sort of loving Church family in which the love and grace of God might be offered to the child, long before this little one is even able to utter the word "God" or begin to understand what the word "God" means. Such is God's grace that works in us and around us before ever we say "Lord, I believe. Help my unbelief."[19]

The grace of God has been provided to his children long before they realize what it is. The children of God experience divine grace before they understand what they do and confess what they believe in. The UCA's recognition of the nature of the grace of God turns the attention to how children experience or sense the presence of God in worship rather than how much they know about God. It does not mean that the UCA views the church's educational program for baptism and the eucharist as not necessary. While traditional eucharistic understanding teaches that participants in the eucharist are to be prepared with a certain level of knowledge and faith before participation, the UCA recognizes that through participating in the eucharist participants can deepen their understanding of the eucharist and faith. This recognition of the UCA echoes the theology of John Wesley

---

17. The Commission on Doctrine, the Commission on Liturgy and the Joint Board of Christian Education.

18. See section 3.1 Baptism and Membership. Bos and Thompson, *Theology for Pilgrims*, 488.

19. See ibid., 489.

who understood the eucharist as a means of grace.[20] The report, *Children and Holy Communion*, expresses this idea in this way:

> We affirm that children can learn the gospel fundamentals at their level by participation in this celebration; the experience of belonging can deepen faith and confirm their place as members; and the traditional Christian education programs can build on what is learned experientially.[21]

The UCA recognizes that through baptism the baptised person is united in one family of God.[22] The membership of the UCA is "open to all who are baptized into the Holy Catholic Church"[23] regardless of age. Through the eucharist, the people of God grow together into Christ. And through the experience of participating in the eucharist their knowledge and faith are strengthened by the Holy Spirit.[24] Based on these understandings, the report announces a clear position regarding the issue of including baptised children in the eucharist:

> The participation of baptised children in Holy Communion is not merely an option the Council of Elders may consider. It is appropriate and desirable in light of our Church's understanding as reflected in the *Basis of Union*.[25]

Likewise, the debate on the issue of including baptised children in the eucharist, which existed before the inauguration of the UCA and was heated around the early 1980s, ended with the reemphasis on the significance of baptism. Paragraphs 7 and 8 of the Basis of Union especially were used for supporting the participation of baptised children in the eucharist as a crucial evidence. In the process, the UCA reasserted that baptism gives children the right to participate in the eucharist.

---

20. For more details on "means of grace" in John Wesley, see the section "The Eucharistic Understanding of John and Charles Wesley" in chapter 5 of this study.

21. See section 3.3 Understanding and participation. Bos and Thompson, *Theology for Pilgrims*, 492.

22. See paragraph 7 "Baptism" of the Basis of Union. The Uniting Church in Australia, *Constitution and Regulations: 2008 Edition*, 23.

23. See paragraph 12 "Membership" of the Basis of Union. Ibid., 24.

24. See paragraph 8 "Holy Communion" of the Basis of Union. Ibid., 23.

25. See section 5 Proposals for action by the Assembly. Bos and Thompson, *Theology for Pilgrims*, 496.

Doctrinal Interpretation of Baptism and the Eucharist under the Basis of Union

The Working Group on Doctrine of the UCA has provided authoritative resources based on the Basis of Union to guide the journey of the UCA. The order of baptism before the eucharist is reaffirmed in the work of the Working Group on Doctrine:

> Who participates?
>
> All baptised Christians are welcome to share the meal (Basis of Union Para. 8), but not all may be permitted by the laws of their Church to receive communion with the Uniting Church. This needs to be respected as we continue to pursue the unity to which Christ calls us.[26]

This statement is quite similar to traditional eucharistic understanding. Baptism is recognized as a prerequisite for the eucharist. Here, paragraph 8 of the Basis of Union is noted to explain the necessity of baptism for the eucharist. However, at the same time, this statement recognizes that there are some churches with church laws admitting only baptism which is conducted within their churches as a valid ordinance.

One of the most recent publications of the Assembly Working Groups on Doctrine and Worship, *Building on the Basis*, was published in 2012. The section "How do we understand Baptism?" clarifies the UCA's doctrinal stance towards the relationship between baptism and the eucharist. This section consists of 24 questions related to baptism. Among them, the nineteenth question asks: "What is the relationship of baptism to the Lord's supper?"[27] For an answer to this question, the Working Group emphasizes the significance of the eucharist which is different from other ordinary meals. The eucharistic practice of the early church, which excluded the unbaptised from the eucharist, is introduced into the argument. Finally, this traditional order of baptism before the eucharist is confirmed by the Basis of Union and the decision of the Assembly of the UCA is as follows:

> The Basis of Union therefore says: "In this sacrament of his broken body and outpoured blood the risen Lord feeds his *baptized* people . . ." (par 8). The Fourth Assembly of the Uniting Church in 1985 recognised this close link between baptism and the

---

26. The Working Group on Doctrine, "Worksheet 8: The Lord's Supper" (sheet prepared for the National Assembly, Sydney, NSW, 2009).

27. Walker, *Building on the Basis*, 192.

Lord's supper when it said that baptised children could receive communion.[28]

2 The UCA's Open Table Policy

Two Types of Open Table in the UCA

Apparently, as a doctrinal principle, the UCA has expressed the view that the eucharist is a sacrament of baptised people. However, in actual practice, the UCA has an open table policy. "Rituals in the Uniting Church" includes one of the most explicit statements disclosing the open table policy of the UCA:

> The Uniting Church practises an "open table policy." This means that an open invitation is usually extended to "all who love the Lord" to share in Holy Communion. Christians from other denominations, or from no denomination, are welcome to participate in the celebration of Holy Communion at a Uniting Church. In contrast to some denominations, it is not necessary to be a confirmed member or even a baptised member to participate in Holy Communion, though it is seen as appropriate that the person or child has been baptised.[29]

This statement writes clearly that the UCA practises an open table. Ostensibly, according to this statement the UCA seems to promote actively the open table including unbaptised persons in the eucharist. However, this statement does not fully explain why the UCA has an open table policy and how the open table might be practised. For a clear understanding of the open table policy of the UCA, a more careful look at the context in which the issue of the open table began to rise in the UCA is needed.

As stated previously, the issue of the open table might be considered in two categories: The first category is related to the question of admission of baptised children to the eucharist. The second category is the question whether church might allow unbaptised people to participate in the eucharist or not. Regarding the first question, the UCA's position is clear. In a doctrinal sense, the UCA recognizes the open table as the eucharistic practice including baptised children in Holy Communion:

---

28. Ibid., 193.

29. See The Uniting Church in Australia, Synod of NSW & ACT, "Holy Communion" in "Rituals in the Uniting Church."

The Uniting Church is very ecumenical. We are part of one Holy Catholic church. The understanding of the eucharist is on the line with *Baptism, Eucharist and Ministry* of WCC. In terms of the open table, we are very much affirmed that baptism is the basis on which one participates in the eucharist. Also in 1985 the UCA took the decision like the Orthodox that if children are baptised they should be able to participate in communion. The open table of the UCA is related to that.[30]

Regarding the first type of open table, the UCA's eucharistic practice is the same as the eucharistic principles based on the Basis of Union. In other words, the UCA's eucharistic practice of including baptised children is emphatically and practically supported. However, the UCA tends to take a cautious approach to the second issue. There are few official and doctrinal documents supporting the reason why the UCA has to practise the second type of open table. Nevertheless, the open table which includes unbaptised persons in the eucharist is a widespread practice in the UCA. How is it possible? An answer might be found in the UCA's understanding of the reason why the church of God exists.

The UCA's Missional Vision Reflected in the Open Table Policy

The UCA recognizes the nature of Jesus' meal practice in which Jesus accepted and welcomed those who were not prepared and even sinners. Moreover, the UCA recognizes the eucharist as a means of grace. These understandings of the eucharist might form the theoretical basis for practising the open table. Yet, there is a significant reason for the UCA's practice of the open table in that the UCA views that the eucharist is central to the light of mission. The union of three churches in 1977 was motivated by missional vision. The passion for the missional vision enabled the three denominations to be united into one church overcoming doctrinal differences.[31] Although officially the Basis of Union has played a role in influencing doctrine in the UCA, it is not recognized as a doctrine in a traditional sense. In other words, the UCA does not hold a legalistic approach to the traditional eucharistic order of baptism before the eucharist.[32] Borrowing from the terms Norman Young used, Dutney describes the Basis of Union as "the

---

30. Chris Walker, an interview, January 21, 2014. Rev. Dr. Chris Walker is currently serving in the Assembly of the UCA as National Consultant for theology, doctrine and worship.

31. Dutney, "Why does the Church Exist?," 60–61.

32. Walker, *Building on the Basis*, 193.

charter under which we agree to go on mission together."[33] The missional vision involves a pastoral approach to those who want to participate in the eucharist. Thornley says:

> In the Basis of Union it is the baptised that receive communion. However, you do not have to produce evidence of baptism. In a missional sense the church would not prevent people from coming forward for communion and ministers are aware that some coming forward may not be baptised. An example would be a 50 year old woman in one of the congregations where I was a minister started to attend worship and participated in the communion. After a year she asked to be baptised as a member of the church. Her comment was that if she had not been included in communion she would have been isolated and would probably not have stayed at the church. If you do not wish to take communion, especially little children, you can go forward and ask for a blessing. This is not unusual.[34]

The Open Table Based on Ecclesiology: A Pilgrim People.

Paragraph 3 of the Basis of Union contains a crucial reason why the church exists. The ultimate purpose of God is the renewal and reconciliation of the whole creation. For the final purpose, God calls the church. The Basis of Union expresses consistently that the promised day on which the final goal of God will be accomplished is coming.[35] Regarding the promised end, the mission of God will be completed. "The church is a pilgrim people, always on the way towards"[36] the end of the mission of God. God washes and feeds his people through the sacraments until they finish the pilgrimage to the promised end. Through the nourishment, the people grow to be disciples who participate in the mission of God. This recognition of a pilgrim people helps the church realize the vulnerability of human beings. The people of God who are on the way to the end are not perfect. The pilgrim people are beings who need care and support. According to this perspective, the priority of the church is not to investigate their qualification for the eucharist but

---

33. Dutney, *Manifesto for Renewal*, 107.

34. Carolyn Thornley, e-mail message to author, December 9, 2013. Carolyn Thornley is Vice Principal and Dean of Candidates at United Theological College which is constituted within the New South Wales Synod of the UCA.

35. Paragraphs 1, 3, 8, 17 and 18 in the Basis of Union.

36. Paragraph 3 in the Basis of Union. See The Uniting Church in Australia, *Constitution and Regulations: 2008 Edition*, 22.

to support them so that they may keep going on to the promised end and live their lives as disciples.

The recognition of the church as a pilgrim people reveals that the main body of mission is not the church but God. During the second half of the 20th century, there has been a crucial awareness of mission as the *missio Dei*.[37] Since then, churches have begun to change their focus from the traditional goal of mission which is to increase the members of a certain denomination to a different goal of how God works in the world for his mission. In the light of the *missio Dei* even a missional work which was thought to be successful or unsuccessful in the past is revaluated. That comes from a realization that God has been working for his mission in other ways. The *missio Dei* requests the church to broaden its perspective of mission. As the Lutheran World Federation writes, "God's own mission is larger than the mission of the church."[38] Similarly, the UCA recognizes that "all of God's actions relate to mission."[39] God created the whole world in his plan. The whole creation moves to the promised end. The scope of the mission of God encompasses not only the church but also the world. The vastness of the *missio Dei* leads the church to realize the limitations the church has. The UCA recognizes that all decisions the church makes have limitations. At this point, there is no perfect church law "since law is received by human beings and framed by them."[40] Furthermore, the law by which the whole world has been led towards the promised end is not the law of a church but the law of grace and love overflowing from the heart of God.[41] This perspective helps the UCA depend more on the law of God's grace than the eucharistic law of the church:

> The emphasis should be to proclaim the undeserved grace of God in encouraging the unbaptised to seek Baptism, and to encompass them in the love and nurture of the Congregation as they are prepared for and invited to participate in the sacrament. The guiding principle is that the sacraments are a means of grace—they do not limit grace. This principle will allow us with integrity to accept that there are situations in the life of the Church in which unbaptised people may participate in Holy Communion.[42]

37. Bosch, *Transforming Mission*, 398–99.
38. Ibid., 401.
39. Walker, *Building on the Basis*, 43.
40. Paragraph 17 in the Basis of Union. See The Uniting Church in Australia, *Constitution and Regulations: 2008 Edition*, 28.
41. Walker, *Building on the Basis*, 43–44.
42. See Section 5 Proposals for Action by the Assembly. Bos and Thompson,

3 The UCA's Perspective of Worship and the Eucharist: The Pattern of Worship

One of the UCA's official resources for the eucharist, *Holy Communion*,[43] which was published in 1980, provides three orders of the eucharist. All three orders follow the fourfold pattern of worship: The preparation, the service of the word, the service of the eucharist, and the dismissal. This fourfold pattern reveals the UCA's basic understanding of worship that word and the eucharist are central in worship.

Eleven years after the inauguration of the UCA, the first worship book *Uniting in Worship* (UiW) was published in 1988. The second and latest worship book, *Uniting in Worship 2* (UiW2), was introduced in 2005, but UiW is still be employed as a useful worship resource for local churches. UiW notes that Christian worship, basically, has a fourfold pattern: The Gathering of the People of God, the Service of the Word, the Sacrament of the Lord's Supper, and the Sending Forth of the People of God.[44] UiW shows the UCA's perception of worship that the eucharist has a central place in worship:

> Since New Testament times, the Lord's people have gathered at the Lord's table on the Lord's day. This is to remember Christ's death and resurrection and to celebrate the sacraments as signs of the last day, the day of consummation. Through the ages the basic structure of Christian worship has remained the same. In Reformed practice, despite variations for historical reasons, this pattern has been maintained.[45]

Regarding the structure of worship, UiW2 follows the fourfold pattern of its predecessor: "The Service of the Lord's Day has four parts, which could be briefly characterised as: gathering, hearing, being fed and being sent."[46] Yet, in explaining Sunday worship, UiW differs slightly from UiW2. As observed in the excerpt above, the former focuses on the eucharist, as the basis of Christian worship, rather than the service of word. On the other hand, the latter tries to balance word and the eucharist which are two central pillars of worship:

> The pattern of worship from New Testament times has been for Christians to gather to hear God's word and to break bread

---

Theology for Pilgrims, 500–501.

43. See Uniting Church in Australia, *Holy Communion*.
44. The Uniting Church in Australia, *Uniting in Worship*, 76–77.
45. Ibid., 76.
46. The Uniting Church in Australia, *Uniting in Worship 2*, 132.

together on the first day of each week, on Sunday, 'the Lord's Day.' . . . In many historical variations, the fundamental order of Christian worship—word and sacrament together—can be recognised.[47]

There are a few differences in describing the nature of worship between UiW and UiW 2. Yet, there is a clear consensus in both books that the eucharist is an essential element in worship. In defining the theology of the UCA, Bos and Thompson write: ". . . worship in which the Lord's Supper is celebrated should be understood as the norm rather than the exception."[48] This UCA's perception of the eucharist is identical with that of the World Council of Churches. Different from Roman Catholic and Greek Orthodox traditions, Protestants, having been influenced by Zwingli who emphasized the eucharist as memory and remembrance and reformers who fought against the misuse of the eucharist by the medieval church, began to develop the so-called preaching-centred worship. Recently, however, there has been an ecumenical convergence with a remarkable academic achievement about the origin of worship proposing that the celebration of the eucharist "continues as the central act of the Church's worship"[49] from the earliest period of church history. Likewise, this eucharistic perception has inherited the early church tradition. The recognition of the eucharist as the central part of worship was firmly entrenched in the early church. One of the earliest Christian literatures, the *Didache* 14:1, depicts the eucharist as an essential part of Sunday worship: "Assembling on every Sunday of the Lord, break bread and give thanks, confessing your faults beforehand, so that your sacrifice may be pure."[50] In addition, the liturgical outline of Sunday service recorded in chapter 67 of *First Apology* of Justin Martyr (100–165 CE) shows the place of the eucharist in worship: Gathering – Scripture reading – Exhortation – Prayer – Offering of the eucharistic elements – Thanksgiving prayer – Sharing of the eucharist – Collection & Dismissal.[51] The Doctrine and Worship working group of the UCA writes:

> In the Uniting Church the sacrament of the Lord's Supper is not always included and monthly is the practice in many churches. Nevertheless, it is important to recognise that it is not an extra.

---

47. Ibid., 138.
48. See Bos and Thompson, *Theology for Pilgrims*, 429.
49. See World Council of Churches, *Baptism, Eucharist and Ministry*, 10.
50. Niederwimmer, *The Didache*, 194.
51. For more details on the order of Sunday service of Justin Martyr, see Johnson, *Worship in the Early Church*, 68–69.

Rather, worship without Holy Communion is less than the fullness of worship.[52]

4 A Reflection on the Structure of the Eucharist of the UCA

The UCA holds up four categories as the basic pattern of worship. However, regarding the composition of each category the UCA provides many options in worship resources so that local churches can freely express their worship within the basic pattern according to various occasions. This "freedom that lies within the form of the Service"[53] is one of the most important values to be found in the UCA's understanding of worship. Based on the fourfold pattern of worship and the freedom in worship order, the UCA provides rich and various resources regarding the eucharist.

The first and second orders in *Holy Communion* present a full liturgy for an ordinary worship in a church, and the third one is designed for the eucharist in small groups and in ministering to the sick.[54] These three orders of Holy Communion reflect the UCA's perspective of worship and the eucharist. The UCA recognizes that Holy Communion does not begin at the Service of the Eucharist. Moreover, the eucharist does not begin merely at the breaking of the bread or invitation to the table. The starting point of the eucharist is the same as that of worship. When the congregation gathers to worship, the eucharist begins. In other words, the eucharist is not a special ritual distinct from an ordinary Sunday service but a different name for worship:

> There are many names for worship. When we call it the Service of the Lord's Day, we remember that Christians began to worship together on the day of Christ's resurrection: Sunday. When we call it liturgy, we are saying that this is our service to God. The word "liturgy" comes from a Greek word meaning "public

---

52. Walker, *Building on the Basis*, 231.

53. Monro and Moore, *Exploring Worship*, 5. Introducing the UCA's worship, Monro and Moore place a deep value on the diversity of ways of worship and meaning of worship elements. For example, regarding the eucharist, they give readers instructions: "Think about some of the different meanings given to the words bread and wine, e.g. bread can signify food generally." Ibid., 17. And they indicate: "Find different forms of greetings used around the world. For example, in Korea, people bow to one another." Ibid., 18. Moreover, regarding the origin of the eucharist, they broaden the eucharistic understanding of the UCA through introducing the institution narrative and the Emmaus story in the Service of the Eucharist. See ibid., 20, 22.

54. Uniting Church in Australia, *Holy Communion*, 1.

service": *leitourgia*. When we call it Holy Communion, we highlight our communion in Jesus. When we call it the Lord's Supper, we recall that what we do has its beginnings in the words and actions of Jesus at the Last Supper. When we call it the Eucharist, we focus on our thanksgiving for all that the Triune God has done for our world and us. We remember especially God's work in Jesus and the Holy Spirit. The word "Eucharist" is Greek for "thanksgiving"![55]

However, at the same time, worship can be categorised functionally. That is why the figure above divides worship into four categories. In this section, this study will focus on the main components of the Service of the Eucharist.

The Peace

First of all, a notable part of the Service of the Eucharist is the passing of the peace. In Holy Communion One and Three, the peace appears as the first order: "The peace of the Lord be always with you. *And also with you.*"[56]

The first written account of the peace as an order of the eucharist is found in Justin Martyr's *First Apology*: "Having ended the prayers, we greet one another with a kiss"[57] (65.2). According to Dix, in the Pre-Nicene period, the greeting words for the kiss of peace would possibly be "peace be with you" like Jesus' greeting in John 20:19. Around the fourth century, the simple words developed into a more elaborate formula: "The peace of God be with you all (in Syria), or The peace of Lord be always with you (in the West)."[58] The UCA follows the western tradition for the peace as observed above.[59] The ways of the peace in the UCA are varied according to local churches' customs. The peace may be shared one another with a sign of peace such as a handshake or hug including greeting words. Regarding the practice of the peace, it would be worth observing a direction that "the manner of the greeting and the words to be used"[60] for the peace should be notified to the congregation. This direction seemingly aims to prevent the peace from being in disorder or tarnishing its meaning. For, the UCA

---

55. Monro and Moore, *Exploring Worship*, 8.
56. Ibid., 9, 31.
57. Bradshaw, *Eucharistic Origins*, 61.
58. Dix, *The Shape of the Liturgy: NEW EDITION*, 103.
59. The Uniting Church in Australia, *Holy Communion*, 9, 31. See also The Uniting Church in Australia, *Uniting in Worship 2*, 162, 209.
60. The Uniting Church in Australia, *Holy Communion*, 3.

recognizes that the peace "is primarily about reconciliation in Christ rather than personal greeting."[61]

Offertory

In Holy Communion One and Two, the offertory is placed between the end of the service of the word and the prayer of consecration. This position of the offertory embraces significant meanings. For some protestants who are based on the preaching-centred worship tradition, the offertory is generally appreciated as a thanksgiving and response to the word. For example, in the first service of the Lord's Day of UiW2, the position of the offering is within the service of the word independent from the eucharist.[62] Thus, the offering as a response to the word is emphasized. On the other hand, when considering the offertory placed within the eucharist, the offertory's meaning is beyond its relationship with the word. One of the crucial actions of the offertory is to bring the eucharistic elements, bread and wine, to the communion table.[63]

The eucharistic bread and wine include a meaning of a remembrance of Christ's saving act as the last supper tradition preserves. Yet, the significance of the eucharistic bread and wine cannot be confined to the sacrificial meaning, expressed as the body and blood. First of all, bread and wine are the products of human efforts. At the same time, fundamentally, everything is from God the Creator. Thus worshippers bring the offerings not with arrogance but with thanksgiving and humbleness. Offertory prayers of the UCA express clearly this point:

> Blessed are you, Lord, God of all creation. Through your goodness we have this bread to offer, which earth has given and human hands have made. It will become for us the bread of life. Blessed are you, Lord, God of all creation. Through your goodness we have this wine offer, fruit of the vine and work of human

---

61. The Uniting Church in Australia, *Uniting in Worship 2*, 136.

62. The order of the Service of the Word: First reading – Psalm – Second reading – Gospel – Hymn – Preaching of the Word – Affirmation of faith – Offering – Notices and concerns of the Church – Prayers of the people. See Ibid., 148, 160.

63. The UCA has two ways of presenting the offertory. One is that the elements may be brought to the table by members of the congregation during the offertory. Another way is to place the elements on the table and cover them with a white cloth before the service. In this case, the action of bringing the elements is replaced by removing the white cloth. Ibid., 142, 162.

hands. It will become for us our spiritual drink. Blessed be God for ever.[64]

Almighty Father, We are unworthy to celebrate this sacrament, but in your Son Jesus Christ you have drawn near to us. It is in his name that we draw near to you. In obedience to his command we offer this bread and this cup. All that we have comes from you and what we give you is your own. *Amen.*[65]

Regarding the offertory, another important eucharistic understanding is that bread and wine are food. According to McGowan, the early church offered more varied foods for the offertory such as oil, cheese, vegetables, olives, salt, milk, and honey along with the main eucharistic elements, bread and wine.[66] Some of them were possibly used with an ascetic purpose[67] and others seem to be used for suggesting certain theological symbolism: Salt symbolizes unity and commensality,[68] and milk and honey are depicted in the Scripture as "the sense of growing in faith . . . and God's free invitation to abundant life."[69] Above all, it should be noted that these varied eucharistic elements were used for a meal by the early church. God nourishes his people with the food not only spiritually but physically. The two dimensions of spirit and physical body are inseparable in the eucharist.

However, since the ritualization of the eucharist,[70] the physical aspect of the eucharist as food has been gradually weakened. The act of eating and drinking in the eucharist has become a symbolic ritual. The richness of food provided in the early eucharistic practices has been replaced by a small cup and a coin size wafer. Since the inauguration of Christianity, for a long time, the bread at the eucharist and the bread used for ordinary meals at home had not been different. Yet, around the ninth century, the church confirmed the use of unleavened bread for the eucharist. Moreover, the way of distribution of the bread was changed from putting it in hands to on tongues. As a result, the type of the bread became flat and round. Spontaneously, the size of the bread became smaller. By the eleventh century, the custom of baking

64. The Uniting Church in Australia, *Holy Communion*, 9.

65. Ibid., 23.

66. For more details on the varied foods for the eucharist of the early church, see McGowan, *Ascetic Eucharists*, 95–127.

67. See chapter 4 of this study.

68. McGowan, *Ascetic Eucharists*, 124.

69. Burns, *Pilgrim People*, 144.

70. It is uncertain when the ritualization began in church history. Yet, according to Murphy-O'Conner, the increase of the number of a congregation would possibly cause the change of the eucharist from full meal to the current form of the eucharist. Murphy-O'Conner, *St. Paul's Corinth*, 183–85.

the eucharistic bread in a small size for lay communicants prevailed in the west.[71] The significance of the physical aspect of the food has gone beyond filling participants' stomach with food or sharing equally the food between participants in the eucharist. In the early church, the food in the eucharist was not only enjoyed by participants but also sent to the absent members,[72] and more importantly, the elements offered on the table were used as daily bread for the poor. Focusing on the relationship between the eucharist and offerings, which were brought by rich members, depicted in *First Apology* 67, Bradshaw says:

> The connection of the Eucharist with giving to those in need continued to be maintained in later Christian tradition, thus re-inforcing the intimate relationship that was understood to exist between the shared meal and the mutual love expected of the participants – the failure of which was the very basis of Paul's criticism of the Corinthians (1 Cor. 11).[73]

The recovery of the physical aspect of eucharistic food helps Christians to turn their attention to those who need the food. In the early church period, the varied foods which were offered and then sent to the poor, orphans and strangers (*First Apology* 67:6) were the fruits of their labour. Today, foods still might be a good offering. Yet, when considering the nature of the offertory, foods are not necessarily confined to an object for the offertory. In the 21st century, for people living in urban areas and even rural areas, money is recognized as the fruits of their labour. As Kavanagh notes, money "is one of the strongest symbols in an industrial and consumer oriented culture."[74] The second service of the Lord's day in UiW2 echoes clearly this perspective on the offertory. Here, the offering of money is placed at the end of the service of the word but definitely connected with the offertory of bread and wine: "A Scripture sentence may be used before the gifts of money are collected. They may be brought forward with the bread and wine."[75]

---

71. See Foley, *From Age to Age*, 83–84, 108.

72. Justin Martyr, *First Apology* 67:5. See Rordorf, *The Eucharist of the Early Christians*, 73.

73. Bradshaw, *Eucharistic Origins*, 68.

74. Kavanagh, *Elements of Rite*, 65.

75. The Uniting Church in Australia, *Uniting in Worship 2*, 208. Also see The Uniting Church in Australia, *Holy Communion*, 9 and 22.

The Dismissal

Ultimately this eucharistic understanding of the offertory is connected with the mission of the dismissal and extended to people outside the church building. As McMichael declares, the offering is "not confined to the liturgy."[76] The eucharist brings Christian communities into the world. To participate in the eucharist is to join the prayer of Jesus: "Your kingdom come. Your will be done, on earth as it is in heaven" (Matt 6:10). The kingdom of God coming on earth engages inevitably in the earthly matters. To share the eucharist is an act of desiring the realization of "the Son's triumph over the political, economic and social powers which dominate the earth."[77] At this point, as the last part of the eucharist, the dismissal needs to include more detailed descriptions to determine where the eucharistic community should reach and what the community should do. The dismissal below helps participants be reminded of the mission:

> Closing Sentences
>
> We must not stay here. Our purpose is among those who cry out for peace. Our place is alongside those who search for justice.
>
> Let us go with trembling hearts and joyful spirits, to sow the seeds of God's kingdom.[78]

The words for a dismissal do not necessarily contain long instructions or lessons to enlighten congregations. A simple expression often becomes more effective than long sentences. The following dismissal is simple but powerful to lead participants to focus on what they should engage in after the eucharist:

> Sending Out
>
> Go in peace. Remember the poor.
>
> In the name of Christ. Amen.[79]

On the contrary, the UCA's "The Dismissal" mainly consists of a blessing towards congregation and closing sentences in which the main theme

---

76. McMichael, *Eucharist*, 125.
77. Sagovsky, "The Eucharist and the practice of Justice," 76.
78. Tirabassi and Eddy, *Gifts in Open Hands*, 143.
79. After the service of the word conducted in the chapel, the assembly processed into the atrium and formed the shape of a circle around the eucharistic table. They shared bread and the cup and processed outside to the main entrance of the buildings where Blessing and Sending Out were conducted. United Theological College, "Eucharist," (This liturgy is used in the eucharist conducted at United Theological College on August 18, 2010).

is a command to serve the Lord. It is interesting to observe that there is no mention of the specific place and object of the mission. In the dismissal of Holy Communion One, after Prayer of Thanksgiving, the minister gives these blessing and sending out words:

> 32 Blessing
> May almighty God bless you, the Father, the Son and the Holy Spirit. *Amen.*
>
> 33 Dismissal
> Go in peace to love and serve the Lord. In the name of Christ. *Amen.*[80]

In "The Sending Forth of the People of God" of UiW2, the themes of the sending words are strengthening congregation with blessing and a command to live of glorifying God in the world:

> Go in peace to love and serve the Lord. In the name of Christ. Amen.
> *or*
> Go in peace refreshed and renewed in the eternal love of God. In the name of Christ. Amen.
> *or*
> Go in peace; may you carry God's Wisdom, speak forth God's Word, and embody God's Presence wherever you are. In the name of Christ. Amen.[81]

The command, "serve the Lord" includes, indeed, everything which the eucharistic community should do. For, to love God embraces to love our neighbours. As John says, those who do not love a brother or sister cannot love God (1 John 4:20). Yet, as observed above, when the dismissal includes more detailed and specified words describing the mission of church into the world the significance of the dismissal might be strengthened.

Thanksgiving Prayer

Since the earliest period of Christian history, the thanksgiving prayer has been a dominant element in the eucharist. Thanksgiving prayer mainly consists of thanksgiving and praise. In the *Didache*, thanksgiving is the main theme penetrating the eucharist. In the prayer, the Didache

---

80. See The Uniting Church in Australia, *Holy Communion*, 15.

81. The Uniting Church in Australia, *Uniting in Worship 2*, 224. In the first liturgy of the Sunday Service, these themes are repeated. See, ibid., 185.

community gives thanks to God for "the holy vine of David" (9:2), and "the life and knowledge" (9:3).[82] In chapter 10 of the *Didache*, the reasons for thanksgiving continue as follows: "your holy name" (10:2), "the knowledge and faith and immortality" (10:2), and giving "food and drink" (10:3) through Jesus. The last reason of thanksgiving in the *Didache* is that "you are powerful" (10:4).[83] The reasons of thanksgiving of the Didache community are closely connected with the work of God for salvation. Another crucial theme in the eucharistic prayer of the *Didache* is praise to God. Most verses in the eucharist of the *Didache* are full of words of praise and glory towards God: "To you be glory forever"[84] (9:2; cf. 9:3, 4, 10:2, 4, 5 and 6). In the thanksgiving prayer of the *Didache*, the image of God as the Creator and Saviour is highlighted. God the Creator is worthy to receive glory and praise (10:3f).[85] Then, worshippers give thanks to God who gives them eternal life (10:3ff).[86] Besides the *Didache*, another important resource regarding the eucharistic prayer of the early church is the so-called *Apostolic Tradition* of Hippolytus. Although the title of this material has the name of Hippolytus of Rome, there has been recently a general recognition that it is a later collection from various sources arising from diverse regions. Nevertheless, there is a consensus that this document contains liturgical sources dating from the second to the fourth century CE.[87] The theme of the eucharistic prayer in the *Apostolic Tradition* is slightly different from the *Didache*. In the *Apostolic Tradition*, the whole life of Jesus from his birth to resurrection is described (4–8), and then followed by an illustration of the last supper (9–11), invocation (12) and praise to the triune God (13).[88] Yet, there is no mention of God the Creator. Regarding the contents of the eucharistic prayer, the UCA follows the *Didache* rather than the *Apostolic Tradition*. The two main themes of the *Didache*, which are praise to God the Creator and thanks for salvation, are observed in the UCA's "The Great Thanksgiving" prayer. Regarding the first theme, Holy Communion One offers praise as follows:

---

82. For the texts of chapter 9 of the *Didache*, see Niederwimmer, *The Didache*, 144.

83. For the texts of chapter 10 of the *Didache*, see ibid., 155.

84. Ibid., 144.

85. "You, almighty Lord, created all things for the sake of your name, and you gave food and drink to human beings for enjoyment, so that they would thank you." Ibid., 155.

86. "But you graced us with spiritual food and drink and eternal life through <Jesus> your servant." Ibid., 155.

87. Bradshaw, *Reconstructing Early Christian Worship*, 50.

88. For the full text, see Bradshaw et al., *The Apostolic Tradition*, 38–40.

> We praise you
> that through your eternal Word
> you brought the universe into image.
> You have given us this earth
> to care for and delight in
> and with its bounty you preserve our life.[89]

The second service of the Lord's Day in UiW2 develops this theme in the Australian context:

> We bless you for this wide, red land,
> for its rugged beauty,
> its changing seasons,
> for its diverse peoples,
> and for all that lives upon this fragile earth.
> You have called us to be the Church in this place,
> to give voice to every creature under heaven.
> We rejoice with all that you have made,
> as we join the company of heaven in their song.[90]

Secondly, the focus of thanksgiving is on the saving work of God through Jesus. In the thanksgiving prayer of UiW2, the whole life of Jesus is described as in the *Didache* and the *Apostolic Tradition*. In order to save the world, God sent his only son to the lowliest part of the earth. During his life, Jesus showed the world what love was. The suffering and death on the cross is remembered in the prayer. Then the anticipation of the second coming of Jesus appears in the prayer.[91] UiW2 provides an acclamation which might be said or sung by the congregation as part of the thanksgiving prayer. Here one can observe three sentences which condense the life of Jesus:

> Christ has died.
> Christ is risen.
> Christ will come again.[92]

In this acclamation, the vision of worshippers does not stay only in the memory of Jesus. They give thanks to Jesus who is present among them and

---

89. The Uniting Church in Australia, *Holy Communion*, 10.
90. The Uniting Church in Australia, *Uniting in Worship 2*, 212.
91. See The Uniting Church in Australia, *Holy Communion*, 10, 26.
92. See The Uniting Church in Australia, *Uniting in Worship 2*, 179, 214, 315, and 319.

at the same time anticipate his second coming. This eschatological sense leads worshippers to have "a real encounter with the Christ who actively works our salvation."[93]

On the other hand, the thanksgiving prayer needs to be reflected in the light of justice. The eucharist is not only a matter of how to share equally the meal in church. It involves justice in much broader dimensions than simply the church.[94] When considering the whole process through which the eucharistic ingredients are produced from the soil and set on the table, it is not difficult to find that there is a widespread injustice based on social, political and economic oppression.[95] Also, in terms of ecology the production of the eucharistic elements might cause injustice. As Moore indicates, deforestation, agricultural chemicals and wastes which are caused in the process of the production of bread and wine contaminate soil and rivers.[96] As a result, the ecosystem is endangered and flora and fauna in such areas are at risk of extinction. At this point, to neglect these unjust situations in the eucharistic prayer would be to evade the responsibility of the church as provided by God. The thanksgiving prayer should confront the injustice and embrace the voices of suffering in the world. It is worth observing Moore's indication of the thanksgiving prayer which does not fully embody the essence[97] of thanksgiving:

> Christian thanksgiving, like the psalms, involves lament. It is the relationship of thanksgiving to lament that ensures that our praise is not simply an escape from taking responsibility through flight into "mystery." Without lament we ignore the pain and suffering of the world, God's world. Conveniently, we also overlook our part in that injustice, whether it is played out as a hunger for food, rights, medicine, education, resources or priority in scientific research. Our prayer becomes just another form of forgetfulness. Without lament, has our faith stood by the cross, whether that of Jesus or one of his many suffering brothers and sisters?[98]

---

93. Adam, *The Eucharistic Celebration*, 65.
94. Power, "Eucharistic Justice," 864.
95. Ibid., 865.
96. Moore, "The Justice Dimension in the Eucharist," 82.
97. Christian thanksgiving is not based on only the moment of success and happiness. The essence of Christian thanksgiving is to give thanks and praise to God even in the midst of suffering (cf. Rom 5:3).
98. Moore, "The Justice Dimension in the Eucharist," 83.

Invocation or Epiclesis

From the very early stages of Christian history, invocation or epiclesis has been offered in the eucharistic prayer. Although there is no mention of the terms, "through/by the Holy Spirit" or "Come Holy Spirit," which are characteristics of the epiclesis observed in the present form of the eucharistic prayer, the *Didache* contains a "forerunner"[99] of epiclesis: "As this broken bread, scattered over the mountains, was gathered together to be one, so may your Church be gathered together in the same manner from the ends of the earth into your kingdom" (9:4).[100] This petition of gathering God's people in the *Didache* might have developed into the idea of "sanctifying the congregation and, further on, to a Spirit-epiclesis."[101] More clearly, the *Didache* prays for the divine presence: "May grace come, and may this world pass away. . . . Maranatha" (10:6).[102] This petition does not specify the Holy Spirit as the divinity who is asked to come. Moreover, "Maranatha" in the early church was used as an acclamation in worship anticipating the second coming of Christ rather than the Holy Spirit (1 Cor 16:22; Rev 22:20).[103] However, when considering that a clear concept regarding the roles of the trinity had not yet developed in the first two centuries, this early form of the petition for the divine presence might have possibly evolved into the epiclesis later.[104] Like the *Didache*, Justin's *First Apology* apparently contains the concept of invocation without a direct use of the terms related to the Holy Spirit: ". . . through the word of prayer that comes from him the food over which the thanksgiving has been spoken becomes the flesh and blood of the incarnate Jesus, in order to nourish and transform our flesh and blood" (66:2).[105]

However, the early third century Christian literature in Syria, known as the *Didascalia Apostolorum*, embraces the eucharistic theology of consecration by the Holy Spirit: "The eucharist is accepted and sanctified through

---

99. McKenna recognizes a possibility that the eucharistic prayer of the *Didache* might contain a forerunner of epiclesis. However, he has been reluctant to ensure it. For, he is not confident that chapters 9 and 10 of the *Didache* are the eucharist rather than an agape meal. See McKenna, *The Eucharistic Epiclesis*, 7. On the other hand, Bradshaw views that there is "the most likely antecedent for an early Christian use of a direct invocation" in the *Didache*. See Bradshaw, *Eucharistic Origins*, 126.

100. This is translated by W. Rordorf and A. Tuilier. See Johnson, *Worship in the Early Church*, 37.

101. Zheltov, "The Moment of Eucharistic Consecration in Byzantine Thought," 268.

102. Johnson, *Worship in the Early Church*, 38.

103. See Fitzmyer, *First Corinthians*, 630–31.

104. Bradshaw, *Eucharistic Origins*, 127.

105. Jourjon, "Justin," 72.

the Holy Spirit" (6:21).¹⁰⁶ Around the same time, in the west, the *Apostolic Tradition* also expresses a well developed version of epiclesis with the term of the Holy Spirit:

> And we ask that you would send your Holy Spirit upon the offering of your holy Church; that, gathering them into one, you would grant to all who partake of the holy things (to partake) for the fullness of the Holy Spirit for the confirmation of faith in truth (4:12).¹⁰⁷

This epiclesis includes two objects which will be transformed by the presence of the Holy Spirit: the eucharistic elements and participants. Since the third century, this basic structure of the epiclesis has pervaded the west and the east. This structure is also observed in the epiclesis of the liturgies of the UCA:

> Father, let your Spirit come upon your holy people, and may he sanctify these gifts of bread and wine. As we share these holy things, may we be nourished and grow in grace to your honour and glory; through Jesus Christ our Lord.¹⁰⁸

In Holy Communion Two, the title of Invocation of the Holy Spirit is changed to Prayer of Consecration. Here, the two structural components of the epiclesis are more clearly expressed:

> O God, by your Word and Spirit bless and sanctify this bread and this wine, that they may be for us the communion of the body and blood of our Saviour Jesus Christ, and that he may ever live in us and we in him. Father, accept us, as we offer and present ourselves, our souls and bodies, to be a holy and living sacrifice, through Jesus Christ our Lord, to whom with you and the Holy Spirit be all honour and glory, now and for ever. *Amen.*¹⁰⁹

The Lord's Prayer

The New Testament has two versions of the Lord's Prayer in Matthew 6:9–13 and Luke 11:2–3. The earliest literal source containing the full text of the Lord's Prayer outside the Scripture is the *Didache* 8:2–3. Matthew and the

---

106. Brock and Vasey, *The Liturgical Portions of the Didascalia*, 32.
107. Jasper and Cumming, *Prayers of the Eucharist*, 23.
108. The Uniting Church in Australia, *Holy Communion*, 11.
109. See ibid., 26. UiW2, also, follows this pattern of the epiclesis. See The Uniting Church in Australia, *Uniting in Worship 2*, 179, 215–16.

Didache share many similarities rather than Luke, but definite differences exist even in them. According to Betz, the textual variation indicates that the Lord's Prayer was written down through the oral tradition. He suggests that there would have been more varied versions of the Lord's Prayer in the early church.[110] In spite of the variation, the early church believed that the Lord's Prayer had come from Jesus. So it is clear that the Lord's Prayer has had a great influence on worship and life throughout Christian history. Besides the three earliest prayers, there are several documents proving that the early Christians had recognized the Lord's Prayer to be crucial in their religious lives. In the second century, Tatian's *Diatessaron* includes the full text of the Lord's Prayer which is presumed to be the version of Matthew with a few alterations. In the third century, the Lord's Prayer appears more broadly in Tertullian's *On Prayer*, Cyprian's *On the Lord's Prayer* and Origen's *On Prayer*.[111] However, it is an interesting fact that the first three centuries' texts containing the Lord's Prayer were written for mainly a catechetical rather than liturgical purpose. The earliest textual proof that the Lord's Prayer was used in a liturgical context is the twenty-fourth Catechetical Lecture of Cyril of Jerusalem in the fourth century. Although some scholars view that the variation of the Lord's Prayer in the Scripture was the consequence of liturgical use of it,[112] there is little textual evidence that the Lord's Prayer had been used in the eucharist prior to Cyril. Thus, it is assumed that the use of the Lord's Prayer in communal service might possibly be a liturgical development by the later church whereas there is obvious evidence that

---

110. Betz, *The Sermon on the Mount*, 370–71.

111. For more details on the Lord's prayer in the first three centuries' Christian literatures, see Hammerling, *The Lord's Prayer in the Early Church*, 11–44.

112. Jeremias argues that the shorter version of Luke is nearer to the original and Matthew expanded it for liturgical use. For more details on his comparison between the versions of Matthew and Luke, see Jeremias, *The Prayers of Jesus*, 90–91. In contrast, Charlesworth, providing literal evidence of abbreviations made by later religious communities, suggests that Luke's version would be abbreviated for liturgical purposes. Charlesworth, "A Caveat on Textual Transmission," 1–5. Also, Willy Rordorf contends that the Lord's Prayer is essentially connected with communal worship in which the word of God is proclaimed and the sacraments are conducted. Rordorf, "The Lord's Prayer," 2–3. Mazza insists a close relationship between the Lord's Prayer and the eucharist with a hypothesis that Jesus offered two prayers at the last supper: the Lord's Prayer and thanksgiving prayer. However, his idea is highly dependent on his hypothesis without any evidence. See Mazza, *The Eucharistic Prayers of the Roman Rite*, 250–80. Based on the *Didache* 10:5, Luz argues that the Lord's Prayer was offered with a doxology in early Greek Christina communities. However, although the clause of the *Didache* 10:5 is identified with the last clause of the Lord's Prayer, there is no evidence that the *Didache* 10:5 was from the Lord's Prayer. See Luz, *Matthew 1–7*, 385.

the Lord's Prayer was used as a model for individual prayer and taught in catechetical instruction.

The position of the Lord's Prayer in the lecture of Cyril comes between the prayer of intercession and the communion.[113] Similarly, in the fifth century, Jerome placed the Lord's Prayer immediately before receiving the communion. His theological point was that all participants need to be forgiven through the petition for forgiveness of the Lord's Prayer:

> Next comes, "Forgive us our debts, as we also forgive our debtors." No sooner do they rise from the baptismal font, and by being born again and incorporated into our Lord and Saviour thus fulfil what is written of them, "Blessed are they whose iniquities are forgiven and whose sins are covered," than at the first communion of the body of Christ they say, "Forgive us our debts," through these debts had been forgiven them at their confession of Christ (*Dialogus adversus Pelagianos* 3:15).[114]

Since Gregory the Great (590–604), in the Roman Mass, the Lord's Prayer has been moved from right before receiving communion to before the rite of Peace, Breaking of the Bread and Communion and after Canon including Sanctus, Anamnesis, Epiclesis and Doxology. This alteration of placement enhances the previous theological focus on forgiveness, and plays a role of completing the Canon.[115]

On the other hand, since the Reformation, Protestants have developed theological meanings of the Lord's Prayer in worship. Generally, in Protestant traditions, the Lord's Prayer is placed after the Sermon and Intercession Prayer and before the Service of the Eucharist. Luther gives an instruction of the order of the Lord's Prayer in the Sunday Service: "After the sermon shall follow a public paraphrase of the Lord's Prayer, with an exhortation to those who are minded to come to the Sacrament."[116] Regarding the position of the Lord's Prayer, Worship orders of Calvin's The Form of Church Prayers 1542, Knox's The Form of Prayers 1556 and the Westminster Directory for the Public Worship of God 1664 are similar to that of Luther.[117] In the period after the Reformation, the Lord's Prayer in the Protestant tradition seems to play the role of completing the service of the word and the intercession prayer. On the other hand, when it comes to the eucharist, congregations

---

113. Jeremias, *The Prayers of Jesus*, 82–83.
114. Schaff and Wace, *Nicene and Post-Nicene Fathers*, 480.
115. Adam, *The Eucharistic Celebration*, 96–97.
116. Luther, "The German Mass," 200.
117. For more details on their worship orders, see Committee on the Book of Common Worship, *The Book of Common Worship* (2008), 111–13.

through the Lord's Prayer are allowed to participate in the eucharist. In this case, the theology of forgiveness in the Lord's Prayer is emphasized. Before long, however, Protestants began to develop freely worship orders according to their denominational theologies. One interesting position concerning the Lord's Prayer is observed in *American Book of Common Prayer* 1790–1979: Opening Dialogue – Proper Preface – Sanctus – Prayer of Humble Access – Anamnesis with *Verba* and Manual Acts – Epiclesis – Oblation – Distribution – Lord's Prayer.[118] In this case, the Lord's Prayer might be interpreted as concluding the whole worship.

In the resources of the eucharist of the UCA, the Lord's Prayer is placed between the eucharistic prayer, which includes epiclesis and thanksgiving, and the Breaking of the Bread which is followed by Lamb of God, Invitation and Distribution.[119] Historically, as observed above, this position of the Lord's Prayer is similar to that of Cyril. This position is, also, found in various contemporary liturgies of denominations engaged in the ecumenical movement such as the Roman Catholic, the Lutheran Church of Australia, the United Methodist, the PCUSA and the PCK.[120] Moreover, the Lima liturgy which is a symbolic icon of the liturgical movement expresses this placement. Theologically, the focus of this position is on completing the eucharistic prayer and signifies God's acceptance and forgiveness. On the other hand, regarding the text of the Lord's Prayer, the UCA uses Matthew's version. There is an interesting fact that the UCA encourages the church to use a variety of forms of language in saying the Lord's Prayer: "Members of the congregation may say the Lord's Prayer in a language of their choice."[121] It shows the commitment of the UCA to embrace people who are familiar with languages other than English in worship.

The Institution Narrative

In the history of eucharistic liturgies, one of the most interesting topics is the institution narrative. Traditionally, the institution narrative has been

---

118. See Byars, *Lift Your Hearts on High*, 38.

119. For more details on the position of the Lord's Prayer in the liturgies of the UCA, see The Uniting Church in Australia, *Holy Communion*, 12–13, 26–27. Also, see The Uniting Church in Australia, *Uniting in Worship 2*, 180, 217.

120. The recent worship book of the PCK gives four examples for the Sunday service including the eucharist (6, 7, 8 and 9). Among them, last two examples place the Lord's Prayer between the eucharistic prayer and the breaking of the bread. See Committee on the Book of Common Worship, *The Book of Common Worship* (2008), 79, 83.

121. The Uniting Church in Australia, *Uniting in Worship 2*, 180. Also see ibid., 334–44.

recognized as informing the church on the origin of the eucharist: Jesus instituted the eucharist at the last supper before he was arrested (Matt 26, Mark 14, Luke 22, and 1 Cor 11). This perspective on the origin of the eucharist based on the so-called last supper tradition, which is closely connected with the death of Jesus, has formed the mainline churches' eucharistic theology and practice. However, as observed in the previous chapters, in the first two centuries' Christian literature, there is no textual evidence advocating the traditional understanding of the eucharist.

The first interpretation of the eucharist within the last supper milieu is found in Tertullian's *Against Marcion* (4.40) in the early third century. However, his teaching of the eucharist in *Against Marcion* seems to be a commentary on the last supper story aiming at refuting Marcionism rather than a depiction of an actual eucharistic practice in his community.[122] A little later, in the middle of the third century, Cyprian of Carthage gives a eucharistic instruction that church should conduct the eucharist according to the last supper tradition (*The Epistles of Cyprian* 62). Although it is evident that in his eucharistic understanding there is a strong connection between the eucharist and the suffering of Jesus, at the same time Cyprian reveals indirectly that the actual practices of the churches in his time were different from the last supper tradition.[123]

The first textual evidence, that the institution narrative was used in the eucharistic liturgy, is found in the anaphora of Serapion in the mid-fourth century. Then, in the late fourth century, Ambrose of Milan's *De Sacramentis* and John Chrysostom's liturgy placed the institution in the eucharist. However, the use of the institution narrative in the eucharist was not a universal feature in the fourth century. For example, in the anaphora of *Addai and Mari*, which is presumed to be used around the fourth century in the east Syria, there is no mention of the institution narrative.[124] Nevertheless, since the fourth century, the institution narrative has become firmly established in the eucharist of the east and the west.

In the UCA's eucharist, the institution narrative is an essential order. The institution narrative is generally placed before the prayer of thanksgiving as an independent order but it is also possible to be read this "as part of The Great Prayer of Thanksgiving."[125] The eucharistic understanding based

---

122. For more details on the actual eucharistic practice of Tertullian's community, see chapter 5 of this study.

123. For more details on the eucharistic understanding of Cyprian, see chapter 5 of this study.

124. For more details on the use of the institution narrative in the eucharist of Serapion, Ambrose, Chrysostom and *Addai and Mari*, see chapter 5 of this study.

125. The Uniting Church in Australia, *Uniting in Worship 2*, 215.

on the institution narrative spontaneously connects the eucharist with the suffering and death of Jesus. In other words, the use of the institution narrative in the eucharist emphasises the point that the UCA recognizes the origin of the eucharist as the last supper.

The Lamb of God

This strong connection between the eucharist and the last supper is reaffirmed in the Lamb of God, *Agnus Dei* in Latin. The Lamb of God is known to have been first introduced in the eucharist by Pope Sergius I (687–701).[126] This special term of Christ, however, is not an invention of Sergius I but is already found in the New Testament. John the Baptist sees Jesus and calls him: "the Lamb of God" (John 1:29, 36). In Revelation, Jesus is called the Lamb (5:6; 19:9). Also, Paul and Peter recognize Jesus as the paschal Lamb (1 Cor 5:7; 1 Pet 1:19). Moreover, the Old Testament prophet Isaiah describes Messiah as a Lamb that is led to slaughter (53:7). The UCA recognizes the Lamb of God as a crucial element in the eucharist. The three orders in *Holy Communion* and UiW2 place the Lamb of God after the Breaking of the Bread.[127] The Lamb of God who takes away the sin of the world is a repetition of the image of Jesus who offers himself for the salvation of the world at the last supper. The Lamb of God which is placed right before receiving the eucharistic elements has important theological meanings. Firstly, it reminds participants of the significance of the death of Christ in the history of redemption. Secondly, the recognition that Jesus was sacrificed as the paschal Lamb for sinners leads people to face the nature of human beings as they are. Eventually, they have to say: "Jesus, Lamb of God, have mercy on us."[128] Lastly, humility based on this recognition of sin impels the church to recognize that all are equal before the table of Jesus. No one can dare come to the table of Jesus because all are sinners. Yet, through his grace, all are invited to his merciful table. The third order of *Holy Communion* expresses this theology of humility. After the breaking of the bread, the minister says:

> Jesus is the Lamb of God, who takes away the sin of the world. Happy are those who are called to his supper. Lord, I am not worthy to receive you. But only say the word and I shall be whole.[129]

---

126. See Baumstark, *On the Historical Development of the Liturgy*, 78, 109. See also Adam, *The Eucharistic Celebration*, 105.

127. See The Uniting Church in Australia, *Holy Communion*, 13, 27–28, 34. See also The Uniting Church in Australia, *Uniting in Worship 2*, 181, 220.

128. The Uniting Church in Australia, *Uniting in Worship 2*, 181, 220.

129. The Uniting Church in Australia, *Holy Communion*, 34.

The Invitation

The Invitation in the UCA's eucharist is placed before receiving the communion in the first order or after the Offertory in the second and third orders.[130] The position of the Invitation in UiW2 follows the latter.[131] The Invitation is a place through which the open table policy of the UCA is disclosed. In the first and second orders of *Holy Communion*, the Invitation emphasizes participants' faith and knowledge of Christ who was sacrificed for salvation. However, there is no mention of baptism as a prerequisite for the eucharist. On the other hand, in the third order of *Holy Communion* the open table theology is clearly reflected:

> Friends, this is the table of the Lord and he calls us to this sacred feast. Come, not because you are strong, but because you are weak; come, not because of any goodness of your own, but because you need mercy and help; come, because you love the Lord a little and would like to love him more; come, because he loves you and gave himself for you.[132]

UiW and UiW2, also, provide rich examples of the Invitation. In UiW2 there are five examples of the Invitation. Two examples are included in Service of the Lord's Day One and Two, and the others are added in Resources for the Service of the Lord's Day. Among them, only one example expresses baptism with regard to the eucharist.[133] Two examples in Service of the Lord's Day contain the terms "repent of their sin"[134] but the focus is not on repentance as a requirement for the eucharist but, rather, that they are unworthy sinners who need the mercy of God.[135] In UiW, there are eight additional examples of the Invitation. Among them, the third and last three Invitations are based on the last supper tradition and its emphasis is on participants' confession and repentance. However, there is no mention of baptism except in the seventh Invitation. On the other hand, the first two and the fourth and fifth examples express Jesus' hospitality and the openness of the table.[136] It is interesting that these four Invitations are not confined

---

130. Ibid., 14, 23, 31.

131. See The Uniting Church in Australia, *Uniting in Worship 2*, 162, 209.

132. The Uniting Church in Australia, *Holy Communion*, 31. See also The Uniting Church in Australia, *Uniting in Worship 2*, 307.

133. This Invitation is based on the statement of the eucharist in Basis of Union. The Uniting Church in Australia, *Uniting in Worship 2*, 307.

134. Ibid., 162, 209.

135. Ibid., 162–63, 209–10.

136. For more details on eight examples of Invitation, see *Uniting in Worship*, 649–52.

to the traditional understanding of the origin of the eucharist, that is, the last supper. The words for Invitation are from Matthew 11, John 6 and Luke 13 in which Jesus is described as the gracious provider and the host of the banquet of the kingdom of God.[137] Moreover, it is notable that the second Invitation illustrates the Emmaus story in Luke 24 as the eucharist:

> According to Luke, when our risen Lord was sharing an evening meal with two friends in a home at Emmaus, Jesus took the bread, and blessed and broke it, And gave it to them Then their eyes were opened and they recognized him. *Luke 24:30, 31*.[138]

The open table theology sheds light on Jesus who is present and provides "for all peoples a feast of rich food, a feast of well-matured wines, of rich food filled with marrow, of well-matured wines strained clear" (Isa 25:6). In the light of the open table theology, Jesus' meal practice was not a mere act of eating. At the table of Jesus, unacceptable people and sinners became children of God. Moreover, the open table theology gives a new meaning to the last supper. At the supper, the twelve participants did not know what they were doing (Luke 22:24). Among them, there was even Judas who was a slave of Satan (John 13:27). Nevertheless, Jesus welcomed all to his table. In this sense, the Invitation is to be a place through which Jesus' hospitality and openness are revealed:

> This is the joyful feast of Jesus; bread for beloved children; a meal for those expecting scraps; and a banquet for last-minute guests! Come, your place is at the table. Here Christ meets you and calls you God's own.[139]

5 Ways of Celebrating the Open Table in the UCA

Strathfield-Homebush Uniting Church (Carrington Avenue Faith Community)[140]

Carrington Avenue Faith Community (CAFC) was established in 1908 at Carrington Avenue in North Strathfield, NSW. CAFC had belonged to Methodist Church originally but in the process of amalgamation there was

---

137. Ibid., 649.
138. Ibid., 650.
139. The Uniting Church in Australia, *Uniting in Worship 2*, 209.
140. This case study is based on an interview with Rev. Leonie Findlay on November 24, 2013.

a considerable influx of Presbyterians and other denominations. The size of the congregation is about fifty to sixty consisting of approximately 50% of Anglo-Celtic Australians and 50% of ethnic groups from Sri Lanka, Pakistan, India, Malaysia and South Korea. This congregation has been led by Rev. Leonie Findlay since March, 2013.

The eucharist of CAFC demonstrates in a general way how a local church in the UCA conducts the eucharist. The eucharist is celebrated on the first Sunday morning of each month. The eucharistic elements are prepared by elders who are in charge of the eucharist of the month. For the eucharistic bread, leavened bread is sliced in a size of two cubic centimetres and placed on plates. For the cup, grape juice is filled in small cups. The eucharistic elements are set on the table before worship and covered with a white cloth.

The service of the eucharist begins after the service of the word. Regarding the structure of the service of the eucharist, Rev. Leonie Findlay refers to the formats of UiW or UiW2 but reconstructs the order and contents, particularly in terms of the prayers and the Invitation, of the eucharist according to the context of the congregation. While the congregation sits on pews, the service of the eucharist begins with her warm invitation. For the Invitation, she refers to resources of UiW and UiW2 and also other denominations' worship books. She recognizes that, in receiving the communion, participants' baptism, beliefs and confession of sins are crucial but not mandatory requirements. Thus, she tries to make the words of the Invitation more inclusive so that all may participate in the eucharist. During the eucharist an organist plays a hymn. The mood of the music is solemn so that participants may ponder on the meaning of the eucharist. Two elders firstly deliver bread to all participants including children. After checking that all have received the bread, they eat it at the same time. Then, the cup is delivered and drunk in the same way. The eucharist of CAFC is based on the last supper tradition. The last supper story and the meaning of the sacrifice of Jesus for salvation are explained in the eucharist. On the other hand, in terms of the tradition of the open table, the minister tries to avoid deliberately exclusive language especially such as "baptised people" and "church members." Moreover, the elders, when they deliver the elements to the congregation, do not ask whether the participants have been baptised or not. The eucharist at CAFC concludes with a hymn and the minister's benediction.

St. Stephens' Uniting Church[141]

St. Stephens' Uniting Church (SSUC) which began with twenty two members in 1842 grew consistently and dedicated its present building on Macquarie Street, Sydney in 1935. SSUC was originally a Presbyterian Church which joined the UCA in 1977. The average number of Sunday service participants is approximately eighty. Since May 2011, Rev. Ockert Meyer has served the congregation.

Similar to other Uniting Churches, the eucharist of SSUC is held on the first Sunday morning of each month. For the eucharistic elements, leavened bread and grape juice are used. Bread is thinly sliced and put on plates. Grape juice is filled in small cups. The eucharistic elements are set on the table before worship and covered with white cloth. The minister generally uses resources from UiW and UiW2 for the eucharist. The worship including the eucharist is quite liturgical.[142] The whole worship order and most of the contents are printed and distributed to the congregation so that even visitors follow the order of worship with ease.

After the service of the word, the congregation stands and the service of the eucharist begins with the minister's invitation. The focus of the invitation is that the eucharist is a place in which participants experience God's provision for his people in the vision of the promised land which flows with abundant milk and honey. Then the minister invites everyone to Great Prayer of Thanksgiving. In the eucharist, not only Jesus' death but also his resurrection and second coming are remembered. SSUC's tradition of distribution is that bread and the cup are simultaneously distributed to the congregation. During the distribution, the choir sings a musical offering with an appropriate theme and tune fitting for the occasion. Participants retain the eucharistic elements until all receive it so that they eat and drink together. It is worth observing the position of the Affirmation of Faith in the eucharist of SSUC. In terms of the open table theology, locating the Affirmation of Faith after the communion echoes the recognition of the

---

141. This case study is based on an interview with Rev. Ockert Meyer and the Chair of Church Council Rosalie Ramsay on December 2, 2013.

142. The first Sunday Advent Service order conducted on December 1, 2013 is as follows: Organ Prelude – Announcements – Introit – Call to Worship – Greeting – The Candle of Hope – Passing of the Peace – Hymn 132 – Prayers of Approach and Confession – Assurance of Pardon – Gloria (singing) – First Reading (Isa 2:1–5) – Gospel Reading (Matt 24:36–44) – Hymn 426 – Sermon – Anthem – Great Prayer of Thanksgiving – Sanctus – Breaking of the Bread – Distribution of the elements – Agnus Dei – Communion – The Lord's Prayer – Prayers of the People – Affirmation of Faith – Offering and Dedication – Hymn 276 – Blessing – Dismissal – Sung Amen – Organ Postlude.

eucharist as a means of grace. The eucharist of SSUC is concluded with a series of strong requests for dedication.[143]

United Theological College[144]

United Theological College (UTC) was established in Enfield in 1974 by a resolution of the Congregational, Methodist and Presbyterian Churches and moved to its present position in North Parramatta, NSW in 1987. Since the union of the three denominations in 1977, UTC, as the theological college of the NSW Synod of the UCA, has provided theological education and ministerial formation.

During semesters, worship including the eucharist is held from 11:30 am each Wednesday in the Chapel of St Andrew which is located at the centre of the main building of UTC. Students, Faculty and Uniting Mission and Education (UME) staff of the Centre for Ministry (CFM) are the main participants and their families and visitors are welcome to join the worship. Groups made up of candidates, Faculty and Adjunct Lecturers plan worship in UTC. The groups take turns to design and prepare worship each week with a presider of the eucharist. The person presiding over the eucharist is generally a minister of the UCA and sometimes a minister from other denominations who has been given permission to preside at the eucharist at UTC. The content of the eucharist and the way of celebrating it are mainly prepared by the presider of the week.

At 11:30 am on Wednesday October 2, 2013, at the sound of a gong people who have been talking together in the atrium begin to enter the Chapel. The space of the Chapel reflects the worship theology of the UTC community. When they enter the chapel the first thing which welcomes them is a baptismal font moderately filled with water: this is symbolic of where a Christian life begins. A lectern, where the word of God is read and preached, stands on the opposite place of the baptismal font. Between the font and the lectern, in the centre of the worship space, there is the eucharistic table where the people of God are nourished.

In a circular configuration, pews for the congregation surround the font, the table and the lectern. There is no special chair for worship leaders.

---

143. The liturgy of the first Advent Sunday Service places Offering and Dedication after the communion. Then, the minister blesses the congregation and Dismissal follows it: "Go in peace to love and serve the Lord. In the name of Christ." St. Stephens' Uniting Church, *Sunday Service Order: Advent 1* (December 1, 2013, printed), 15.

144. This case study is based on an interview with Rev. Carolyn Thornley, who is Vice Principal and Dean of Candidates at UTC, on December 13, 2013.

They arise from the pews of congregation. This arrangement reminds worshippers of the nature of Christian life and the identity of the worshipping community. In explaining the worship space, Rev. Carolyn Thornley says:

> The focus of our community is that we are the people of God together. We need to be looking at each other. . . . The circle is inclusive of all people. There are no sharp edges. It is about gathering community. It is about how we share with one another. We share our vulnerability and fragility in this place. But we support each other. And pastorally we care for each other.[145]

Following the UCA's theology of worship, UTC's worship contains four parts: the Gathering of the People of God, the Service of the Word, the Sacrament of the Lord's Supper and the sending Forth of the People of God. After the Service of the Word, the Sacrament of the Lord's Supper begins with the Offertory which is followed by Great Prayer of Thanksgiving. The institution narrative is placed at the end of the prayer. Then, participants gather around the table for sharing the Peace. For the eucharistic bread, a loaf of bread and some wafers[146] are used. One loaf of bread symbolizes one community. Sharing one loaf of bread symbolizes that they participate in and share one loaf of bread together. For the cup, a cup of wine and a cup of grape juice are separately prepared so that children and those who do not want wine choose grape juice. On this particular children's day communion took place so that the bread was firstly passed to the children. The children, by themselves or with the help of their parents, broke the bread in a proper size and ate it after dipping it in the cup. Adult participants break the bread by themselves and ate it after dipping it in the cup. After the communion, the Sacrament of the Lord's Supper is completed by the Lord's Prayer and then the whole worship comes to an end with the Sending Forth of the People of God.[147]

---

145. Carolyn Thornley, Interview by author, UTC, North Parramatta, NSW, December 13, 2013.

146. Wafers are prepared for people who need a gluten free diet.

147. The order of the service held at 11:30 am on October 2, 2013 was as follows: 1 The Gathering of the People of God (Call to Worship – Prayers – Song); 2 The Service of the Word (Readings – Sermon – Silence – Song – Affirmation of Faith – Prayers of Intercession); 3 The Sacrament of the Lord's Supper (Great Prayer of Thanksgiving – Sharing of Peace – Breaking of Bread – Communion – Prayer after Communion – The Lord's Prayer); 4 The Sending Forth of the People of God (Song – Blessing – Dismissal).

6 Reflection of the Eucharistic Theology and Practice of the UCA

The Pursuit of Balance of the Word and the Eucharist in Worship

The UCA recognizes that the eucharist is an essential element in worship. However, in practice celebrating the eucharist on Sunday service is not a compulsory regulation in the UCA. Thus, most churches in the UCA celebrate the eucharist once a month.[148] UiW and UiW2 give directions for worship without the eucharist: "when the section entitled 'The Sacrament of the Lord's Supper' is omitted, other acts of thanksgiving and dedication are used."[149] In this statement, the UCA does not seem to use thanksgiving and dedication as a mere substitute for the eucharist. Such an interpretation might lead the church to rationalize their worship omitting the eucharist. Also, that consequence is contrary to the UCA's understanding of worship. Rather, it would be a more appropriate interpretation of the statement that even in worship omitting the eucharist in which there are no eucharistic elements and actions, worshippers can still embody the nature of the eucharist through acts of thanksgiving and dedication. In this sense, it is worth noting the significance of thanksgiving and dedication in the eucharist. The term "eucharist" which derives from the Greek "*eucharistia*" might be best translated as "thanksgiving." In the New Testament, all of the precursors of the eucharist contain the term "thanksgiving" or its synonym "blessing."[150] The *Didache* and the early church fathers such as Justin Martyr, Ignatius, Irenaeus, Clement and Origen recognized thanksgiving as the central part of the eucharist.[151] This early church's eucharistic tradition has been preserved in an ecumenical document of contemporary churches, BEM:

> [The eucharist] is the great thanksgiving to the Father for everything accomplished in creation, redemption and sanctification, for everything accomplished by God now in the Church and in the world in spite of the sins of human beings, for everything that God will accomplish in bringing the Kingdom to fulfilment.

---

148. The Uniting Church in Australia, Synod of NSW & ACT, "Rituals in the Uniting Church,"

149. The Uniting Church in Australia, *Uniting in Worship 2*, 138. See also The Uniting Church in Australia, *Uniting in Worship*, 76.

150. Luke 9:16; Matt 14:19; Mark 6:41; John 6:11; Matt 15:36; Mark 8:6; Luke 24:30; Acts 27:35; 1 Cor 11:24. See Davies, *Bread of Life and Cup of Joy*, 20–21.

151. For more details on the use of the term eucharist in the early church documents, see Ibid., 24–25.

Thus the eucharist is the benediction (*berakah*) by which the Church expresses its thankfulness for all God's benefits.[152]

The eucharist is the place where the reciprocal offerings between God and his people occur.[153] In the eucharist Jesus the host provides the food of life and the people of God receive the gifts of grace. The eucharist is based on the initiating offering of God. At the same time, however, in the eucharist the recipients are called to respond to God with thanksgiving, praise and offering themselves to be a living sacrifice. After the eucharist, the people of God are sent into the world where they are to dedicate themselves. Thus, the idea of dedication, that is human offering, occupies an important place in the eucharist. At this point, the UCA tries to respect the meaning of the eucharist through thanksgiving and dedication in worship omitting the service of the eucharist. In a recent study on UiW 2, *Pilgrim People*, Burns says:

> In the vision of *Uniting in Worship 2*, worship should therefore *always* have a *eucharistic* aspect: expressing thanksgiving and offering, as much when the meal of holy communion is not part of what happens as when it is.[154]

The Pursuit of Diversity

The second paragraph of the Basis of Union declares that "The Uniting Church recognises that it is related to other Churches."[155] The UCA's passion for ecumenism goes beyond such a simple statement. The ecumenism asks the UCA to learn from other WCC churches and to pursue a strong relationship with them. In explaining this paragraph of the Basis of Union, Andrew Dutney insists that a sign of the true church is to involve the diversity of church traditions.[156] The diversity based on the UCA's pursuit of ecumenism is embodied in its worship resources and practice. The UCA introduces rich sources of the eucharist from various church traditions in UiW 2. In the preface in UiW 2, there is a statement:

---

152. World Council of Churches, *Baptism, Eucharist and Ministry*, 10.

153. McMichael, determining the meaning of the sacrificial nature of the eucharist, says: "The full participation of Christians in Christ's priesthood and sacrifice permits the understanding that an offering of Christ takes place in the Eucharist; there is a mutuality between Christ offering us and we offering him." McMichael, *Eucharist*, 74.

154. Burns, *Pilgrim People*, 40.

155. Paragraph 2 in The Basis of Union of the Uniting Church in Australia (1992 edition). The Uniting Church in Australia, *Constitution and Regulations: 2008 Edition*, 21.

156. Dutney, *The Uniting Church in Australia and the Ecumenical Movement*, 65.

It has been open to new insights in studies in Scripture, theology, liturgy and ritual, including ecumenical learning, new perspectives on our liturgical inheritance and denominational histories, and a widespread debate about theological and liturgical language. It uses material from beyond our shores, as part of a generous exchange with overseas Churches, as well as much original material.[157]

The diversity is also found regarding methods of distribution of the eucharist. The UCA recognizes the value of diverse eucharistic traditions which local churches preserve. There is no one way of distribution preferred in the UCA. Some churches in the UCA practise the Methodist tradition having altar rails at which participants receive the elements. Others follow the Presbyterian style that elders distribute the elements to the congregation sitting on pews. In enhancing the meaning of personal participation and experience in the eucharist some churches lead the participants to directly take the elements at the table. This eucharistic policy of the UCA is well described in UiW2:

> It is the responsibility of the minister with the church council to determine whether the bread used is leavened or unleavened, pre-cut or an unbroken loaf; and whether the wine used is fermented or unfermented, offered in individual cups or in a common cup. They also decide how the elements are to be distributed during the service, and how the elements remaining after the service are to be disposed, whether by eating and drinking or some other reverent means. Respect for these means of grace, as well as sensitivity to ecumenical visitors, requires this care.[158]

Regarding the diversity in worship of the UCA, "Ordered Liberty" which is the UCA's particular policy for worship needs to be mentioned. UiW2 gives an explanation of "Ordered Liberty":

> Our approach [to worship] has great freedom, which is exercised within a broad framework. In some places, the freedoms will be emphasised over the framework; in others, the people will find that an ordered style enables them to be free before God.[159]

What is the framework for worship in the UCA? According to the Doctrine and Worship Groups, the basic framework consists of four parts: Gathering as God's People, Receiving God's Word, Celebrating the Lord's

---

157. The Uniting Church in Australia, *Uniting in Worship 2*, 7.
158. The Uniting Church in Australia, *Uniting in Worship 2*, 143.
159. Ibid., 13.

Supper and Being Sent on God's Mission.[160] Within this framework, local churches can freely develop a worship service "to focus on God."[161] In designing the eucharist, the UCA recognizes that there are essential orders in the eucharist such as the Great Prayer of Thanksgiving, the institution narrative and the breaking of the bread.[162] However, in organizing the eucharist, also, "Ordered Liberty" is applied:

> Even with the core elements there is liberty in relation to how they are performed or expressed or lived out. Creative worship in whatever form or style can make use of drama, video, photography, music, silence, and symbols. Those devising the worship can decide how the space is set up and how people are to be invited to participate.[163]

The pursuit of diversity involves an effort to embrace various ethnic languages and cultures in the UCA. In 1985 the Fourth Assembly of the UCA adopted "the statement 'The Uniting Church is a Multicultural Church' as a declaration of the intention and nature of the Uniting Church in Australia."[164] Seongja Yoo-Crowe comments that "this was an historic, bold commitment to respond to a new reality."[165] Through this statement, ethnic worshipping communities came to have a new identity in the UCA and confirm that they are members of the UCA.[166] Since then, there has been concern for the embodiment of multiculturalism in the UCA. Sang Taek Lee indicates that egalitarianism has played a crucial role in the course of the UCA's declaration of its multicultural identity.[167] Egalitarianism is not upheld to assimilate non-mainstream cultures to the mainstream but in order that cultural minorities are equally recognized and the value of diversity is enhanced.

On the basis of egalitarianism, the UCA has developed some meaningful implications of multiculturalism in worship. The UCA's worship policy 'Ordered Liberty' contains the statement that "Worship will be offered in a variety of tongues, and in a variety of styles."[168] In UiW2, one of the most prominent multicultural implications is found in the Lord's Prayer in the

160. Walker, *Building on the Basis*, 230.
161. Ibid., 231.
162. Ibid., 231.
163. Ibid., 231.
164. Minutes of the Fourth Assembly, 85.89.1.
165. Yoo-Crowe, "Life with Members," 106.
166. Lee, *New Church New Land*, 176.
167. Lee, "Multiculturalism," 120.
168. The Uniting Church in Australia, *Uniting in Worship 2*, 13.

eucharist. For the Lord's Prayer, UiW2 provides four indigenous languages in Australia and nine languages other than English. The Lord's Prayer in UiW2 contains a guide that a congregation may choose a language to use.[169] The pursuit of cultural diversity in worship includes not only languages but also liturgical sources and styles.[170] The Assembly Working Groups on Doctrine and Worship recognizes that multiculturalism in worship as not only an aspect of the UCA today but also something to be proud of:

> The Uniting Church has become increasingly culturally and linguistically diverse so that worship is now conducted in many languages and forms, from Korean to Pacific Island worship. Special worship events are making use of their contribution to the richness of worship.[171]

The UCA's Open Table Policy Strengthening the Sacraments

In the UCA which practises widely the open table, sometimes an anxiety has been expressed about whether the open table might weaken the relationship between baptism and the eucharist and diminish the significance of the two sacraments. Bos indicates:

> Many ministers now found it difficult to deny unbaptised children Holy Communion, whilst welcoming baptized children. An unintended consequence of the decision was that, increasingly, unbaptised persons received the Lord's Supper, thus weakening the historical and theological link between the sacraments.[172]

At the same time, the National Working Groups on Doctrine and Worship also indicated that the admission of unbaptised children to the eucharist "weakened even further the nexus between baptism and the Lord's supper."[173] In a sense, the traditional order of "baptism before the eucharist" might be regarded as being undermined by the open table. However, the alteration of the order of the sacraments does not necessarily imply a diminishing relationship between baptism and the eucharist or a weakening

---

169. Ibid., 180.

170. See Assembly Minutes 85.99.1 "To encourage ethnic ministers and their congregations where appropriate to maintain their relationships with their church of origin while exercising membership in the Uniting Church." Also see Assembly Minutes 85.99.2 "To encourage ethnic congregations to use liturgies familiar to them."

171. Walker, *Building on the Basis*, 232.

172. Bos, "That Other Controversy," 5.

173. Walker, *Building on the Basis*, 193.

of the significance of the sacraments. Rather, the open table theology of the UCA enhances the significance of baptism. The PCK's eucharistic regulation prohibits children under fifteen years old from receiving communion although they have received infant baptism.[174] Conversely, in the eucharist of the UCA, all baptised children are encouraged to receive the communion. For this, UiW2, referring to a resolution resolved in the Fourth Assembly, introduces a new direction encouraging the church to allow baptised children to receive the eucharist.[175] While children in the PCK, in spite of being baptised, cannot receive the communion until the age of fifteen, children in the UCA can be part of the eucharist because of baptism.

In addition, even in the case that the UCA allows those who are not baptised to receive communion, the eucharist is not dissociated from baptism. The UCA does not argue that baptism is an unnecessary sacrament for a Christian life or irrelevant to the eucharist. UiW2 gives a direction regarding the issue of allowing those who are not baptised to participate in the eucharist:

> People not receiving the bread and wine may come forward a blessing. Children and adults who wish to receive the bread and wine, but are not yet baptised, should be encouraged to prepare for baptism (Article 19).[176]

This article reflects clearly the eucharistic perspective of the UCA. Based on the Basis of Union, because it clarifies literally that in the eucharist "the risen Lord feeds his baptised people,"[177] it would mean that people should be baptised before receiving the eucharist. Such an interpretation is identical to other mainstream churches' eucharistic understanding. However, at the same time, the UCA does not have a legalistic approach to church laws and more importantly missional perspective plays a decisive role in the UCA's worship and life. In the light of the UCA's missional perspective, the article would mean that church would not prohibit unbaptised people from participating in the eucharist but would encourage them to be baptised. This means that the relationship between baptism and the eucharist is not disconnected.

---

174. For more details on the PCK's eucharistic regulation, see part one of this study.
175. The Uniting Church in Australia, *Uniting in Worship 2*, 143.
176. Ibid., 143.
177. The Uniting Church in Australia, *Constitution and Regulations*, 23.

7. Summary and Evaluation

The UCA's eucharistic theology and practice suggest a moderate way through which a Christian community might practise the open table in preserving the traditional eucharistic understanding and at the same time in responding to pastoral needs for the open table on the basis of a missional perspective. In the eighth paragraph of the Basis of Union, the UCA defines that the eucharist is a sacrament of baptised members. Although recently some scholars have attempted to interpret paragraph 8 of the Basis of Union as not opposing the open table, this statement literally reflects an ecumenical consensus on "baptism before the eucharist." This eucharistic understanding invests the UCA with a doctrinal orthodoxy. As a result, that understanding leads the UCA to keep conversing with other mainline churches. On the other hand, in practice, the UCA follows the open table policy so that a local church might conduct the open table according to diverse situations in ministry. This open table theology is based on the recognition of the eucharist as a means of grace, and the UCA's mission-oriented identity. This two-dimensional approach to the eucharist enables the UCA, on one hand, to secure its orthodox status and, on the other hand, to respond to its missional task.

However, the UCA's open table theology still has a weakness in terms of the authority of the open table which includes unbaptised people in the eucharist. Besides the missional emphasis, where can a church find the authority for practising the open table? Regarding this question, the answer of the UCA's open table theology seems to be less than satisfactory. In the previous chapters, this study has explored historical, biblical and theological grounds for the open table. This study has found that there is substantial and reliable evidence supporting the open table especially in the meal practices of Jesus and the early churches' eucharist in the first two centuries CE.

Moreover, in terms of the origin of the eucharist, the UCA emphasizes the last supper. However, as Norman Young indicates, the eucharistic theology immersed in the last supper might lead the eucharist to be confined in the death of Jesus.[178] As a result, the eucharist based on the last supper might hinder the church from experiencing the eucharist as not only the joyful banquet of the kingdom of God with the risen Lord but also the meal shared with the poor, gentiles, strangers and sinners as Jesus did during his public life.

The UCA's eucharistic theology and practice would be a challenge to those who try to adhere to the traditional eucharistic order, "baptism before

---

178. Young, "Sacrament," 99.

the eucharist." Conversely, for those who want to practise more actively the open table, the UCA's approach to the eucharist seems to be somewhat passive. However, the UCA's approach to the eucharist would, also, be a good guide for those who have a vision of the open table while recognizing the significance of both baptism and the eucharist in the life of a Christian and the value of church tradition.

Conclusion

THE STUDY HAS SET out to explore the PCK's eucharistic tradition and to research the shape of the study of the open table. The PCK has developed its unique eucharistic tradition over about 120 years in Korea. In the process of development, the PCK has formulated some eucharistic practices: (1) The PCK has kept strictly a eucharistic regulation which allows only baptized members who are over fifteen years old to participate in the eucharist; (2) even though recently some churches in the PCK try to hold the eucharist more often, the eucharistic frequency of the majority is still four times a year; (3) theologically, the eucharist of the PCK is based on the last supper tradition. Thus, the meaning of the death of Jesus is emphasized in the eucharist. In addition, the words of the institution from the Synoptic Gospels and 1 Corinthians 11 which are based on the last supper tradition play an essential role in the eucharist of the PCK.

There were several factors which affected the formation and development of the PCK's eucharistic tradition. Firstly, the PCK's eucharistic tradition was formed under the influence of Korean culture. When Protestantism was introduced in Korea at the end of the nineteenth century, there were three representative religions: Shamanism, Buddhism and Confucianism. Of these three, Korean society was mainly controlled by Confucianism. As a result, Confucianism made a bigger impact on the formation of the PCK's eucharistic tradition than the other two. Under the influence of Confucianism, the division between men and women, adults and children, and social classes was a crucial principle supporting the social system of Korea. The PCK's eucharistic regulation which gave permission for the eucharist to only baptized members who were over fifteen years old was accepted easily by a society accustomed culturally to social divisions.

Secondly, regarding the frequency of the eucharist in the PCK, it is this practice was influenced partly by ancestor worship. However, the most direct effect on the frequency was the worship tradition of the early American missionaries. The worship tradition introduced by the missionaries to the

PCK was preaching centred worship omitting the eucharist. According to this worship tradition, the eucharist was recognized as not part of ordinary Sunday service but a sacrament. As a result, the eucharist was held three or four times a year. This worship recognition had been preserved for many decades. However, from the end of the twentieth century the PCK began to express the view that the eucharist is part of worship and needs to be held more frequently. The change of the PCK's recognition of the eucharist came as the PCK began to participate actively in the ecumenical movement. The PCK's worship books BCW 1997 and BCW 2008 reflected the eucharistic theology contained in WCC documents such as BEM and the Lima liturgy, and expanded its theological horizons of the eucharist.

Thirdly, regarding the last supper tradition, in spite of the theological expansion of the PCK in recent years, it remains fundamental to the eucharistic understanding of the PCK. When the Jeonnam Synod made a decision in its regular meeting in 2001 that unbaptized people can participate in the eucharist, other synods of the PCK viewed the decision as a challenge to the PCK's eucharistic tradition. Soon, influential theologians in the PCK began to write editorials and essays concerning the issue of the open table. However, almost all the studies were a reassertion of the PCK's traditional eucharistic understanding rather than a study of the open table. The PCK's traditional eucharistic understanding reaffirmed in the studies was closely connected with its perception of the eucharistic origin. The PCK has had a strong belief that the origin of the eucharist is the last supper. The PCK's adherence to the last supper tradition has been further reinforced by some international scholars. For example, Dix has sought the origin of the eucharist through his structural approach and Baumstark has tried to reconstruct the origin of the eucharist by comparing eucharistic liturgies. Jeremias and many other scholars have attempted to explore the theological meanings and the prototype of the eucharist through an exegetical approach. Although their methodologies and the results of the studies were different, there was a common presupposition that the eucharist was instituted by Jesus at the last supper. These studies led the PCK to stand firmly in the last supper tradition. As a consequence, the PCK came to emphasize theologically the paschal meaning of the eucharist.

Recent studies, however, have challenged the belief of the traditional eucharistic understanding that the origin of the eucharist is the last supper, leading to new understandings of the eucharist. There is a scholarly consensus that the early church conducted the eucharist with a variety of content and in different ways. The traditional eucharistic understanding has tried to explain that the eucharistic diversity of the early church was a development from the last supper. However, if the last supper is the origin of the eucharist, why did the eucharistic documents of the early church consistently exclude the critical features of the last supper tradition? With the exception of the Synoptic Gospels and 1 Corinthians 11 which are based on the last supper tradition, all the early church eucharistic documents, especially those estimated to be from the first two centuries, do not mention the time and context of the last supper. In addition, the theological foci in these early eucharistic documents are thanksgiving, the presence of Christ and the kingdom of God rather than the paschal interpretation of the eucharist which is emphasized in the last supper tradition. An interesting fact is that even the biblical texts based on the last supper tradition fail to illustrate the same last supper in terms of the words and ways of the eucharist. Furthermore, there is no mention of the institution narrative and the breaking of the bread in the Fourth Gospel's illustration of the last supper (John 13). Instead, the Fourth Gospel locates the eucharistic sayings of Jesus in its chapter 6 where Jesus feeds the multitude on a mountain.

The first attempt to explain the eucharist in the context of the last supper is observed in *Against Marcion* written by Tertullian in the third century. Before long, around the middle of the third century, Cyprian introduced the last supper tradition as the proper way of conducting the eucharist into his community. These documents have two significant meanings. Firstly, around the third century the last supper tradition began to be introduced and recognized as the proper eucharist in the communities of Tertullian and Cyprian. Secondly, before the introduction of the last supper tradition as the proper form, the actual practice of the eucharist in their communities was still different from the last supper tradition. The influence of the last supper tradition began to rapidly expand in the fourth century. Around the late fourth century, the institution narrative based on the last supper tradition came to be an essential part of the anaphora even though the anaphora of *Addai and Mari*, presumed to be used by the east Syrian churches even after the fourth century, does not contain the institution narrative. In the process, the early eucharistic diversity gradually disappeared and the last supper tradition became widespread. According to the church tradition in the middle age, Reformers also recognized the last supper tradition as the proper eucharist. As a result, most mainline churches today have a traditional eucharistic understanding based on the last supper tradition.

This historical approach to the eucharistic origin leads the church to rethink the traditional eucharistic understanding adhering to the last supper, and to ponder on the significance of Jesus' meal practice towards the kingdom of God. Jesus' meal practice was a symbolic action beyond an ordinary meal. Following out of his vision of the kingdom of God, Jesus invited all people to his table. There was no discrimination in the banquet of the kingdom of God realized by Jesus. There was no prerequisite to be prepared by participants. In the table of Jesus, children and women came to be valuable, gentiles be his people, and sinners be forgiven. There was only the hospitality and love of Jesus, the host of the banquet. The value pursued by the open table theology is the inclusivity based on the generous love of Jesus rather than exclusivity based on rigid eucharistic regulation. Even in the last supper, the open table theology lays theological emphasis on the love of Jesus who willingly allowed Judas the betrayer to come to the table rather than drawing on certain eucharistic principles of exclusion.

The purpose of the open table theology is not to destroy the traditional way of the eucharist and build a new tradition. Rather, the open table theology analyzes the context of the traditional eucharistic understanding and explores the reasons why the church developed such traditional eucharistic regulations. The results of such open table studies could help the church possess a deeper knowledge of its eucharistic tradition and expand its understanding of other eucharistic traditions, through providing a reinterpretation of the last supper and emphasizing the eucharistic value of other meals of Jesus. The reflection of the meals of Jesus could lead church to come closer to the teaching and example of Jesus for the eucharist, and broaden its eucharistic understanding.

The open table theology could help church recognize that the focus of the eucharist is on the risen Christ. The eucharist is the place that all participants experience the presence of Christ and his abundant grace. The encounter with the risen Christ in the eucharist strengthens participants' faith and spirituality. The growth of personal faith will refresh worship and revitalize church ministry. Also, the centrality of the presence of the risen Christ renews the meaning of sacramentality. In the debates in the past on "how Christ is present in the eucharistic elements," the focus was on the eucharistic elements rather than Christ. In the debates on the number of sacraments, also, the focus was not on Christ but rituals. However, in the eucharist based on the open table theology the risen Christ cannot be confined to bread or wine. The risen Christ the host is among people and provides them with spiritual and physical food. In the eucharist participants meet the risen Christ the primordial sacrament.

By highlighting the inclusivity of the meals of Jesus and the diversity of the early Christian eucharistic traditions, I hope this study can contribute to enhancing the ecumenical movement towards Christian unity. Although the ecumenical movement has made considerable progress in finding common eucharistic theology and practice in various eucharistic traditions, there are still limitations. When churches maintain the distinctive features of their eucharistic traditions to be more important than the common eucharistic features, this will continue to hinder the goal of the ecumenical movement. The open table theology views diversity and inclusivity as fundamental features of the eucharist. If there has been a common feature in the history of the eucharist, it is the risen Christ not certain eucharistic traditions. The risen Christ is the sole authority of the eucharist beyond every doctrine and regulation made by human beings. When the church meets truly the risen Christ in the eucharist and views eucharistic diversity as the divine gift, that experience will enable the church to overcome its long history of separation and enjoy the richness of eucharistic diversity.

Bibliography

1 English Language Sources

Adam, Adolf. *The Eucharistic Celebration: The Source and Summit of Faith*. Translated by Robert C. Schultz. Collegeville, MN: Pueblo, 1994.

Ahn, Byung Mu. "Jesus and the Minjung in the Gospel of Mark." In *Minjung Theology: People as the Subjects of History*, edited by Yong Bok Kim, 136–51. Singapore: A CTC-CCA, 1981.

Anderson, Paul N. "The Sitz im Leben of the Johannine Bread of Life Discourse and Its Evolving Context." In *Critical Readings of John 6*, edited by R. Alan Culpepper, 1–59. Leiden: Brill, 1997.

Aquinas, Thomas. *Summa Theologica: Volume V - Part III, Second Section & Supplement*. Translated by Fathers of the English Dominican Province. New York, NY: Cosimo, 2007.

Bagchi, David, and David C. Steinmetz, eds. *The Cambridge Companion to Reformation Theology*. Cambridge: Cambridge University Press, 2004.

Barrett, Charles K. *Essays on John*. London: SPCK, 1982.

Bauckham, Richard. "The Restoration of Israel in Luke-Acts." In *Restoration: Old Testament, Jewish, & Christian Perspectives*, edited by James M. Scott, 435–88. Leiden: Brill, 2001.

Baumstark, Anton. *Comparative Liturgy*. Translated by F. L. Cross. London: A. R. Mowbray & Co. Limited, 1958.

———. *On the Historical Development of the Liturgy: Foreword by Robert F. Taft; Introduction, Translation, and Annotation by Fritz West*. Translated by Fritz West. Collegeville, MN: Pueblo, 2011.

Best, Thomas F., and Dagmar Heller, eds. *Eucharistic Worship in Ecumenical Contexts: The Lima Liturgy - and Beyond*. Geneva: WCC, 1998.

Betz, Hans Dieter. *The Sermon on the Mount*. Minneapolis, MN: Fortress, 1995.

Betz, Johannes. "The Eucharist in the Didache." In *The Didache in Modern Research*, edited by Jonathan A. Draper, 244–75. Leiden: E. J. Brill, 1996.

Bieler, Andrea, and Luise Schottroff. *The Eucharist: Bodies, Bread, & Resurrection*. Minneapolis, MN: Fortress, 2007.

Bingham, Dwight Jeffrey. *Irenaeus' Use of Matthe's Gospel: In Adversus Haereses*. Leuven: Peeters, 1998.

Bock, Darrell L. *A Theology of Luke and Acts: A Biblical theology of the New Testament*. Grand Rapids, MI: Zondervan, 2012.

Bond, Helen K. *The Historical Jesus: A Guide for the Perplexed*. New York, NY: T.&T. Clark, 2012.

Borg, Marcus J., and Nicholas T. Wright. *The Meaning of Jesus: Two Visions*. New York, NY: HarperCollins, 1999.

Bos, Rob, and Geoff Thompson, eds. *Theology for Pilgrims: Selected Theological Documents of the Uniting Church in Australia*. Sydney: Uniting Church Press, 2008.

Bos, Robert. "That Other Controversy: Debates Over Baptism in the UCA 1979–2003." *Uniting Church Studies* 11, no. 1 (2005) 1–20.

Bosch, David J. *Transforming Mission: Paradigm Shifts in Theology of Mission*. Maryknoll, NY: Orbis, 2011.

Box, G. H. "The Jewish Antecedents of the Eucharist." *Journal of Theological Studies* 3 (1902) 357–69.

Boyd, Robin. "Twenty Years A-Growing - Are We Still Uniting?" In *Marking Twenty Years: The Uniting Church in Australia 1977–1997*, edited by William W. Emilsen and Susan Emilsen, 82–90. North Parramatta, NSW: UTC Publications, 1997.

Brackenridge, R. Douglas. *The Presbyterian Church (U.S.A.) Foundation: A Bicentennial History, 1799–1999*. Louisville, KY: Geneva, 1999.

Bradshaw, Paul F. *Eucharistic Origins*. London: SPCK, 2004.

———. *Reconstructing Early Christian Worship*. Collegeville, MN: Liturgical Press, 2009.

———. *The Search for the Origins of Christian Worship: Sources and Methods for the Study of Early Liturgy*. Oxford: Oxford University Press, first published in 1992, 2002.

Bradshaw, Paul F., and Maxwell E. Johnson. *The Eucharistic Liturgies: Their Evolution and Interpretation*. Collegeville, MN: Liturgical Press, 2012.

Bradshaw, Paul F., et al. *The Apostolic Tradition*. Minneapolis, MN: Fortress, 2002.

Breidenthal, Thomas E. "The Festal Gathering: Reflections on Open Communion." *Sewanee Theological Review* 54:2 (2011) 142–58.

Bretherton, Luke. *Hospitality as Holiness: Christian Witness Amid Moral Diversity*. Burlington, VT: Ashgate, 2006.

Brock, Sebastian, and Michael Vasey. *The Liturgical Portions of the Didascalia*. Bramcote, Notts: Grove, 1982.

Brown, Arthur J. *The Mastery of the Far East: The Story of Korea's Transformation and Japanese Rise to Supremacy in the Orient*. New York, NY: Charles Scriber's Son, 1919.

Brown, John P. "The Australian Mission in Korea since 1977." In *Tales of Two Churches: Australia and Korea*, edited by The General Assembly of Presbyterian Church of Korea, 89–103. Seoul: Publishing House of the PCK, 2012.

Brown, Raymond E. *The Gospel According to John, Volume 1, I-XII*. London: Geoffrey Chapman, 1984.

Bruner, Frederick Dale. *The Gospel of John: A Commentary*. Grand Rapids, MI: Wm. B. Eerdmans, 2012.

Bultmann, Rudolf. *The Gospel of John: A Commentary*. Translated by G. R. Beasley-Murray. Oxford: Basil Blackwell, 1971.

Burns, Stephen. "The Treasures of the Bible." In *Renewing the Eucharist Volume 2: Word*, edited by Stephen Burns, 1–14. Norwich: Canterbury, 2009.

———. *Pilgrim People: An Invitation to Worship in the Uniting Church.* Unley, SA: Mediacom, 2012.
Buxton, Richard. "The Shape of the Eucharist: A Survey and Appraisal." In *Liturgy Reshaped*, edited by Kenneth Stevenson, 83–93. London: SPCK, 1982.
Byars, Ronal P. *Lift Your Hearts on High: Eucharistic Prayer in the Reformed Tradition.* Louisville, KY: John Knox, 2005.
Byfield, Ted, ed. *Renaissance: God in Man, A.D. 1300 to 1500: But Amid Its Splendors, Night Falls on Medieval Christianity.* Edmonton, AB: The Society to Explore and Record Christian History, 2010.
Calvin, John. *Catechism of the Church of Geneva: Being a Form of Instruction for Children, 1545.* http://www.reformed.org/documents/calvin/geneva_catachism/geneva_catachism.html.
———. *Institutes of Christian Religion.* Vol. 2. Edited by John T. McNeill, translated by Ford Lewis Battles. London: SCM, 1960.
———. *Short Treatise on the Holy Supper of our Lord Jesus Christ, 1540.* http://www.the-highway.com/supper1_Calvin.html.
Carson, D. A. *The Gospel According to John.* Grand Rapids, MI: Wm. B. Eerdmans, 1991.
Charlesworth, James H. "A Caveat on Textual Transmission and the Meaning of *ABBA*: A Study of the Lord's Prayer." In *The Lord's Prayer and Other Prayer Texts from the Greco-Roman Era*, edited by James H. Charlesworth, 1–14. Valley Forge, PA: Trinity, 1994.
Chauvet, Louis Marie. *Symbol and Sacrament: Sacramental Reinterpretation of Christian Existence.* Translated by Patrick Madigan. New York, NY: Pueblo, 1995.
Chilcote, Paul Wesley. *John & Charles Wesley: Selections from Their Writings and Hymns - Annotated & Explained.* Woodstock, VT: SkyLight Paths, 2011.
Chilton, Bruce. *A Feast of Meanings: Eucharistic Theologies from Jesus through Johannine Circles.* New York, NY: Brill, 1994.
———. *Jesus' Prayer and Jesus' Eucharist: His Personal Practice of Spirituality.* Valley Forge, PA: Trinity, 1997.
———. *The Temple of Jesus: His Sacrificial Program Within A Cultural History of Sacrifice.* University Park, PA: The Pennsylvania State University Press, 1992.
Ciampa, Roy E., and Brian S. Rosner. *The First Letter to the Corinthians.* Grand Rapids, MI: Eerdmans, 2010.
Clark, Allen D. *History of the Korean Church.* Seoul: The Christian Literature Society of Korea, 1961.
Clark, Charles A. *Moksa Jibup.* Seoul: Chosen Yesu Kyo Seohoe, 1919.
Cooke, Bernard J. *Sacraments & Sacramentality.* 7th ed. New London, CT: Twenty-Third, 2006.
Countryman, Louis William. *Dirt, Greed and Sex: Sexual Ethics in the New Testament and Their Implications for Today.* London: SCM, 1989.
Cox, Harvey G. *Fire from Heaven: The Rise of Pentecostal Spirituality and the Reshaping of Religion in the Twenty-first Century.* Reading, MA: Addison-Wesley, 1995.
Crockett, William R. *Eucharist: Symbol of Transformation.* New York, NY: Pueblo, 1989.
Crossan, John Dominic. *The Historical Jesus: The Life of A Mediterranean Jewish Peasant.* New York, NY: HarperSanFrancisco, 1991.
Cullmann, Oscar. *Early Christian Worship.* Translated by A. Stewart Todd and James B. Torrance. London: SCM, 1973, first published in 1953.

Cummings, Owen F. *Eucharistic Doctors: A Theological History.* New York, NY: Paulist, 2005.
Davies, Horton. *Bread of Life and Cup of Joy: Newer Ecumenical Perspectives on the Eucharist.* Eugene, OR: Wipf and Stock, 1999.
Deming, Charles S. "The Korean Christian." *The Korea Mission Field* 2, no. 8 (1906) 153.
Dix, Dom Gregory. *The Shape of the Liturgy.* 3rd ed. Westminster: Dacre Press, 1947.
———. *The Shape of the Liturgy: NEW EDITION with an introduction by Dr Simon Jones.* New York, NY: Continuum, 2007.
Dix, Gregory, and Henry Chadwick, eds. *The Treatise on the Apostolic Tradition of St Hippolytus of Rome: Bishop and Martyr.* New York, NY: Routledge, 2013, first published in 1937.
Donahue, John R., and Daniel J. Harrington. *The Gospel of Mark.* Collegeville, MN: Liturgical Press, 2002.
Dutney, Andrew. "It Was Like They'd Had A Vision." In *Swimming between the Flags: Reflections on the Basis of Union,* edited by Walter Abetz and Katherine Abetz, 3–10. Bendigo, VIC: Middle Earth, 2002.
———. "Why does the Church Exist?" In *Swimming between the Flags: Reflections on the Basis of Union,* edited by Walter Abetz, and Katherine Abetz, 57–62. Bendigo, VIC: Middle Earth, 2002.
———. *Manifesto for Renewal: The Shaping of A New Church.* Melbourne: Uniting Church Press, 1986.
Easton, Burton S. *The Apostolic Tradition of Hippolytus.* Michigan, MI: Cambridge University Press, 1962.
Edmondson, Stephen. "Opening the Table: The Body of Christ and God's Prodigal Grace." *Anglican Theological Review* 91:2 (2009) 213–34.
Eliade, Mircea. "Shamanism: An Overview." In *The Encyclopedia of Religion.* Vol. 13, edited by Mircea Eliade, 202–8. Chicago, IL: University of Chicago Press, 1987.
Emilsen, William W., and Susan Emilsen, eds. *The Uniting Church in Australia: The First 25 Years.* Armadale, VIC: Melbourne, 2003.
Fabian, Richard. "The Scandalous Table," In *The Art of Tentmaking: Essays in Honour of Richard Giles,* edited by Stephen Burns, 137–58. Norwich: Canterbury Press, 2012.
Farmer, William R., and Denis M. Farkasfalvy. *The Formation of the New Testament Canon: An Ecumenical Approach.* New York, NY: Paulist, 1983.
Farwell, James. "Baptism, Eucharist, and the Hospitality of Jesus: On the Practice of 'Open Communion.'" *Anglican Theological Review,* 86:2 (2004) 215–38.
Feeley-Harnik, Gillian. *The Lord's Table: the Meaning of Food in Early Judaism and Christianity.* Philadelphia, PA: University of Pennsylvania Press, 1981.
Fisk, Bruce N. *First Corinthians.* Louisville, KY: John Knox, 2000.
Fitzmyer, Joseph A. *First Corinthians: A New Translation with Introduction and Commentary.* New Haven, CT: Yale University Press, 2008.
Foley, Edward. "Eucharist, Postcolonial Theory and Developmental Disabilities: A Practical Theologian Revisits the Jesus Table." *International Journal of Practical Theology* 15 (2011) 57–73.
———. *From Age to Age: How Christians Have Celebrated the Eucharist.* Chicago, IL: Liturgy Training, 1991.
Gale, James S. *Korea in Transition.* New York, NY: Eaton & Mains, 1909.
Gamble, Harry Y. *The New Testament Canon: Its Making and Meaning.* Philadelphia, PA: Fortress, 1985.

Garland, David E. *First Corinthians: Baker Exegetical Commentary on the New Testament.* Grand Rapids, MI: Baker, 2003.
Gese, Hartmut. *Essays on Biblical Theology.* Translated by Keith Crim. Minneapolis, MN: Augsburg, 1981.
Greer, Rowan A. *Origen: An Exhortation to Martyrdom Prayer and Selected Works.* Mahwah, NJ: Paulist, 1979.
Hamman, Adalbert. "Irenaeus of Lyons." In *The Eucharist of the Early Christians.* Edited by Willy Rordorf, translated by Matthew J. O'Connell, 86–98. New York, NY: Pueblo, 1990.
Hammerling, Roy. *The Lord's Prayer in the Early Church: The Pearl of Great Price.* New York, NY: Palgrave Macmillan, 2010.
Harrison, John. *Baptism of Fire: The First Ten Years of the Uniting Church in Australia.* Melbourne: Uniting Church Press, 1986.
Hays, Richard B. *First Corinthians: Interpretation: A Bible Commentary for Teaching and Preaching.* Louisville, KY: John Knox, 2011.
Higgins, Angus J. B. *The Lord's Supper in the New Testament.* London: SCM, 1956, firstly published in 1952.
Hill, Charles E. *The Johannine Corpus in the Early Church.* Oxford: Oxford University Press, 2004.
Hulbert, Homer B. *The Passing of Korea.* New York, NY: Doubleday, 1906.
———., ed. *The Korea Review.* Seoul: Methodist Publishing House, 1902.
Hultgren, Arland J. *The Parables of Jesus: A Commentary.* Grand Rapids, MI: Eerdmans, 2002.
Hylen, Susan E. *Imperfect Believers: Ambiguous Characters in the Gospel of John.* Louisville, KY: WJK, 2009.
Hylen, Susan. *Allusion and Meaning in John 6.* Berlin: Walter de Gruyter, 2005.
Irenaeus, Saint. *St. Irenaeus of Lyons: Against the Heresies.* Edited by John L. Dillon, translated by Dominic J. Unger. Mahwah, NJ: Newman, 1992.
Irwin, Kevin W. "A Sacramental World - Sacramentality As The primary Language for Sacraments." *Worship* 76 (2002) 197–211.
Jagessar, Michael N., and Stephen Burns. *Christian Worship: Postcolonial Perspectives.* Oakville, CT: Equinox, 2011.
Jasper, R. C. D., and G. J. Cuming. *Prayers of the Eucharist: Early & Reformed.* London: Collins, 1975.
Jeffrey, David L., ed. *Dictionary of Biblical Tradition in English Literature.* Grand Rapids, MI: Eerdmans, 1992.
Jenson, Robert W. *Systematic Theology: The Works of God.* Vol. 2. New York, NY: Oxford University Press, 1999.
Jeremias, Joachim. *The Eucharistic Words of Jesus.* Translated by Norman Perrin. London: SCM, 1966.
———. *The Prayers of Jesus.* Norwich: SCM, 1976, first published in 1967.
Johanny, Raymond. "Ignatius of Antioch." In *The Eucharist of the Early Christians*, edited by Willy Rordorf, translated by Matthew J. O'Connell, 48–70. New York, NY: Pueblo, 1990.
———. "Cyprian of Carthage." In *The Eucharist of the Early Christians*, edited by Willy Rordorf, translated by Matthew J. O'Connell, 156–82. New York, NY: Pueblo, 1990.
Johnson, Lawrence J. *Worship in the Early Church: An Anthology of Historical Sources Volume One.* Adelaide, SA: ATF, 2009.

Johnson, Luke Timothy. *Religious Experience in Earliest Christianity: A Missing Dimension in New Testament Studies*. Minneapolis, MN: Augsburg, 1998.

Johnson, Maxwell E., ed. *Sacraments and Worship: The Sources of Christian Theology*. Louisville, KY: John Knox, 2012.

Joncas, Jan Michael. "Tasting the Kingdom of God: The Meal Ministry of Jesus and Its Implications for Contemporary Worship and Life." *Worship*, 74:4 (2000) 329–65.

Jones, Bayard H. "The History of the Nestorian Liturgies." *Anglican Theological Review* 46 (1964) 155–76.

Jones, Paul H. *Christ's Eucharistic Presence: A History of the Doctrine*. New York, NY: Peter Lang, 1994.

Jourjon, Maurice. "Justin." In *The Eucharist of the Early Christians*, edited by Willy Rordorf, translated by Matthew J. O'Connell, 71–85. New York, NY: Pueblo, 1990.

Jungmann, Joseph A. *The Mass of the Roman Rite: Its Origins and Development, Volume Two*. Translated by Francis A. Brunner. Westminster: Christian Classics, 1986.

Karris, Robert J. *Eating Your Way through Luke's Gospel*. Collegeville, MN: Liturgical Press, 2006.

Kavanagh, Aidan. *Elements of Rite: A Handbook of Liturgical Style*. Collegeville, MN: The Order of St. Benedict, 1990.

Kearns, Carl E. "A Collection in Days of Preaching." *The Korea Mission Field* 2, no. 1, (November 1905) 7–8.

———. "Itineration." *The Korea Mission Field* 2, no. 12, (1906) 225–26.

Kennedy, David. *Eucharistic Sacramentality in an Ecumenical Context: The Anglican Epiclesis*. Burlington, VT: Ashgate, 2008.

Kerr, Alan R. *The Temple of Jesus' Body: The Temple Theme in the Gospel of John*. New York, NY: Sheffield, 2002.

Khoo, Lorna. *Wesleyan Eucharistic Spirituality*. Hindmarsh, SA: ATF, 2005.

Kodell, Jerome. *The Eucharist in the New Testament*. Wilmington, DE: Michael Glazier, 1988.

LaVerdiere, Eugene. *Dining in the Kingdom of God: The Origin of the Eucharist According to Luke*. Chicago, IL: Liturgy Training, 1994.

———. *The Eucharist in the New Testament and the Early Church*. Collegeville, MN: Pueblo, 1996.

Lee, Graham. "How the Spirit Came to Pyeng Yang." *The Korea Mission Field* 3, no. 3 (1907) 33–37.

Lee, Sang Taek. "Multiculturalism Yesterday, Today and Tomorrow in the Uniting Church." In *Marking Twenty Years: The Uniting Church in Australia 1977–1997*, edited by William W. Emilsen, and Susan Emilsen, 114–21. North Parramatta, NSW: UTC Publications, 1997.

———. *Religion and Social Formation in Korea: Minjung and Millenarianism*. Berlin: Mouton de Gruyter, 1996.

———. *The Kingdom of God in Korea: A Study of Korean Church History from the Perspectives of Both Conservative and Liberal*. Seoul: Yangsuh, 1988.

Leon-Dufour, Xavier. *Sharing the Eucharistic Bread: The Witness of the New Testament*. Translated by Matthew J. O'Connell . New York, NY: Paulist, 1987.

Lietzmann, Hans J. *Mass and Lord's Supper: A Study in the History of the Liturgy*. Translated by Dorothea H. G. Reeve, edited by Robert Douglas Richardson. Leiden: Brill, 1979.

Loades, Ann. "Table." In *Journey: Renewing the Eucharist*, vol. 1, edited by Stephen Burns, 62-80. Norwich: Canterbury, 2008.
Luther, Martin. "The German Mass and Order of Divine Service, January 1526." In *Documents Illustrative of the Continental Reformation*, edited by B. J. Kidd, 193-202. Oxford: Clarendon, 1911.
———. *Three Treatises: From the American Edition of Luther's Work*. Edited by Helmut T. Lehmann. Philadelphia, PA: Fortress, 1970.
Luz, Ulrich. *Matthew 1-7: A Commentary*. Edinburgh: T.&T. Clark, 1989.
Macquarrie, John. *A Guide to the Sacraments*. London: SCM, 1997.
Maier, Paul L. *Eusebius: The Church History*. Grand Rapids, MI: Kregel, 2007.
Marshall, I. Howard. *Last Supper and Lord's Supper*. Homebush West, NSW: Paternoster, 1980.
Maxwell, William D. *An Outline of Christian Worship: Its Development and Forms*. London: Oxford University Press, 1936.
Mazza, Enrico. *The Celebration of the Eucharist: The Origin of the Rite and the Development of Its Interpretation*. Translated by Matthew J. O'Connell. Collegeville, MN: Pueblo, 1998.
———. *The Eucharistic Prayers of the Roman Rite*. Collegeville, MN: Liturgical Press, 2004.
———. *The Origins of the Eucharistic Prayer*. Collegeville, MN: Liturgical Press, 1995.
McCaughey, J. Davis. *Commentary on the Basis of Union of the Uniting Church in Australia*. Melbourne: The Uniting Church Press, 1980.
McCune, George S. "The Holy Spirit in Pyeng Yang." *The Korea Mission Field* 3, no. 1 (1907) 1-2.
McGowan, Andrew. *Ascetic Eucharists: Food and Drink in Early Christian Ritual Meals*. Oxford: Clarendon, 1999.
McKenna, John H. *The Eucharistic Epiclesis: A Detailed History from the Patristic to the Modern Era, Second Edition*. Chicago, IL: Liturgy Training, 2009, first published in 1975.
McMichael, Ralph N. *Eucharist: A Guide for the Perplexed*. New York, NY: T.&T. Clark, 2010.
Methodist Conference Office. *The Methodist Hymn-Book: For Use in Australasia and New Zealand*. Aylesbury, BUKS: Hazell Watson and Viney, 1954.
Methodist Episcopal Church. *Methodist Church Doctrine and Discipline*. Edited by E. M. Cable. Kyeongseong: Yasogyo Seohoe, 1910.
Methodist Episcopal Church Board of Foreign Missions. *Annual Report of the Board of Foreign Missions of the Methodist Episcopal Church: for the Year*. New York, NY: Society, 1906.
Metzger, Marcel. *History of the Liturgy: The Major Stages*. Collegeville, MN: Liturgical Press, 1997.
Mick, Lawrence E. *Eucharist: Understanding the Sacraments*. Collegeville, MN: Liturgical Press, 2007.
Milavec, Aaron. *The Didache: Text, Translation, Analysis, and Commentary*. Collegeville, MN: Liturgical Press, 2003.
Mills, Watson E., ed. *Mercer Dictionary of the Bible: The Mercer Commentary on the Bible Series*. Macon, GA: Mercer University Press, 1997.
Minns, Denis. *Irenaeus: An Introduction*. New York, NY: T.&T. Clark, 2010.

Moloney, Francis J. *The Gospel of John*. Edited by Daniel J. Harrington. Collegeville, MN: Liturgical Press, 1998.

Monro, Anita, and Gerard Moore. *Exploring Worship*. Unley, SA: MediaCom, 2010.

Moore-Keish, Martha L. *Do This in Remembrance of Me: A Ritual Approach to Reformed Eucharistic Theology*. Cambridge: Eerdmans, 2008.

Moore, Gerard. "The Justice Dimension in the Eucharist." In *The Eucharist: Faith and Worship*, edited by Gerard Kelly, 75–89. Sydney: Pauls, 2001.

Morris, Loen. *The Gospel According to John: Revised Edition*. Cambridge: Eerdmans, 1995.

Murphy-O'Conner, Jerome. *St. Paul's Corinth: Texts and Archaeology*. Collegeville, MN: Liturgical Press, 2002.

Mutschler, Bernhard. "John and his Gospel in the Mirror of Irenaeus of Lyons: Perspectives of Recent Research." In *The Legacy of John: Second-Century Reception of the Fourth Gospel*, edited by Tuomas Rasimus, 319–44. Leiden: Brill, 2010.

Nevius, John L. *Methods of Mission Work*. Shanghai: The American Presbyterian Mission, 1886.

Newman, Elizabeth. *Untamed Hospitality: Welcoming God and Other Strangers*. Grand Rapids, MI: Brazos, 2007.

Niederwimmer, Kurt. *The Didache: A Commentary on the Didache*. Minneapolis, MN: Fortress, 1998.

Nisbet, Anabel Major. *Day In and Day Out in Korea*. Richmond, VA: Presbyterian Committee of Publication, 1919.

O'Day, Gail R., and Susan E. Hylen. *John*. Louisville, KY: John Knox, 2006.

Oesterley, W. O. E. *The Jewish Background of the Christian Liturgy*. Oxford: Clarendon, 1925.

Osborne, Kenan B. *The Christian Sacraments of Initiation: Baptism, Confirmation, Eucharist*. Mahwah, NJ: Paulist, 1987.

Outler, Albert C. ed. *John Wesley*. New York, NY: Oxford University Press, 1980, first published in 1964.

Paik, Lak-geoon G. *The History of Protestant Missions in Korea: 1832–1910*. Pyong Yang: Union Christian College Press, 1929.

Park, Hendrick. *The Roman Catholic Church: A Critical Appraisal*. Longwood, FL: Xulon, 2008.

Park, Seong-won. *Worship in the Presbyterian Church in Korea: Its History and Implications*. New York, NY: Peter Lang, 2001.

Perrin, Nicholas. *Jesus the Temple*. Grand Rapids, MI: SPCK, 2010.

Perry, John Michael. *Exploring the Evolution of the Lord's Supper in the New Testament*. Kansas City, MO: Sheed & Ward, 1994.

Power, David N. "Eucharistic Justice." *Theological Studies* 67 (2006) 856–79.

Presbyterian Church (U.S.A.). *Invitation to Christ: A Guide to Sacramental Practices*. KY, Louisville: Office of Theology and Worship, 2006.

Presbyterian Church in the U. S. A. Board of Foreign Missions. *The Annual Report of the Board of Foreign Missions of the Presbyterian Church in the U. S. A.* New York, NY: Board of Foreign Missions, 1908.

Reid, J. K. S. *Calvin: Theological Treatises*. Westminster: John Knox, 2000.

Richardson, Robert D. "A Further Inquiry into Eucharistic Origins with Special Reference to New Testament Problems." In *Mass and Lord's Supper: A Study in the History of the Liturgy with Introduction and Further Inquiry by Robert Douglas*

Richardson, edited by Hans Lietzmann, translated by D. H. G. Reeve, 219–700. Leiden: Brill, 1979.

Roberts, Alexander, et al., eds. *The Ante-Nicene Fathers: Volume III - Latin Christianity*. New York, NY: Cosimo, 2007.

———. *The Ante-Nicene Fathers: Volume V - Fathers of the Third Century*. New York, NY: Cosimo, 2007.

Rordorf, Willy. "Does the Didache Contain Jesus Tradition Independently of the Synoptic Gospels?" In *Jesus and the Oral Gospel Tradition*, edited by Henry Wansborough, 394–423. London: T.&T. Clark, 2004.

———. "The Didache." In *The Eucharist of the Early Christians*, edited by Willy Rordorf, translated by Matthew J. O'Connell, 1–23. New York, NY: Pueblo, 1990.

———. "The Lord's Prayer in the Light of Its Liturgical Use in the Early Church." *Studia Liturgica* 14, no. 1 (1980–1981) 1–19.

Sagovsky, Nicholas. "The Eucharist and the practice of Justice." *Studies in Christian Ethics* (2002) 75–96.

Saxer, Victor. "Tertullian." In *The Eucharist of the Early Christians*, edited by Willy Rordorf, translated by Matthew J. O'Connell, 132–55. New York, NY: Pueblo, 1990.

Schaff, Philip, and Henry Wace, eds. *Nicene and Post-Nicene Fathers: Jerome: Letters and Select Works*. Vol. 6. Peabody, MA: Hendrickson, 1995.

Schillebeeckx, Edward. *Christ the Sacrament of the Encounter with God*. Lanham, MD: Sheed & Ward, 1963.

Schreiner, Thomas R., and Matthew R. Crawford. *The Lord's Supper: Remembering and Proclaiming Christ Until He Comes*. Nashville, TN: B&H, 2010.

Schwiebert, Jonathan. *Knowledge and the Coming Kingdom: The Didache's Meal Ritual and Its Place in Early Christianity*. New York, NY: T.&T. Clark, 2008.

Small, Joseph. D. "A Church of The Word and Sacrament." In *Christian Worship in Reformed Churches Past and Present*, edited by L. Vischer, 311–23. Cambridge: Eerdmans, 2003.

Smith, Dennis E. *From Symposium to Eucharist: The Banquet in the Early Christian World*. Minneapolis, MN: Fortress, 2003.

Smith, Dennis E., and Hal E. Taussig. *Many Tables: The Eucharist in the New Testament and Liturgy Today*. Eugene, OR: Wipf and Stock, 1990.

Spinks, Bryan D. *Addai and Mari - the Anaphora of the Apostles: A Test for Students with Introduction, Translation, and Commentary*. Bramcote, Notts.: Grove, 1980.

———. "Mis-Shapen. Gregory Dix and the Four-Action Shape of the Liturgy." *Lutheran Quarterly Review* 4 (1990) 161–77.

St. Stephens' Uniting Church. *Sunday Service Order: Advent 1*. (Paper prepared for Sunday Service, Sydney, NSW, December 1, 2013).

Stamm, Mark W. "Open Communion as a United Methodist Exception." *Quarterly Review* 22, no. 3 (2002) 261–72.

———. *Extending the Table: Guide for a Ministry of Home Communion Serving*. Nashville, TN: Discipleship Resources, 2009.

———. *Let Every Soul be Jesus' Guest: A Theology of the Open Table*. Nashville, TN: Abingdon, 2006.

Stookey, Laurence Hull. *Eucharist: Christ's Feast with the Church*. Nashville, TN: Abingdon, 1993.

Stringer, Martin. *Rethinking the Origins of the Eucharist*. London: SCM, 2011.

Stubbs, David L. *The Open Table: What Gospel Do We Practice?: Theology and Worship Occasional Paper No. 22.* Louisville, KY: Presbyterian Church (U. S. A), 2009.

Stutzman, Paul Fike. *Recovering the Love Feast: Broadening Our Eucharistic Celebrations.* Eugene, OR: Wipf & Stock, 2011.

Suh, David Gwang-seon. "Minjung and Theology in Korea: A Biographical Sketch of an Asian Theological Consultation." In *Minjung Theology: People as the Subjects of History*, edited by Yong Bok Kim, 17–40. Singapore: A CTC-CCA, 1981.

Tanner, Kathryn. "In Praise of Open Communion: A Rejoinder to James Farwell." *Anglican Theological Review* 86:3 (2004) 473–85.

The General Council. "A Call to A Special Effort." *The Korea Mission Field* 2, no. 2, (1905) 30.

The Presbyterian Church in Canada. "Worship and the Sacraments." http://presbyterian.ca/about/more/#worship-and-the-sacraments.

The Uniting Church in Australia. *Constitution and Regulations: 2008 Edition.* Sydney: Uniting Church Press, 2008.

———. *Holy Communion: Three Orders of Service.* Melbourne: The Joint Board of Christian Education of Australia and New Zealand, 1980.

———. Minutes of the Fourth Assembly (1982). Uniting Church Archives NSW/ACT.

———. Minutes of the Fourth Assembly (1985). Uniting Church Archives NSW/ACT.

———. *Uniting in Worship 2.* Edited by Paul Walton. Sydney: The Assembly of the Uniting Church in Australia, 2005.

———. *Uniting in Worship: Leader's Book.* Edited by Hugh McGinlay. Melbourne: Uniting Church Press, 1988.

The Uniting Church in Australia, Synod of NSW & ACT. "Holy Communion." In "Rituals in the Uniting Church." http://nsw.uca.org.au/schoolprojects/ucarituals.htm.

The Working Group on Doctrine. "Worksheet 8: The Lord's Supper." (Sheet prepared for the National Assembly, Sydney, NSW, 2009).

Theissen, Gerd. "Social Stratification in the Corinthian Community: A Contribution to the Sociology of Early Hellenistic Christianity." In *Christianity at Corinth: The Quest for the Pauline Church*, edited by Edward Adams, and David G. Horrell, 97–105. Louisville, KY: John Knox, 2004.

———. *The New Testament: A Literary History.* Translated by Linda M. Maloney. Minneapolis, MN: Fortress, 2012.

Thurian, Max, and Geoffrey Wainwright, eds. *Baptism and Eucharist Ecumenical Convergence in Celebration.* Geneva: World Council of Churches, 1983.

Thurian, Max, ed. *Churches Respond to BEM: Official Responses to the "Baptism, Eucharist and Ministry" Text Vol. 2, Faith and Order Paper 132.* Geneva: World Council of Churches, 1986.

Tirabassi, Maren C., and Kathy Wonson Eddy. *Gifts in Open Hands: More Resources for the Global Community.* Cleveland, OH: Pilgrim, 2011.

Trumbower, Jeffrey A. *Born from Above.* Tubingen: Mohr, 1992.

Underwood, Horace G. *The Call of Korea: Political - Social - Religious.* New York, NY: Revell, 1908.

United Theological College. "Eucharist," (Liturgy used in the eucharist conducted at United Theological College, North Parramatta, NSW, August 18, 2010).

Uniting Church in Australia. *Holy Communion: Three Orders of Service.* Melbourne: The Joint Board of Christian Education of Australia and New Zealand, 1980.

Vinson, Richard B. *Luke: Smyth & Helwys Bible Commentary*. Macon, GA: Smyth & Helwys, 2008.

Vischer, Lukas, ed. *Christian Worship in Reformed Churches Past and Present*. Grand Rapids, MI: Eerdmans, 2003.

Von Wahlde, Urban C. *The Gospel and Letters of John: Volume 1 Introduction, Analysis, and Reference*. Cambridge: Eerdmans, 2010.

Wainwright, Geoffrey. *Eucharist and Eschatology*. London: Epworth, 1973.

Walker, Christopher C., ed. *Building on the Basis: Papers from the Uniting Church in Australia Assembly Working Groups on Doctrine and Worship 2000–2011*. Sydney: MediaCom, 2012.

Walker, P. W. L. *Jesus and the Holy City: New Testament Perspective on Jerusalem*. Cambridge: Eerdmans, 1996.

Wandel, Lee Palmer. *The Eucharist in the Reformation: Incarnation and Liturgy*. New York, NY: Cambridge University Press, 2006.

Watts, Rikk E. "The Lord's House and David's Lord: The Psalms and Mark's Perspective on Jesus and the Temple." *Biblical Interpretation* 15 (2007) 307–22.

Wawrykow, Joseph. "The Heritage of the Late Empire: Influential Theology." In *A Companion to the Eucharist in the Middle Ages*, edited by Ian Christopher Levy, Gary Macy, and Kristen Van Ausdall, 59–92. Leiden: Brill, 2012.

Wesley, John, and Charles Wesley. *Hymns on the Lord's Supper*. Bristol: Felix Farley, 1745. http://www.canamus.org/Enchiridion/Xtrs/brevint.htm.

White, James F. *Documents of Christian Worship: Descriptive and Interpretive Sources*. Westminster: John Knox, 1992.

———. *Protestant Worship: Traditions in Tradition*. Louisville, KY: John Knox, 1989.

———. *The Sacraments in Protestant Practice and Faith*. Nashville, TN: Abingdon, 1999.

Winter, Bruce W. *After Paul Left Corinth: The Influence of Secular Ethics and Social Change*. Grand Rapids, MI: Eerdmans, 2001.

World Council of Churches. *Baptism, Eucharist and Ministry: 25th Anniversary Printing, Faith and Order Paper No. 111*. Geneva: World Council of Churches, 1982.

Wright, N. T. *Luke for Everyone*. Louisville, KY: John Knox, 2004.

———. *The Challenge of Jesus: Rediscovering Who Jesus Was and Is*. Madison, WI: InterVarsity, 1999.

Yoo-Crowe, Seongja. "Life with Members of Different Cultural Traditions during the Twenty Years since Union." In *Marking Twenty Years: The Uniting Church in Australia 1977–1997*, edited by William W. Emilsen, and Susan Emilsen, 104–13. North Parramatta, NSW: UTC, 1997.

Young, Norman. "Sacrament, Sign, and Unity: An Australian Reflection." In *Ecumenical Theology in Worship, Doctrine, and Life: Essays Presented to Geoffrey Wainwright on His Sixtieth Birthday*, edited by David S. Cunningham, et al., 95–105. New York, NY: Oxford University Press, 1999.

Zheltov, Michael. "The Moment of Eucharistic Consecration in Byzantine Thought." In *Issues in Eucharistic Praying in East and West: Essays in Liturgical and Theological Analysis*, edited by Maxwell E. Johnson, 263–306. Collegeville, MN: Pueblo, 2010.

2 Korean Language Sources

Ahn, Byung Mu. *Galilee Yesu (Galilee Jesus)*. Seoul: Han Gil Sa, 1993.
Andong Church History Committee. *Andong Gyohoe 90 Nyeon Sa (Andong Church History 90 Years)*. Seoul: Handl, 2001.
Bae, Gyeong-nae. "Geundae Jabonju-eui Sahoe-wa Adong: Adong Ingwon-eui Wanjeonhan Silhyon-eul Wihan Jogeon-eui Tamsaek (Society and Child of Modern Capitalism: Exploration of the Condition for the Full Realization of Children's Right)." *Jin Bo Pyeong Ron* 17 (2003) 195–216.
Barr, John. "PCK-UCA Partnership from A Uniting Church Perspective." In *Tales of Two Churches: Australia and Korea*, edited by The General Assembly of Presbyterian Church of Korea, 98–110. Seoul: Publishing House of the PCK, 2012.
Cho, Ki-yeon. *Hanguk Gyohoe-wa Yebae Gangsin (Korean Church and Renewal of Worship)*. Seoul: The Christian Literature Society of Korea, 2004.
Choi, Joon-sik. *Choi Joonsik-eui Hanguk Jonggyosa Barobogi: Yubulseon-eui Tleul Ggaera (Joonsik Choi's Proper View on the History of Korean Religions: Break the Category of Confucianism, Buddhism and Taoism)*. Seoul: Hanul Academy, 2007.
———. *Hanguk-eui Jeontong Mingan Sinang (Korea's Customs People's Faith)*. Seoul: Ewha Womans University Press, 2005.
Committee on the Book of Common Worship. *Pyojun Yesikseo (The Book of Common Worship)*. Seoul: Publishing House PCK, 1997.
———. *Yebae Yesikseo (The Book of Common Worship)*. Seoul: Publishing House PCK, 2008.
Dutney, Andrew. *The Uniting Church in Australia and the Ecumenical Movement*. Edited and translated by Seong Gi Cho. Seoul: Publishing House PCK, 2012.
Ewha Institute for the Humanities. *Gender-wa Tal/Gyeonggye-eui Jihyeong (The Landscape of Gender and Post/Boundary)*. Seoul: Ewha Womans University Press, 2009.
Goh, Eun. "Miruk-gwa Minjung (Miruk and Minjung)." In *Han-guk Geun-dae Minjung Jong-gyo Sa-sang*, edited by Sun-myeong Whang, 225–70. Seoul: Hakminsa, 1983.
Gu, Mi-rae. "Palgwanhoe-eui Gukga Chukjae-jeok Seong-gyeok (National and Festival Feature of Pal-Gwan-Hwoe)." *Yeok-sa Min-sok Hak* 16 (2003) 253–85.
Gum, Jang-tae. *Guisin-gwa Je-sa: Yugyo-eui Jonggyo-jeok Seigye (Ghost and Ancestor Worship: Religious World of Confucianism)*. Seoul: JNC, 2009.
Han, Ja-kyeong. *Hanguk Cheolhak-eui Mak (Context of Korean Philosophy)*. Seoul: Ewha Womans University Press, 2008.
Han, Queen So-heon. *Shin-Wan-Yeok Nae-Hun, Ge-Nyeo-Seo*. Edited by Si-yeol Song and Jong-kwon Kim. Seoul: Myeongmundang, 1987.
Im, Sok-jae. *Mu-ga: The Ritual Songs of Korean Mu-dangs*. Translated by Alan C. Heyman. Seoul: Jain, 2003.
Ji, Jae-hee. *Ye-Gi*. Seoul: Jayu Mungo, 2000.
Jo, Soo-hyun. "Minjung Sinhak-eui Meotgaji Gwajae (Several Tasks of Minjung Theology)." *Sinhak Gwa Hyeonjang* 6 (1996) 286–306.
Joo, Hak-seon. *Hanguk Gamrigyoheo Yebae (Korean Methodist Worship): 1885–1931*. Seoul: KMC, 2005.
Jung, Jang-bok. "Hanguk Jonggyo Munhwa-eui Gidosimseong-gwa Gidokgyo Gido-eui Jae-ihae (A New Understanding of the Mental Image of Prayer in Korean

Religion and Culture and the Prayer of Christianity)." *Jangsin Nondan* 9 (1993) 124–54.

———. "Sadojeonseung-e Natanan Seongchan Seongryejeon Yeon-gu-eui Hyeonjae-jeok Jomyeong (The Current Illumination of the Study on the Eucharist in the Apostolic Tradition)." *Jangsin Nondan* 13 (1997) 270–96.

———. "Jangrogyo-eui Goyuhan Seongryejeon-eul Malhanda (The Original Sacrament of Presbyterian Church)." *Gidokgongbo*, May 26, 2001.

———. *85 Yebae-wa Seolgyo Handbook (Handbook of Worship and Preaching)*. Seoul: Yang Seo Gak, 1984.

———. *Yebae-wa Seolgyo Gyehoek-eul Wihan Calendar (Calendar for the Plan of Worship and Preaching)*. Seoul: Kyo Moon Sa, 1981.

Kang, Seong-gu. *MBC Hanguk Minyo Daejeon (MBC Korea Minyo Contest) - Chungcheong-Namdo Minyo Commentary*. Seoul: Sambo Munwhasa, 1995.

Kim, Bu-sik. *Sam-guk Sa-gi: A Historical Record of Three Kingdoms*. 2 vols. Translated by Byeong-do Lee. Seoul: Eulyoo, 1988.

Kim, Gi-jeon. "Mit-myeo-neu-ri Hak-dae Mun-je-eh Dae-ha-ya." In *So-choon Gi-jeon Kim Jeonjib (The Complete Works of So-choon Gi-jeon Kim)*. Vol. 2, edited by Young-bok Lee, et al., 541–44. Seoul: Gook-hak Ja-ryo-won, 2010.

Kim, In-hoe. *Hanguk Mu-sok Sasang Yeon-gu (Study on Shamanism of Korea)*. Seoul: Jib Mun Dang, 1987.

Kim, In-soo. *Ganchurin Hankuk Gidok Gyoheo-eui Yeoksa (A Brief History of the Christian Church in Korea: for the Laity and the Church School Teachers)*. Seoul: The Presbyterian Church of Korea, 1998.

———. *Hanguk Gidok Gyohoesa (Korean Church History)*. Seoul: Korean Presbyterian Publishing, 2005.

Kim, Kyeong-jin. "Chogi Hanguk Jangro Gyohoe Yebae Ihae (The Early Korean Presbyterian Church Worship), 1879–1934." In *Modern Society and Worship - Preaching Ministry*, edited by Committee of Essays in Celebration of Dr. Jang-bok Jung's 60th Birthday, 517–38. Seoul: Worship and Preaching Academy, 2002.

Kim, Tae-gon. "Min-gan Sinang-eui Silsang (Realities of Folk Believes in Korea)." *In-mun Gwa-hak Yeon-gu* 1 (1982) 69–90.

Kim, Yeol-gyu. "Mu-sok Sinang-gwa Gidokgyo Sinang (Mu-sok faith and Christian faith)." *Gi-dok-gyo Sa-sang* 10 (1988) 14–21.

Kim, Young-tae. *Yebae Yesikseo-e Natanan Juil Yebae-eui Hyeongseong Gwajeong Yeon-gu (The Study of Formation of Sunday Service Presented in Worship Book): Focused on Methodist Church in Korea*. PhD diss., Baekseok University, 2007.

Kim, Eui-hwan. *Seonggyeong-jeok Chukbok-gwan (Biblical View on Blessing)*. Seoul: Seong Gwang Munwhasa, 1981.

Lee, Gyu-seong. *Dongyang Cheolhak Gu Bulmyeol-eui Munjaedeul (Eastern Philosophy the Everlasting Questions)*. Seoul: Ewha Womans University Press, 1994.

Lee, Hay-soon, et al., *Joseon Jung-gi Yeh-hak Sasang-gwa Ilsang Munwha (Yeh-hak Philosophy and Everyday Culture in the Middle of Joseon): focused on Ju-ja-ga-rye*. Seoul: Ewha Womans University Press, 2008.

Lee, Hyeon Woong. *Jangrogyo Yebae Mobum-eui Yeoksa-wa Jeonmang-e Gwanhan Yeon-gu (A Study of History and Prospect of the Presbyterian Directory for Worship)*. Seoul: Presbyterian Theological Seminary, 2004.

Lee, Man-yeol, ed. *Appenzeller: Hanguk-e On Cheot Seon-gyo-sa (The First Missionary Sent to Korea)*. Seoul: Yeonsei University, 1985.

Lee, Sang-gyu. "The Presbyterian Church of Australia and Korean Church." In *Tales of Two Churches: Australia and Korea*, edited by The General Assembly of Presbyterian Church of Korea, 25–60. Seoul: Publishing House of the PCK, 2012.
Lee, Sang Taek. *Sae Gyohoe-wa Sae Ddang (New Church New Land)*. Seoul: Publishing House of the PCK, 2011.
Lee, Sook-in. "Ju-Ja-Ga-Rye and Culture of Ancestral Worship in the Middle of Joseon." *Jeong-sin Mun-wha Yeon-gu*, vol. 29, no. 2 (2006) 35–65.
Moffett, Samuel. *Wui Won Ip Kyo In Kyu Do*. Seoul: Chosen Yesukyo Seohyoe, 1895.
Mun, Ok-pyo. "Gajok Nae Yeoseong Jiwi-eui Byeonwha (The Change of Women's Position in Family): Centered on Confucian Tradition." *Jeong-sin Mun-wha Yeon-gu* 19, no. 2 (1996) 59–78.
Ohk, Seong-deuk. "Hanguk Jangrogyo Chogi Seongyo Jeongchek (The Early Mission Policy of Korean Presbyterian): 1884–1903." *Hangook Gidokkyo Wa Yeoksa* 9 (1998) 117–88.
Park, Hae-jeong. "Hanguk Chogi Gamri Gyohoe-eui Seongmanchan Ihae (Understanding on Holy Communion of the Early Methodist Church in Korea): 1885–1935." *Sinhak Gwa Silcheon* 10 (2006) 135–74.
Park, Jae-soon. *Yesu Wundong-gwa Bapsang Gongdong-che (Jesus Movement and Table Community)*. Seoul: Cheon Ji, 1988.
———. "Yesu-eui Bapsang Gondong-che Wundong-gwa Gyohoe (Jesus' Table Community Movement and Church)." In *Sinyak Seongseo-neun O-neul Wuri-egye Ireoke Jeungeonhanda (The New Testament Testifies This to Us Today)*, edited by Weolyo Sinhak Seodang, 87–120. Seoul: Hanguk Sinhak Yeonguso, 1992.
Park, Keun-won. *Yebae-wa Gangdan (Worship and Pulpit)*. Seoul: Yang Seo Gak, 1987.
Park, Kyeong-soo. "Hanguk Gaesingyo Chogi Gyohoe Yeonhab Wundong-eui Yusan (The Legacy of Early Korean Protestant Church's Union Movement)." *Jangro-Gyohoe wa Shin-hak* 8 (2011) 201–28.
Park, Seong-heum. "Seongchan Nonran, Nohoeseo Il Nyeon Yeonguro Ildanrak (Debates on the eucharist, decided as one year study in Presbytery)." *Gidokgongbo*, June 23, 2001.
Ryu, Dae-young. *Chogi Miguk Seon-gyo-sa Yeon-gu (Early American Missionaries in Korea, 1884–1910: Understanding Missionaries from their middle-class background*. Seoul: Hanguk Gidokgyo Yeoksa Yeonguso, 2007.
Saemoonan Church History Committee. *Saemoonan Gyohoe 100 Nyeonsa (Saemoonan Church History 100 years) 1887–1987*. Seoul: Saemoonan Church, 1995.
Shin, Hyeong-sik, and Bae-yong Lee. *Hanguksa-eui Saerowun Ihae (A New Understanding of the History of Korea)*. Seoul: Ewha Womans University Press, 1997.
Suh, Gwang-seon. *Jong-gyo-wa Ingan (Religion and Humans)*. Seoul: Ewha Womans University Press, 2009.
The General Assembly of the Presbyterian Church of Korea. *Heonbup (Constitution)*. Seoul: Daehan Gidokgyo Seohoe, 1934.
———. *Heonbup (Constitution)*. 2nd ed. Seoul: Publishing House PCK, 2001.
———. *Heonbup (Constitution)*. Seoul: Publishing House PCK, 1983.
The Institute of Korean Church History. *Hanguk Gidokgyo-eui Yeoksa (A History of Korean Church)*. Vol. 1. Seoul: Gi Dok Gyo Mun Sa, 1989.

The Korean Methodist Church Mission. *Gidokgyo Daehan Gamrihoe Yebaeseo (The Korean Methodist Church Worship Book)*. Seoul: The Korean Methodist Church, 1992.

Yeo, Ik-gu. *Miruk Gyeong-eui Saegye (The World of Miruk Gyeong)*. Seoul: Jiyangsa, 1986.

Yoon, Kyeong-no. *105 In Sageon-gwa Sinminhoe Yeon-gu (The Study on The 105-Man Incident and Sinminhoe)*. Seoul: Iljisa, 1990.

Yu, Dong-sik. "Hanguk Munwha-eui Jong-gyo-jeok Giban (Religious Basis of the Korean Culture)." *Hyundai Wa Sinhak* 6, no. 1 (1970) 111–22.

———. "Hanguk *Mu-gyo*-eui Jongyo-jeok Teukseong (Religious Character of Korean *Mu-gyo*)." In *Hanguk Munwha-wa Poong-ryu Sinhan (Korean Culture and Poong-ryu Theology)*, edited by Hanguk Munwha Shinhakhoe, 37–52. Seoul: Handl, 2002.

Name Index

Allen, Horace N., 29
Ambrose, 122–23, 125–26, 209
Anderson, Paul N., 88
Appenzeller, Henry G., 28–32, 38
Aquinas, Thomas, 127–29
Augustine, 125–26, 128

Barr, John, 182n7
Barrett, Charles K., 90n34
Baumstark, Anton, 66–69, 79, 210n126, 226
Berengar, 127
Betz, Hans Dieter, 206
Betz, Johannes, 93–95
Bickell, J. W., 61
Billerbeck, P., 71–72
Bock, Darrell L., 144
Bond, Helen K., 148–49
Box, G. H., 72
Bradshaw, Paul F., xvi, 53n90, 61n1, 62, 66, 69, 89, 93, 95, 100, 102–105, 110n123, 113n1, 118, 198, 201n88, 204n99
Brown, John P., 182n5
Brown, Raymond E., 84n1, 88
Bruner, Fredrick Dale, 92
Bryennios, Philotheos, 61, 93
Bultmann, Rudolf, 84–85
Burns, Stephen, 117, 178, 218
Buxton, Richard, 66
Byars, Ronal P., 132n85, 208

Callistus, 62, 115–16
Calvin, John, 22, 30, 35, 53–58, 129, 131–32, 168

Carson, D. A., 87–88, 152–53
Chauvet, Louis Marie, 75–76
Chilton, Bruce, xvi, 70, 102, 142, 147n33, 148–49, 154, 156–57, 162
Clark, Charles Allen, 35–39
Cooke, Bernard J., 176n44
Countryman, Louis William, 147
Cox, Harvey, 16
Crockett, William R., 133
Crossan, Dominic, 138–40, 143, 148
Cullmann, Oscar, 86–87, 90–92
Cummings, Owen F., 98n66, 100, 103n87, 107, 115n11, 127, 131n77, 135n98
Cyprian, 107, 119–21, 135, 206, 209, 227

Davies, Horton, 145n28, 217n150
Dix, Dom Gregory, 59, 62–66, 73, 79, 93, 102, 104, 159, 195, 226
Dutney, Andrew, 182n8, 189–90, 218

Easton, Burton Scott, 62, 116n13
Edmonson, Stephen, 141n13, 175n41, 177n49
Engberding, Hieronymus, 62

Fabian, Richard, 144, 146
Farwell, James, 155, 172n35
Feeley-Harnik, Gillian, 147
Fitzmyer, Joseph, 166n7, 204n103
Foley, Edward, 141n11, 198n71

Gese, Hartmut, 75
Goh, Eun, 8

NAME INDEX

Harrington, Daniel J., 158n83
Higgins, Angus, 69, 73
Hippolytus, of Rome, 52–53, 59, 61–62, 74, 115–16, 201
Hultgren, Arland J., 143–44
Hus, Jan, 129

Ignatius Antioch, 89, 90n33, 93n44, 98–103, 111, 119, 158n78, 217
Irenaeus, 108–12, 114–15, 158, 217
Irwin, Kevin W., 175

Jasper and Cumming, 122n37, 205n107
Jenson, Robert W., 159n86
Jeremias, Joachim, 59, 70–71, 73–75, 77–79, 87, 93, 206n112, 207n113, 226
Johanny, Raymond, 90n33, 98n64, 119n26, 121n31
Johnson, Lawrence J., 94n45, 100n70, 101n76, 103n88, 110n120, 193n51, 204n100
Johnson, Maxwell E., xvi, 62, 125n51, 127n59, 128n61, 131n81
Joncas, Jan Michael, 147, 160–61
Jones, Paul H., 126–29
Jourjon, Maurice, 105n95, 204n105
Jung, Jang-bok, 40, 52–53
Jungmann, Joseph A., 123
Justin Martyr, 47, 89, 103–104, 111, 158n78, 193, 198n72, 217

Karris, Robert J., 160n90
Kerr, Alan R., 152–53
Kodell, Jerome, 89
Kuhn, K. G., 74–76

Lagarde, Paul de, 61
Lanfranc, 127
LaVerdiere, Eugene, 85–86, 98n68, 141n10, 159, 160n89
Lee, Sang Taek, 173–74, 220
Lee, Soo-jeong, 28–29
Leon-Dufour, Xavier, 75–76, 88
Lietzmann, Hans, 73–74, 76, 102
Loades, Ann, 169n24, 176n48
Lorentz, Rudolf, 62
Luther, Martin, 129–31, 207

Macquarrie, John, 176
Marshall, Howard, 71–72
Maxwell, William D., 72
Mazza, Enrico, 77–78, 96, 117, 119, 122n35, 125n50, 206n112
McCaughey, J. Davis, 183–84
McGowan, Andrew, 107–108, 197
McMichael, Ralph N., 132, 199, 218n153
Metzger, Marcel, 62, 121n33
Mick, Lawrence E., 170n25
Milavec, Aaron, 95
Minns, Denis, 108n111
Moffett, Samuel, 31, 35, 37–39
Moloney, Francis J., 91
Moore-Keish, Martha L., 132n88
Moore, Gerard, 194n53, 195n55, 203
Morris, Leon, 87–88
Mutschler, Bernhard, 108

Nevius, John L., 32–33, 37
Niederwimmer, Kurt, 52n87, 95, 97, 201n82
Nisbet, Anabel Major, 164n1

Oesterley, W. O. E., 73
Origen, of Alexandria, 114–16, 206, 217

Perrin, Nicholas, 140, 151–52
Perry, John Michael, 89–90
Phillips, Edward, 62
Probst, Ferdinand, 67

Radbertus, 126
Ratramnus, 126
Richardson, Robert D., 104, 106
Rordorf, Willy, 94, 96–97, 198, 204n100
Ross, John, 27–28

Saxer, Victor, 117–19
Schillebeeckx, Edward, 176
Schwiebert, Jonathan, 89n24, 99–100, 105–106
Scotus, John Duns, 128–29
Serapion, 74, 122–23, 209
Small, Joseph, 160n92
Smith, Dennis E., xv–xvi, 102, 154, 158, 167n16

Spinks, Brian, 66, 124
Stamm, Mark, 133n90, 143n20, 145, 170n27, 171
Stookey, Laurence Hull, 129, 131n78, 167n14
Stringer, Martin, 89, 93n41, 98n67
Suh, Sang-ryoon, 27–28

Tanner, Kathryn, 141n12, 156n71
Tertullian, of Cartage, 102, 117–19, 135, 206, 209, 227
Theissen, Gerd, 114, 116, 165
Trumbower, Jeffrey A., 155

Underwood, Horace G., xiii, 28–30, 32n20

Vinson, Richard B., 144

Wahlde, Urban C. Von, 85
Wainwright, Geoffrey, 46n70, 158n81, 169n22
Walker, Chris, 187n27, 189n30, 191n39, 194n52, 220–21
Walker, P. W. L. 151–53
Watts, Rikk E., 151
Wesley, John, xviii, 133–35, 137, 172n31, 173, 185, 186n20
White, James F., 54, 131
William of Occam, 129
Winter, Bruce W., 166
Wright, N. T., 138, 145, 147–50
Wyclif, John, 129

Yerkes, R. K., 76
Young, Norman, 189, 223

Zwingli, Ulrich, 129–31, 193

Subject Index

Addai and Mari, 123–24, 209, 227
Agape, 64, 93, 101–103, 118–19, 204
Age, 13, 18, 21–22, 26, 49, 56–59, 79, 92, 133, 163, 169, 184–86, 222
Ancestor Worship, 13–15, 23–24, 26, 225
Andong Church, 37–39
Apostolic Church Order, 61
Apostolic Constitutions 8, 61
Apostolic Tradition, 52–53, 59, 62, 116, 201–202, 205

Banquet. *See* Feast.
Basis of Union, xviii, 181n3, 182–87, 189–91, 211n133, 218, 222–23
BCW 1997, xiv, 41, 43, 47–49, 57–58, 226
BCW 2008, xiv, 43, 45–50, 57–58, 69, 226
BEM, xiv, 40–41, 58, 169, 217, 226
Berakah, 76, 102, 218
Birkat Ha-Mazon, 77, 96
Buddhism, xvii, 3, 6–9, 18, 24–25, 225

Canons of Hippolytus, 61–62
Catechism, 28, 33, 54, 56, 168n18
Chaburah, 63–65, 73–74, 79, 102
Children, 4, 10, 12–13, 19, 21–22, 25–26, 44, 48–49, 56n105, 58, 94, 121, 131, 138, 141, 170, 178, 181–82, 184–86, 188–90, 212–13, 216, 221–22, 225, 228
Confirmation, 56–57, 139, 168–69, 172, 175, 184, 205

Confucian. *See* Confucianism.
Confucianism, xvii, 3, 6, 9–14, 19–26, 181n3, 225

Death of Jesus, 23, 41, 71, 74, 79, 89–90, 92, 94, 105, 119, 134, 152–56, 159–60, 174, 209–10, 223, 225
Didache, 51–53, 59, 61, 64, 74, 77–78, 90, 93–98, 111, 114, 116, 158n78, 193, 200–202, 204–206, 217
Didascalia Apostolorum, 61, 204, 205n106
Discriminated. *See* Discrimination.
Discrimination, 10–12, 18, 20, 97, 161–62, 166–67, 227
Distinction, 9, 11, 19–20, 24–26, 38, 97

Easter, 29, 31, 43–44, 46–47, 50, 116
Eastern Orthodox. *See* Greek Orthodox.
Ecumenical Movement, xiv, 35, 38, 40, 45, 47, 58, 182, 208, 218, 226, 228–29
Ecumenism. *See* Ecumenical Movement.
Egyptian Church Order, 61–62
Emmaus, 44–45, 50, 156, 159–60, 169, 194, 212
Essenes, 74–75

Feast, xvi, 43–44, 55, 70n39, 72–73, 86–87, 93, 102–103, 108–109, 117–19, 132–33, 142–46, 149–50, 154, 156–62, 211–12, 223, 227–28

SUBJECT INDEX

First Apology, 47, 103–106, 193, 195, 198, 204
Fourth Gospel, xvi, 44, 63n10, 84–85, 87, 90–91, 100, 111, 118, 141, 152, 154–55, 157–58, 227

Goryeo, 6, 12, 24
Greek Orthodox, xiv, 45, 46, 58, 123, 183n12, 193
Gut, 4–5, 16, 18, 24–25

Infant Baptism, 48, 184, 222
Institution Narratives, xvi, 44, 49–51, 65, 78, 84, 86–88, 99, 104, 121–25, 128–30, 132, 135, 194n53, 208–10, 216, 220, 225, 227

Je-sa. See Ancestor Worship.
Jeonnam Synod, xiv-xv, 49–50, 58, 226
Jesus' Meal. *See* Meals of Jesus.
Johannine, 71–72, 85–86, 88–90, 92, 94–95, 98–99, 101n77, 108–12
Joseon, 6, 8–15, 18–19, 22, 24–26

Kiddush, 62, 72–74, 77–79, 154
Kingdom of God, xvi, xviii, 18, 43, 64, 93, 96, 138, 140–42, 144–47, 149–62, 171, 177, 199, 212, 223, 227–28

Last Supper, xiv-xviii, 19, 41, 44–45, 50–51, 60, 63–65, 69–79, 83–84, 86–88, 90, 92–97, 99–100, 104–106, 110–13, 117–22, 125, 130, 132, 134–38, 154–59, 161, 163, 167, 169, 178, 195–96, 201, 206n112, 209–10, 212–13, 223, 225–28
Liturgical Movement, 40, 208

Manchuria, 27–29
Meals of Jesus, xvi, xviii, 18, 74, 76, 136, 138, 141–42, 154, 157, 159, 161–62, 169, 178, 189, 212, 227–28
Means of Grace, xviii, 131, 133, 135, 149, 160, 171–73, 178, 186, 189, 191, 215, 219, 223

Membership, 14–15, 24, 145, 155–56, 168, 177, 185–86, 221n170
Minjung, 8–9, 17–19, 25
Miruk, 7–9, 17–18, 25
Moksa Jibup, 35, 37, 39
Moral. *See* Morality.
Morality, 9, 23–24, 133, 149, 164–65, 171
Mu-gyo, 3–5, 15–17, 24–25

Open Table, xiv-xviii, 21–22, 49–50, 58, 79, 133, 136, 146, 163, 168, 172–78, 181–85, 188–89, 211–14, 221–26, 228–29

Paschal, xiii, xv, 42, 44, 49, 51, 70, 77, 79, 117, 210, 226–27
PCK, xiii-xviii, 3, 15–17, 19–27, 30, 34–35, 37, 39–60, 69, 77–79, 163, 165, 168–69, 172, 175, 181–82, 208, 222, 225–26
PCUS, xiii
PCUSA, 21n64, 181, 208
Pentecostal Church. *See* Pentecostalism.
Pentecostalism, 16, 46

Qumran, 74–75

Rigorism, 22, 116
Roman Catholic, xiv, 29, 45–46, 53–54, 58, 175, 183n12, 193, 208

Sa-kyeong-hoe, 16–17, 25, 33–34
Samil Movement, 37
Seong-ri-hak, 9, 25
Sex, 11, 18–19, 26, 92, 147n31, 155, 184
Shamanism, xvii, 3, 8, 17n48, 18n58, 24, 225
Silla, 3, 6, 8
Skyamuni, 7–9
Synaxis, 63
Synoptic Account. *See* Synoptic Gospels.
Synoptic Gospels, xv-xvii, 44, 63, 71–72, 84, 86–89, 94–95, 100, 105, 109–12, 117, 119–21, 130, 135, 137, 146, 154, 156

Testamentum Domini, 62

UCA, xvii-xviii, 21n64, 181–96, 199, 201, 205, 208–24

WCC, xiv, 47, 189, 218, 226

Westminster Confession of Faith, xiii, 39, 41, 53–54, 56, 132, 168–69

Yang-ban, 9–10, 12, 14

Zebah Todah, 75–76, 79

www.ingramcontent.com/pod-product-compliance
Lightning Source LLC
Chambersburg PA
CBHW050435240426
43661CB00055B/2396